HAITI
IN THE
BALANCE

HAITI
IN THE
BALANCE

WHY FOREIGN AID HAS FAILED
AND WHAT WE CAN DO ABOUT IT

TERRY F. BUSS
WITH ADAM GARDNER

NATIONAL ACADEMY OF PUBLIC ADMINISTRATION

BROOKINGS INSTITUTION PRESS
Washington, D.C.

ABOUT BROOKINGS
The Brookings Institution is a private nonprofit organization devoted to research, education, and publication on important issues of domestic and foreign policy. Its principal purpose is to bring the highest quality independent research and analysis to bear on current and emerging policy problems. Interpretations or conclusions in Brookings publications should be understood to be solely those of the authors.

Copyright © 2008
THE BROOKINGS INSTITUTION
1775 Massachusetts Avenue, N.W., Washington, D.C. 20036
www.brookings.edu

Library of Congress Cataloging-in-Publication data

Buss, Terry F.
    Haiti in the balance : why foreign aid has failed and what we can do about it / Terry F. Buss with Adam Gardner.
        p.   cm.
    Includes bibliographical references and index.
    Summary: "Tackles such questions as why has assistance been so ineffectual and what can be learned from Haiti's plight concerning foreign aid in general, by analyzing nearly twenty years of Haitian history, politics, and foreign relations"— Provided by publisher.
    ISBN 978-0-8157-1391-3 (pbk. : alk. paper)
    1. Haiti—Politics and government. 2. Economic assistance—Haiti. I. Gardner, Adam. II. Title.
    F1921.B88 2008
    972.94—dc22   2008025536

9 8 7 6 5 4 3 2 1

The paper used in this publication meets minimum requirements of the American National Standard for Information Sciences—Permanence of Paper for Printed Library Materials: ANSI Z39.48-1992.

Typeset in Minion and Lithos

Composition by Cynthia Stock
Silver Spring, Maryland

Printed by R. R. Donnelley
Harrisonburg, Virginia

To the Haitian people

May they someday secure their freedom

CONTENTS

FOREWORD

The publication of this book is timely, and urgently needed, because it adds fresh insights into ongoing discussions regarding what is an appropriate development assistance approach for Haiti. If Haiti is considered a failed state, this may be a reflection of what happens when development actors become politicized in an already fragile environment and when the commitment to the national good of a country's political and business elites—supposedly the natural gatekeepers of the welfare of the state—is nonexistent or dysfunctional. The putative leaders of the Republic of Haiti continue to view the country and its resources in the way of foreigners, much as the colonial masters viewed it from its inception: worthy only of exploitation.

This book documents how efforts to effect change in Haiti are often undertaken without taking into account local mores. Policy questions raised here ought to be starting points for all actors aiming to effect change for a new Haiti. Understanding the image of "mountains beyond Haiti's mountains" may also add much needed insight into the deep-seated conflicts based on race, color, class, and political affiliations; these need immediate intervention, even as meaningful attempts at sustainable change in the traditional sectors of the economy take place. Eliminating disparities in access to commercial opportunities, health, and education among Haiti's 8 million citizens, for whom civil and human rights continue to be elusive, is of paramount importance in the effort to bring political stability to what many consider a post-conflict environment.

A key finding of this book is that a paradigm change is needed on the part of both the local Haitian actors, who are primarily consumed with attaining power or in some cases survival, and the international community. The

United States—arguably the most influential player on the Haitian landscape since its occupation of the country from 1915 to 1934—has to allow for the true genius of Haitians to surface so that democracy and free enterprise can grow roots there. A partnership between Haiti and the international donor community called the Interim Cooperation Framework (ICF) is a good start for identifying development priorities and marshaling resources. But allowing for a broader cross section of the society to comment on and contribute to the development framework process to forge a better future for Haiti will increase popular buy-in to the process.

Dwight Waldo, professor emeritus at the Maxwell School of Public Administration at Syracuse University, has said that administration is the core of all government. That is, no government can do what a government by definition does without creating and maintaining some apparatus to make some decisions, carry out decisions, and enforce norms. A finding of this book is that there has been in Haiti a general failure to reinforce the capacity of government institutions at the national, departmental, and municipal level, which has contributed to the country's underdevelopment. Civil society, however robust, cannot, will not, and likely should not do the work of government. In moving forward, development actors will need to deviate from efforts to foster nation building independent of government institutions—indeed, long regarded as corrupt and ineffective—and instead invest in long-term activities to counter the deviant administrative culture and provide assistance to restructure a system based on principles of good governance through recruitment and training of Haitian civil servants. Haiti, arguably one of the world's most economically deprived states, should benefit from some of the most innovative development assistance activities. A right mix of technical assistance and capacity-building needs to dominate nation-building efforts. Reconstructing the beleaguered government institutions ought to be a priority. Lending institutions need to explore relaxed lending measures.

Haiti is like no other country in the hemisphere—and that is why this book is long overdue. It raises the level of the debate on Haiti and in addition may give practitioners, researchers, and the public new insights on aid to other fragile and postconflict nations. Terry Buss's expansive firsthand knowledge and experience of fragile states is evident. He has stated, "Above all, poor people need jobs—but without security, nothing positive is likely to happen in the country." It is now up to development actors to take heed of his findings.

Eric Walcott
Managing Partner
OrgDevelopment Investments (ODI)
May 2008

PREFACE

The National Academy of Public Administration offers an opportunity for some of the finest minds in the country occasionally to congregate to discuss pressing issues of the day. In 2004, at a meeting of the Reconstruction Partnership/Fragile Nations Project, Ambassador Terence Todman, a former special envoy to Haiti for the Organization of American States and an Academy fellow, raised the question: "Why, after the expenditure of so much foreign aid in Haiti, has that country so little to show for it?" At about this time, Carlos Pascual, a former ambassador to Ukraine, then at the U.S. State Department's newly formed Office of Reconstruction and Stabilization, which is charged with developing Bush administration policy in fragile states, solicited the Academy for some advice on how to deal with the challenges posed by Haiti. (Pasqual is now the vice president for foreign policy studies at the Brookings Institution.) The Academy's Standing Panel on International Affairs asked the authors to undertake a fact-finding mission and provide some tentative answers. After visiting Haiti, talking with dozens of experts on Haiti and foreign assistance and development, and reviewing voluminous documents on aid efforts to Haiti, we arrived at the findings and conclusions presented in this volume. Some of these were known, but perhaps not too widely. Others are new and may generate considerable debate. We believe that Haiti is worth learning about, not only in its own right but as an important case in development policy. It is the Academy's hope that this book will stimulate renewed enthusiasm for inquiry into aid provision to developing countries, especially fragile ones.

This book focuses on foreign assistance to Haiti during a period spanning about two decades: from the beginning of the dictatorship of the military junta in 1987 through the Transition Government, which stepped down after parliamentary elections in February 2006 so that the democratically elected government under President René Préval could assume power in May 2006. We take a brief look at Préval's accomplishments and foreign assistance and foreign policy in his first year in office, until spring 2008. Préval's tenure already has augured well for a new era for Haiti, and is a much needed break with the past. With a new democratic start, perhaps Haitians will be able to join the world community as an exemplar of a country that goes from rags to riches. Only time will tell, as Haiti enters yet another phase in its development.

There is a Haitian saying, "beyond these mountains, more mountains," which aptly captures the Haitian experience: it seems that the Haitian people conquer one set of challenges, only to confront new ones. In their journey to attain democracy, good government, and a good life, these goals have proved ever elusive. Let us hope that now their time is near.

ACKNOWLEDGMENTS

The authors would like to thank Jenna Dorn, the president of the National Academy of Public Administration, Howard Messner and Morgan Kinghorn, former Academy presidents, Bill Gadsby, a vice president of the Academy, and Scott Belcher, a former Academy executive vice president, for their support and encouragement in undertaking this research. Terence Todman, an Academy fellow, originally ignited the Academy's interest in foreign assistance to Haiti. Ambassador Todman shared with us his experience in Haiti and his vast knowledge of numerous developing countries in which he served as ambassador. We would like to thank the following Academy fellows for their help in bringing this project to fruition: Enid Beaumont, chair of the International Standing Panel, and Ralph Widner, director of the Reconstruction Partnership/Fragile States Project, a cooperative venture with Princeton University. Our gratitude goes to Ann Marie Walsh for reviewing the manuscript. Sy Murray, chair of the African Working Group, also deserves a special thank-you for his continued efforts to ensure that issues of concern to Haiti as well as to Africa remain high priorities in the Academy. We thank Eric Walcott, an Academy associate who is an expert on Haiti, for piquing our interest in Haiti in 2005, encouraging our efforts ever since, and contributing the foreword to this volume. Fareed Hassan, then at the World Bank, provided valuable insights on aid in Haiti, many of which we have incorporated. Members of a panel on foreign aid at the International Studies Association in 2007 in Chicago—Derick Brinkerhoff, Louis Picard, Steven Hook, and Randall Newnham—offered helpful comments on the manuscript. Dan Spikes, at the State Department, and Steve Redburn, at the Office of Management and Budget, also offered valuable perspectives. Josh DeWind, at the Social Science

Research Council, was kind enough to make his study of foreign assistance to Haiti in the mid-1980s available to us and to comment on a preliminary version of this manuscript. Adam Gardner provided expert support in formatting the text, creating the graphics, and tracking down difficult-to-find references and facts. Three anonymous reviewers made significant contributions to the final manuscript. Ambassador Edward Perkins, who served with distinction in the career U.S. Foreign Service, wrote the book's afterword. No one knows more about U.S. operations in developing countries than Ambassador Perkins.

Last but definitely not least, we thank Phil Rutledge, an Academy fellow, an icon in public administration, and our longtime mentor on all issues of importance, who passed away on January 26, 2007.

The views expressed here do not represent those of the Academy as an institution, and errors of commission and omission are solely those of the authors.

HAITI

IN THE

BALANCE

1 | INTRODUCTION

Beyond these mountains, more mountains.

—Traditional Haitian saying

Why explore foreign assistance failures in Haiti? A country of 8 million people, about the size of Maryland, just 600 miles off the coast of Florida (it shares the island of Hispaniola with the Dominican Republic)—Haiti is one of several extreme cases: it has received billions in foreign assistance, yet persists as one of the poorest and worst governed countries in the world. At the same time, Haiti is of strategic importance to the United States because of its location, perpetual state of violence, and instability, its role as a base for drug trafficking, its potential as a trading partner, its strong ties to a large Haitian-American diaspora, and its relationship with the Latin American and Caribbean community. The country's troubles can potentially affect the surrounding region. Undoubtedly, the Haitian experience can inform our knowledge of foreign assistance and public-sector reform in other countries because, unhappily, Haiti is not unique among developing countries.

Haiti proudly lays claim to the distinction of being the second-oldest republic in the Western Hemisphere and the only nation whose slave population defeated a colonial power to become free, yet it is the poorest country in that very same hemisphere, and one of the poorest worldwide. This has been so for decades. In this book we explain why, after the expenditure of at least $4 billion in Haiti over the past decade—much of it in assistance to develop democracy, foster rule of law, force demilitarization, encourage free and fair elections, expand civil society, and promote public-sector reform and fight corruption—the average Haitian survives on $1 a day; is unemployed and has no prospects of a job; is unable to read, access potable water, or turn on the lights; and will die prematurely, most likely by violence. Why has Haiti throughout its history been among the worst governed and most undemocratic countries on earth?

The international donor community classifies Haiti as a "fragile state," meaning that the government cannot or will not deliver core functions to the majority of its people, especially the poor. Royal Canadian Mounted Police Chief Superintendent David Beer (Sorenson 2006, p. 1) has stated: "We must not lose sight of the fact that there may be no aspect of Haitian society that is not in crisis. Haiti may be the quintessential example of . . . a fragile state." Haiti is also a state where conflict is resolved through violence, ranging from street crime through rioting to coups d'état. Some believe that Haiti is now a "postconflict" state, meaning it is "rebuilding the socioeconomic framework of society and reconstruct[ing] the enabling conditions for a functioning peacetime society to include the framework of governance and rule of law" (Hamre and Sullivan 2002, p. 89). Others have characterized Haiti variously as a nightmare, predator, collapsed, failed, failing, parasitic, kleptocratic, phantom, virtual, or pariah state, and, under the Transition Government, an orphan democracy. In many ways, Haiti is all of these things.

Three Decades of Instability

To understand the failure of aid to help Haiti, one needs to look in part at Haiti's politics and American foreign policy over three decades. From 1957 to 1971, François ("Papa Doc") Duvalier ruled Haiti under a highly repressive dictatorship; government institutions were intentionally weakened to enable the continued power of the dictatorship. Duvalier's son, Jean-Claude ("Baby Doc"), took over on his father's death and continued many of his policies. The Haitian people, with a little help from the United States, forced Duvalier to leave Haiti in 1986. A military junta established a dictatorship in Duvalier's place. For three years, the military repressed the population. Jean-Bertrand Aristide, a former priest seemingly guided by a philosophy of "liberation theology," attacked both the military and the Duvalierists, not to mention Haiti's economic elite, capitalism, and the United States, in an effort to establish a democratic, populist government. He was duly elected president in 1990. At that time, the government was in shambles, as was the country's economy, society, and the environment.

Seven months into his term, the military overthrew Aristide, installing yet another dictatorship. The military became even more repressive than in the past and allowed the country to further sink into despair. The country suffered extreme economic, social, and environmental disaster, from which it has yet to recover. The United States, and other nations, blockaded Haiti in protest against the military dictatorship. From exile in the United States, Aristide lobbied first the Bush, then the Clinton, administration to intervene militarily to restore him to power. In 1994 Clinton did just that. Aristide had only a year left in his original term, and was replaced as president by his former prime minister, René Préval in 1996. Aristide then ran for and won another term as president from 2000 to 2005. During Aristide's second administration Haiti was steeped in violence as political factions and economic interests jockeyed for power, the country became ungovernable, and the economy all but imploded. Aristide's government was threatened by deeply entrenched economic elites and was never accepted as legitimate by these powerful opposition forces; they encouraged factions seeking power to overthrow it. In February 2004, a coalition of ex-military, neo-Duvalierists, paramilitaries, economic aristocrats, and many of Aristide's once-loyal supporters overthrew Aristide in another violent coup.

As of March 2008, Aristide remained in exile in South Africa. The new Transition Government in turn was replaced by a democratically elected government in February 2006, under President Préval, who was sworn in May 2006. During the past three decades, foreign aid from all sources has been suspended, reduced, or redirected, then restored, only to be suspended again. In 2005 and 2006 aid donors invested $1.3 billion in Haiti in an attempt to reconstruct and develop the country yet again. In 2006 and 2007 donors pledged another $750 million in assistance.

Aristide was *the* key actor in Haiti over two decades, and views on his role diverge dramatically, his supporters saying that he was a genuine democrat and warded off overwhelming reactionary forces, his detractors asserting that he was just another in a long line of undemocratic, incompetent leaders. Others say that he was simply a victim of circumstances that are or have been endemic to Haiti. Regardless of one's view of Aristide, four points are clear: First, Haiti has been virtually ungovernable since 1987 (even longer, depending on one's perspective). There was no functioning parliament or judiciary system, there was no political compromise or consensus, and there was extreme violence, perpetrated by paramilitaries, gangs, and criminal organizations. Second, the international economic blockade of Haiti all but destroyed the economy, already on its knees from decades of poor management and exploitation. Third, for better or worse, U.S. administrations suspended, reduced, or delayed U.S. foreign aid to pressure Aristide and the opposition to stop the conflict and blocked aid assistance from multilateral and bilateral donors, which would have contributed to economic and political stability. And fourth, U.S. foreign policy, influenced by powerful factions in Congress, international organizations, the Haitian diaspora, and advocacy groups—with intentions both good and bad—all effectively fostered instability in Haiti.

Policy Questions

Aid failure in Haiti will likely continue unless two things occur: Haitians have long-term success in reducing extreme poverty, curbing violence, and solving problems of governance and politics; and the international community improves foreign policy approaches to, aid policies for, and aid program management on the ground in Haiti. Several major policy questions suggest themselves:

Do extreme poverty, perpetual violence, and poor governance make Haiti a special case for reconstruction and development? Multilateral, bilateral, and charitable donor agencies all consider Haiti one of the most difficult development challenges among the least developed and most fragile and conflict-plagued countries, a group that includes Somalia, Sudan, Ethiopia, and Zimbabwe. Consequently, provision of foreign aid, difficult to deliver even in the most hospitable environments, has been severely tested in Haiti. Sadly, what went on in Haiti has been replicated all too often from time to time in other places. Haiti, although an extreme case, is not unique.

Does Haiti's dysfunctional, unstable political system—in place for 200 years—affect the country's foreign assistance prospects? Throughout its history Haiti has been one of the most politically unstable countries. Of the fifty-four elected presidents since 1806, only nine completed a full term. The rest were overthrown, were killed, or died in office. Many presidents attempted to extend their terms of office to life by imposing highly repressive authoritarian rule. This in turn led to at least a hundred revolts, coups, and uprisings, many successful. The United States has played a determining role in Haiti, dispatching the Navy or Marines dozens of times to restore order, protect Americans and their business interests, or meddle in political affairs. The United States occupied the country from 1915 to 1934. Since 1915, five presidents have been forced out of office by the United States—sometimes with the support of the Haitian people, sometimes not. Since the 1980s, the United States has manipulated Haitian governments with foreign aid and "coercive diplomacy" as leverage over Haitian affairs. Haiti has been steeped in perpetual violence, civil unrest, political instability, and tyranny, and has been unable to escape its past. Haiti's leaders have fomented violence in the streets and by the military, police, and militias to punish adversaries, create chaos, or instill fear, and thugs, gangs, and criminals have been all too willing to employ violence for their own ends. Haiti's leaders, especially among the economic elite, care more for politics and personal aggrandizement than about the people or the country. Its population has paid a terrible price—extreme poverty and loss of hope.

Haiti's political history tends to reinforce the racist notion among some that Haiti, simply, is a black republic and hence unable to govern itself. Consequently, goes this view, Haiti is the product of its own self-made destiny. But this view ignores the fact that foreign nations have meddled extensively in Haitian affairs and have not made much effort to bring Haiti into the world community, or to help the Haitian people. In fact, assistance to and intervention in Haiti have made it worse off in many respects.

How much aid has flowed to Haiti and how have donors targeted that aid? Since 1944, when the Roosevelt administration began its aid program, Haiti has relied heavily upon on-again, off-again foreign assistance from the United States and the international community. Before 1990 this assistance was meager, by today's standards. In 1980 aid was about $131 million. In 1983 the UN Development Program (UNDP) estimated that foreign assistance to Haiti was at least $167 million, and the United States Agency for International Development (USAID) placed it closer to $200 million. From 1990 to 2003, though, Haiti received more than $4 billion in foreign assistance from bilateral and multilateral sources. (In addition to that, remittances from Haitian expatriates amount to $1 billion annually.) From 2005 to 2006 foreign aid rose by another $1.3 billion or so. But how much good did the aid dollars do? For example, some of the money paid for U.S. Coast Guard interdiction of Haitian refugees, refugee support, drug trafficking curtailment, and military expenditures. These are costly, and they are not considered by many to be aid, though they have been included in the aid totals. In many cases, it remained unclear where aid was spent. Donors funded just about everything in Haiti except democratization, governance, and public sector reform, yet these were key because they determine the effectiveness of all the rest. It may be that a shortage of aid for Haiti was not the problem but how the money was spent.

How has U.S. foreign policy affected aid to Haiti? Virtually throughout the country's history, Haitian politics has tended to run afoul of U.S. foreign policy interests, even under sympathetic U.S. administrations. As a consequence, the United States has felt compelled to embargo and restrict assistance, and also to influence assistance offered by bilateral, multilateral, and to some extent charitable organizations. Haitian politics has also precipitated intransigent cleavages within the U.S. Congress, political parties, advocacy groups, ideologues on the political right and left, and Haitian expatriate communities, depending on whether they supported or criticized the official U.S. position, and this has made consensus building on Haiti all but impossible. U.S.-backed embargoes, interventions, and aid suspensions have reflected major policy swings, creating considerable instability, making development problems worse, and reducing prospects for aid effectiveness.

Why did aid to Haiti fail? In addition to development problems precipitated by the embargo, aid suspensions, and military intervention, at least four drivers within Haiti itself contributed to aid ineffectiveness: lack of government capacity generally and in aid administration specifically; lack of government support for or ownership of programs funded by foreign assistance; excessive aid dependency; and widespread dissension between president and parliament, so that Haitian governments seemed consumed by politics rather than focusing on good governance. Foreign assistance programs did not comport with governing elites' desire to acquire power and aggrandize themselves, often through undemocratic and corrupt practices. When aid flowed, Haitian governments took little interest in it and failed to support gains made. Haitian governments abdicated responsibility for meeting the needs of the people—especially the poor, who make up the vast majority of the country—by deferring to bilateral and multilateral donors and the Haitian diaspora, through remittances. Furthermore, there was no shared vision or consensus as to where the country should be headed and who should lead it.

When one looks at past provision of aid, it seems that most things that could go wrong in the provision of aid did go wrong for multilateral, bilateral, and charitable donors (for example, the Red Cross) and nongovernmental organizations (for example, the International Republican Institute). Aid shortcomings likely originated because donors collectively failed to deal with political instability and poor governance as the most important drivers of failure, from which all other negative consequences would follow. Having failed to assign highest priority to politics and governance, donors seemed to go on to adopt an assistance model more appropriate to Latin America. Such a model assumed economic, social, and political stability. In reality, Haiti was more like a least-developed, fragile, postconflict sub-Saharan African country. Haiti represented a case of some of the worst practices in aid assistance. Again, these practices were not unique to Haiti.

What can Haiti teach us about aid to fragile, postconflict nations? Donors seemed to view the aid process in component parts that lead to separate, loosely related policy and program decisions, rather than as a system where each component affects all of the rest. Donors needed to rethink democratization programs that build civil society organizations and political parties, fund elections, promote grassroots participation, support individual politicians, impose change through military intervention, and create legitimacy. Few efforts worked in Haiti because, in spite of the best intentions, they were likely done in the wrong way, at the wrong time, and in the wrong place.

Public-sector reform typically was targeted toward the civil service, anti-corruption efforts, decentralization—devolving authority, fiscal capacity and administration from national to local government—and privatization of government-owned enterprises. Donors should not have confused reconstruction of the civil service system with civil service reform. Civil service reform involves downsizing bloated bureaucracies, creating human resources policies, raising salaries, classifying workers, and the like. Civil service reconstruction involves getting the country started up again after the civil service has been decimated. Corruption is endemic in fragile states and it must be eradicated. Top leadership must put anticorruption high on the public agenda, violators must be identified, tried, and punished, and the culture that makes corruption acceptable must be changed. Decentralization was a laudable goal, but it tends to fail when undertaken during reconstruction. Local officials, like their national counterparts, lacked management capacity. Decentralization must be carefully timed. Privatization of government enterprises makes them more efficient and effective and reduces their use for patronage and pass-through funnels for public monies into corrupt hands. But in countries where there is strong suspicion about business and markets and politicians are corrupt, privatization might have to wait until support for it can be developed.

Unfortunately, democratization and public-sector reform can not be dealt with in a vacuum. They exist in a much broader arena where security, growth and development, and job creation are important preconditions for reconstructing a country. Without security, nothing positive was likely to happen in Haiti. Likewise, unless fragile countries establish the necessary structural reforms, economies cannot grow and develop. Above all, poor people need jobs. If they do not see any positive gains from democratization and foreign assistance, they will likely be manipulated by those who disingenuously promise a better life. Regional relations, especially with Haiti's neighbor, the Dominican Republic, were poor and still must be resolved.

What are the prospects for Haiti's future? In spite of past problems in Haitian governance and the donor community's inability to make a difference in Haiti, we are cautiously optimistic about Haiti's future. The Transition Government seemed somewhat more serious than earlier administrations about breaking away from Haiti's past, although fragments of dysfunctional, undemocratic practices remained under that regime. At the same time, the donor community, in partnership with the Transition Government, appeared for the most part to have recommitted itself to Haiti's reconstruction. On February 7, 2006, Haitians democratically elected a new president.

As of May 2008 President Préval has completed two years in office, and the signs are encouraging. Security has greatly improved, and violence has markedly declined. Préval is practicing the politics of moderation, trying to build compromise and consensus in the country. He has successfully extricated himself from the shadow of Aristide, a divisive figure associated with many of the current issues plaguing Haiti. The Haitian economy has made an impressive recovery in a very short period of time. And Préval has done a masterful job in foreign policy, tiptoeing over a minefield of dictatorships in Cuba and Venezuela, the Caribbean nations, the Latin American nations, and the United States, France, Canada.

The United States, which has always played the lead role in what goes on in Haiti, has managed to build support for Haiti not only within the Bush administration but also in a bipartisan way in Congress. This is an amazing turn of events, given cleavages between the president and Congress and within Congress, and it bodes well for Haiti. Congress passed a bipartisan bill, enthusiastically supported by the administration, offering generous trade preferences to Haiti.

Foreign aid, initially provided to the Transition Government, has been renewed and expanded for Préval. He has made a convincing case for aid, has continued the positive initiatives under the Transition Government, and has been busy reengineering government.

It is too early to tell whether the effectiveness of aid under Préval will improve as a result of lessons learned in the past. Only one recent (through 2006) analysis of aid provision has been completed, by the Inter-American Development Bank (2007a); it shows that aid policy and administration have not changed much.

Methodology

We grounded our analysis in a multipronged methodology. Academy researchers assembled extensive documents covering every aspect of foreign assistance to Haiti. Academy researchers also reviewed voluminous material drawn from other countries on problems, lessons learned, and best practices in providing assistance to developing, fragile, weak, failed, low-income countries under stress, and collapsed, and postconflict countries. The Haitian and international experiences were then combined. The Academy study team visited Haiti in January 2005 on a fact-finding tour as part of this project. (Ironically, we had attempted an earlier trip in February 2004 but were forced to abandon those travels because of the coup against Aristide.) We met with key stakeholders in the government at all levels, as well as representatives of multilateral and bilateral donors and charitable organizations. Eric Walcott visited Haiti again in July 2007 on a humanitarian and trade mission and in the process gathered much additional information on Préval's first year in office. We maintain contact with several leaders in Haiti. We prepared a draft of this book and had it reviewed by experts, policymakers, and practitioners in the fields of foreign assistance generally and Haiti specifically.

The Plan of the Book

In this volume we look at causes, or "drivers," of foreign assistance failure attributable both to Haitian governance problems and to poor practices of multilateral and bilateral aid donors.

First we look at Haiti's economy, society, and environment, then at the governmental system and governance as a way to set the context for aid provision (chapter 2). Haiti's economy, society, and environment gave ample evidence of how extreme poverty had become on the island. Haiti was among the worst-governed countries in the world. In chapter 3 we examine the previous 200 years of Haitian political history, pointing out that Haiti has always been poorly governed and its people exploited by political rulers and elites. Such traditions were difficult to supplant. In chapter 4 we summarize foreign assistance to Haiti from the United States, Canada, multilateral donors, and charities. Over the decade between 1998 and 2007, Haiti received about $3.5 billion in foreign assistance and $5 billion to $7 billion in remittances, not to mention billions in military interventions and drug interdictions—but had little to show for the effort. Foreign policy for Haiti has been a political football not only for the United States but also for regional organizations and multilateral and bilateral donors, as revealed in chapter 5.

Next we turn our attention to the international context (chapter 6), then extrapolate lessons learned from the Haitian experience to current thinking about aid effectiveness generally (chapter 7) and on assistance programs promoting governance and democracy (chapter 8).

The book concludes with an assessment of President Préval's first two years in office, looking first at accomplishments, then at how U.S. foreign policy has changed and how foreign assistance has been reengineered. Finally, what does all this portend for Haiti's future (chapter 9)?

2 | HAITI IN EXTREMIS

Haiti: The Silent Emergency
—United Nations Development Program, 2003

Haiti's economy, society, and environment have rendered it a basket case among nations: Haiti is the poorest country in the Western Hemisphere, and one of the poorest in the world.[1] Successive Haitian governments have been either unwilling or unable to govern or to alleviate poverty. Consequently, Haiti has been of grave concern to the international community for humanitarian reasons.

Haiti's Economy, Society, and Environment

In 1954 the novelist Graham Greene wrote: Haiti is "distressed, tropical, ramshackle, overcrowded, poor and on the brink of civil war." The facts of Haitian poverty are startling (UN–Government of Haiti 2004; see also Lundahl 1979). About three-fourths of the population lives on less than two dollars a day. More than half live in extreme poverty—on less than one dollar a day (Inter-American Development Bank 2007a). To Haitians in this predicament, this means living by, for example, acquiring a pack of cigarettes and selling them one cigarette at a time to make a dollar a day. The annual gross domestic product (GDP) per capita as of 2007 was $360 to $400, roughly equivalent to the income of Haitians in 1955, when controlling for inflation. The GDP per capita growth rate for Haiti from 1990 to 2005 averaged 0 (World Bank 2006a). In some regions in the country, the poverty rate stands at 93 percent (Inter-American Development Bank 2007a).

Gross domestic product is a measure of the wealth of an economy, and is one of the traditional ways of understanding economies over time (World

Bank 2006a, 2006b). Haiti's growth in GDP over nearly two decades—or, rather, the lack of it—reflects the effects of political instability (see figure 2-1). In 1990, the last year of the military dictatorship, GDP grew 0 percent. When Aristide was elected president in 1991, GDP growth jumped nearly 5 percent. During the second military dictatorship, 1991 to 1994, a time of international boycott when foreign aid was suspended, growth rates were actually negative; the lowest, in 1992, was –13 percent. On Aristide's restoration in 1994, growth rates sustained themselves at 3 percent to 4 percent, in large part because of an Emergency and Economic Recovery Program (EERP) imposed by the donor community through foreign assistance. Growth stood still as political problems developed under Aristide's successor, René Préval, then dropped to –1 to –2 percent when Aristide once again was president. In 2005, when Aristide was overthrown for the second time and a Transition Government took over and managed the economy, growth jumped to 3 percent. The economy is now rebounding nicely (see chapter 9).

Half of the population has no access to potable water. One-third has no sanitary facilities. Only 10 percent has electrical service. In some areas children read their school books outside under streetlights because they have no other way to do homework. Only 5 percent of Haiti's roads are in good repair. There are only 150,000 fixed telephone lines in the country to serve 8 million people— a penetration rate of 1.8 percent. Although cell phones are rapidly making landlines outmoded, Haiti lags behind other developing countries in their usage. (This is rapidly changing, however: Digicel, a mobile phone company, invested $260 million in Haiti to offer that country cell phone services in May 2006.) By 2007 more than one million Haitians had subscribed to the service. One-half of the population is less than eighteen years of age. Life expectancy is fifty-three years. Maternal mortality, at 523 deaths per 100,000 live births, is the second leading cause of death in Haiti (in first place is HIV/AIDs). More than half of the population is illiterate. Eighty percent of schools are private, and many Haitians cannot afford to attend them—and they are of dismal quality anyway. Less than one-quarter of rural children attend elementary school. In 2000 the U.S. Agency for International Development (USAID) fed a half million people daily through food aid.

Official unemployment rates range from 50 percent to 70 percent, but no one really knows how many are employed or unemployed. Some two-thirds of entrepreneurs operate outside the law (Institute for Liberty and Democracy 2006), and ninety-five percent of employment in Haiti exists in the underground economy, where workers pay no taxes, receive no employment or unemployment benefits, and engage in illegal activity. About four-fifths of people hold real estate assets without legal title. Real per capita GDP fell at an

Figure 2-1. *Growth of GDP, 1990–2005*

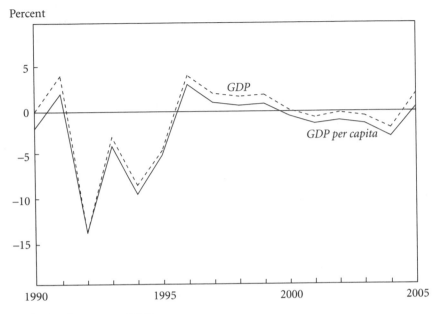

Source: Government of Haiti.

annual rate of 2 percent during the 1980s and at 2.5 percent in the 1990s. The preponderance of poor people live either in remote rural areas or in massive slums in and around Port-au-Prince. Haiti's private sector is made up mostly of subsistence farmers and microbusinesses. About 4 percent of the population owns 66 percent of the country's wealth. Some 10 percent owns nothing. A small elite organized in family groupings controls all exports and imports, tourism, construction and manufacturing (U.S. General Accounting Office 1988, p. 37). Haiti has the second largest income disparity of any country in the world (see UN Conference on Trade and Development 2006).

Only 28 percent of Haitians have access to health care, and only 3 percent have health insurance. Nongovernmental organizations (NGOs) account for 70 percent of health-care services offered in rural areas, and NGOs deliver four-fifths of public services. Haiti is the most severely affected by HIV/AIDS outside sub-Saharan Africa: 3 to 5 percent of the population has HIV/AIDS, and that percentage is rising. Only an estimated 5 to 10 percent of those with HIV/AIDS receive treatment (Franco 2005b). HIV/AIDS reduces life expectancy in Haiti by ten years; about 16,000 people died of HIV/AIDs in 2005. More recently, tuberculosis and polio have emerged as epidemics.

Women, children, and adolescents are especially vulnerable. It has been estimated by the government of Haiti and the UN Children's Fund that 90,000 to 300,000 children work as unpaid servants in homes where they have been placed by their biological parents who cannot afford to care for them. These children are often mistreated and abused. Around 2,000 children annually are victims of human trafficking, primarily to the Dominican Republic (Inter-American Development Bank 2003a, p. 2), as slave labor. Haiti is on a "watch list" established under the Trafficking Victims Protection Act of 2000 for failing to exert sufficient effort to combat trafficking (U.S. Trade Representative 2005). In 2006 the UN Children's Fund issued an alert because the plight of children was so extreme. One-third of women have been violently sexually abused, the highest percentage in the hemisphere.

Violence, especially in poor urban areas, appears to be endemic. In 2006 there were 34 homicides per 100,000 population, as compared to 22.9 per 100,000 for the whole Caribbean region.

Haiti ranks among the worst countries environmentally: 141st out of 155, according to a 2004 study by Yale University that was based on the Environmental Sustainability Index (Center for International Earth Science Information Network 2005). A follow-up study in 2005 did not show any improvement for Haiti.[2] Haiti ranks low on every aspect of environmental quality: stress on environment, human vulnerability, social and institutional capacity, global stewardship, and environmental systems. Because Haitians are forced to use wood for fuel—it is the source of 70 percent of energy used—and because of excessive wood harvesting by private companies and public mismanagement of natural resources, Haiti is now 97 percent deforested.[3] Of Haiti's thirty watersheds, twenty-five are now without natural forest cover. Deforestation leads to repeated catastrophic flooding and extensive loss of life. In two separate floods in 2004, 2,500 and 3,000 people, respectively, died, and 6,500 dwellings were destroyed. In July 2007, four people in Port-au-Prince died in flooding caused by a tropical storm.

In 2004 tropical storm Jeanne caused property damages estimated to be 3.5 percent of the country's GDP. According to the UN Development Program's Disaster Risk Index, Haiti is one of the most vulnerable of countries to natural disasters. From 1900 to 1999, Haiti experienced sixteen hurricanes, twenty-five major floods, one earthquake, and seven droughts. On average, 100 people perish every year in natural disasters in Haiti.

Haiti is still 60 percent rural, but that is rapidly changing. Each year about 75,000 people migrate from very rural areas to Port-au-Prince and other urban areas in search of jobs—which are not, however, generally available. In

---

Box 2-1. *HDI Scores, Haiti versus Other Regions, 2004*

Haiti	0.475
Average developing countries	0.694
Average least-developed	0.518
Average Latin America	0.797
Average sub-Saharan Africa	0.515
Average OECD countries	0.892

Source: United Nations (2006).

1982 only 25 percent of Haitians lived in cities, and there is still a great rift between rural people and city dwellers. Cities get the wealth and attention—Haiti's capital is known as the Republic of Port-au-Prince—whereas rural villages get virtually nothing (Inter-American Dialogue 2005). Even the Creole language shows the cultural and political disparity: *mounn andewò* means "rural," but the literal translation is "outsider." *Lita* means "state," but it literally means "bully." The only interaction the rural poor have with government is with tax collectors, soldiers, and occasional militias or rebel bands (Millett 2001). Living in Port-au-Prince does not improve the quality of life for Haitians: some 75 percent live in shanty towns—*bidonvilles*—in extreme poverty (De Soto 2000).

The UN Development Program reports annually to the international community on human development in every nation, using the UN Human Development Index (HDI) to measure life expectancy, education attainment, and standard of living. The HDI ranks Haiti as the 153rd least developed of the world's 177 countries in 2003 and 154th in 2004. Every country ranking below Haiti is in sub-Saharan Africa, and Haiti ranks at the average of all sub-Saharan African countries. No other Latin or Caribbean country is classified as "least developed." Haiti has had this low ranking for decades, as evidenced by its consistent HDI scores (1.000 is the best possible score): 1980—.451; 1985—.458; 1990—.446; 1995—.451; 2002—.463; 2003—.475; 2004—.475. By contrast, the average score for Latin America in 2004 was .797. According to one 2003 poll, 67 percent of Haitians would emigrate if they could (Dailey 2003a). A 1999 U.S. embassy poll showed that 70 percent of Haitians were thinking of leaving. Many already have: 2 million Haitians live in the United States; 75,000, in the Bahamas; and 500,000, in the Dominican Republic. An Organization for Economic Cooperation and Development (OECD) study

Figure 2-2. *U.S. Coast Guard Interdictions of Haitians, 1982–2004*

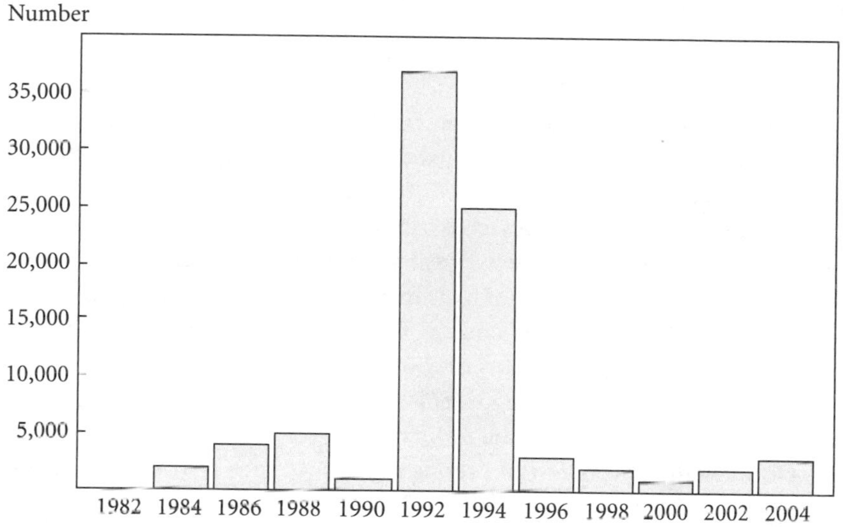

Number

Source: Wasem (2005).

found that 80 percent of Haiti's college-educated citizens live outside of the country, a figure that includes some 35 percent of Haiti's physicians.

Because of political unrest and violence in Haiti, refugees periodically attempt to flee the country, to the United States, the Dominican Republic, or other Caribbean countries.[4] In 1991 and 1992, during the military junta, the U.S. Coast Guard intercepted 41,000 Haitian "boat people" fleeing the country. In 1994 and 1995, during the restoration of Aristide, some 25,000 boat people were intercepted (see figure 2-2).

Haitians themselves have commented on the "transient" nature of their people. The historian Roger Gaillard has observed, "The bourgeoisie most of the time have in their pockets a residence visa for the United States. The middle class who have education think in terms of using it abroad. The peasant's culture tells him that when he dies, he returns to Africa" (quoted in Robinson 1993).

Governance

Haiti's system of government and the country's governance over the past twenty years have fueled political instability and severely retarded growth and development. Understanding Haiti's governance issues is essential in making sense of aid failures.

CONSTITUTIONAL GOVERNMENT

The 1987 constitution, the fundamental law of the land, is roughly modeled on those of France and the United States (Gros 1997).[5] The constitution calls for election of a president and a bicameral parliament. The president appoints a prime minister, subject to confirmation by parliament. Presidents are limited to one consecutive five-year term but are allowed a second nonconsecutive five-year term. Presidents may not dissolve parliament and cannot call "snap" elections or referenda. They cannot veto bills. They may be impeached or toppled by means of a vote of no confidence. The president controls the judiciary, with the consent of parliament, and is the titular—and often the de facto—head of the military and police. The constitution also provides for the devolution of presidential power into provincial councils. Although the form of government in theory creates a weak presidency, few presidents throughout Haitian history have let that stand in their way (discussed further in chapter 3). Hubert de Ronceray, a former Duvalierist, is reputed to have said in 1995, "Since the constitution's promulgation, it seems to have impeded good governance. The Constitution will make the President a puppet in the hands of Parliament and the provisional councils will institutionalize civil war."

According to some jaundiced observers, the only way for presidents to move an agenda forward is by winning majorities in both houses of parliament—through fraud or intimidation; by engaging in widespread corruption, patronage, and influence peddling; by ignoring the legislature and constitution; or by eliminating any opposition posing a challenge. The administrations that have ruled since the constitution's approval in 1987 appear, like previous administrations, to have engaged in all four behaviors. In Haiti, constitutions have been vehicles for enhancing the credibility of dubious regimes. Haiti has had thirty constitutions (Perito and Jocic 2008). When they become inconvenient, they are abandoned. Perhaps a Creole saying summarizes Haiti's situation best: "Constitutions are paper, but bayonets are steel."

QUALITY OF GOVERNANCE

Numerous organizations rank countries on various governance indicators. Despite the fact that ranking methodologies are problematic and hence controversial (especially for countries who do not fare well), it is notable that all ranking systems place Haiti at or near the bottom.

The World Bank biennially ranks countries against six indicators of good governance:

1. Voice (freedom of expression) and accountability: political, civil, and human rights

2. Political instability and violence: the likelihood of violent threats to, or changes in, government, including terrorism

3. Government effectiveness: competence of the bureaucracy and quality of public service delivery

4. Regulatory burden: incidence of market-unfriendly policies

5. Rule of law: quality of contract enforcement, police, and courts, including judiciary independence, and the incidence of crime

6. Control of corruption: level of abuse of public power for private gain, including petty and grand corruption and the capture of state power by elites.

As of 2006, Haiti ranked in the bottom 2 percent of all countries on absence of corruption and 6 percent on government effectiveness, slight improvements over 2004 rankings. Transparency International (TI) ranked Haiti and Bangladesh as the two most corrupt countries in the world in 2004.[6] TI listed Haiti as one of the five most corrupt in 2005; in 2006, as the fifth most corrupt nation in a field of 163, immediately behind Sudan, Guinea, Iraq, and Myanmar. An official U.S. estimate of corruption concluded that 90 percent of Haitian police superintendents were involved in drug trafficking (Robinson 2000). Despite the pervasiveness of corruption, no judge has ever been prosecuted for corruption (International Crisis Group 2007a, p. 10; International Crisis Group 2007b).

A survey by La Fondation Héritage pour Haiti, an affiliate of Transparency International, showed that the perception of corruption in Haitian society was not only widespread but also much tolerated by Haitians. Nonetheless, the Haitian business community believes that corruption is the leading constraint on economic growth and investment. According to a 2006 report from the UN Office of Drugs and Crimes, some 90 percent of entrepreneurs believed corruption had been increasing (International Crisis Group 2007b). Poor Haitian households suffer much more than better-off ones from corruption because it exacts a higher percentage of their meager disposable household income.

In 2005 and 2006 the World Bank Institute began surveying the population on its perception of corruption in the country. Ninety-one percent of households, 87 percent of enterprise managers, and 88 percent of public officials cited corruption in the public sector as a major or serious problem. Seventy percent of public officials reported that bribes were a common practice in avoiding taxes or customs duties.

Haiti fares only slightly better on the rule of law, voice and accountability, and political stability indexes than the most dysfunctional countries. Although Haiti's rankings on each indicator were somewhat worse in 2004 than in 1996, all indicators show only gradual improvement over the past eight years.

The World Bank's annual Country Policy and Institutional Assessment program for assessing a country's economic performance rated Haiti in the bottom fifth of all developing countries, where it kept company with Angola, Central African Republic, Congo, Sudan, Tajikistan, Uzbekistan, and Zimbabwe in 2004.[7] The World Economic Forum in 2002 and 2003 ranked Haiti eightieth on its growth competitiveness index and microeconomic competitiveness index (Haiti was not ranked for 2006).

The Heritage Foundation uses fifty indicators to rank the economic freedom of 161 countries. In 2006 the index showed Haiti in 147th place, ahead of Turkmenistan, Laos, Cuba, Belarus, Venezuela, Libya, Zimbabwe, Burma, Iran, Bangladesh, Guinea Bissau, Syria, Congo, and North Korea,[8] but in 2008 Haiti improved its ranking somewhat, to 138th. All Latin American and Caribbean countries except Cuba and Venezuela enjoy much more economic freedom than Haiti.

Doing business in Haiti is a challenge. According to the World Bank (2006e, p. 14, n. 20), "In Haiti, the process of business regulation is complex and unclear and customs procedures are lengthy. The World Bank's 2005 Doing Business indicators assess the transparency of transaction (Extent of Disclosure Index), the liability for self-dealing (Extent of Director Liability Index), the shareholders' ability to sue officers and directors for misconduct (Ease of Shareholder Suits Index), and the strength of investor protection. Combining these indexes, Haiti ranks 139th poorest out of 175 countries in supporting business. Haiti proves to be a particularly challenging place to open a business: on average, it takes 203 days to start a new business, compared to 73.3 in Latin America or the Caribbean and 16.6 days in the Organization for Economic Cooperation and Development (OECD) countries. It takes 683 days to register a property, compared to 77.4 days in Latin America and the Caribbean region and 31.8 days in the OECD countries. It takes five years of slowly moving through sixty-five bureaucratic steps for a private person to purchase government land (De Soto 2000). Haiti ranks low in terms of investment protection. The World Bank ranks Haiti 142 out of 175.

Technically, the international community classifies Haiti as a "fragile state"—a country where government cannot or will not deliver core functions to the majority of its people, especially the poor.[9] An advocacy organization, Fund for Peace, reporting annually in *Foreign Policy* magazine, ranks seventy-seven countries on a Failed State Index (FSI) on twelve indicators: mounting demographic pressures, massive movement of refugees, legacy of vengeance, chronic human flight, uneven economic development along ethnic or racial lines, severe economic decline, delegitimization of the state, deterioration of public services, widespread violence, security apparatus of a state within a state, rise of factionalized elites, and intervention by external actors.[10] On this index Haiti was among the most fragile, ranking tenth in 2006 and eleventh in 2007 out of the seventy-seven states, behind Côte d'Ivoire, Congo, Sudan, Iraq, Somalia, Sierra Leone, Chad, Yemen, and Liberia (the lower the number on this scale, the worse off the state is). On the Brookings Institution's "weak state index" for 2007, Haiti ranks thirteenth from the bottom on a list of 143 developing or transitional countries (Rice 2007). Using different measures, the World Bank, under its Low Income Countries Under Stress (LICUS) program, categorized Haiti as one of twenty-five LICUS countries (World Bank 2006d).

Some analysts also classified Haiti as a "postconflict" country—one recovering from civil war or rebellion—even though many observers suggest that violence, conflict, and disorder are ongoing.

Impact on Aid Effectiveness

Haiti presents aid donors with one of the most challenging environments for reconstruction and development. Even if foreign assistance had been well conceived, well financed, and well executed, it would have been difficult to realize unqualified successes in Haiti, given the magnitude of the problems to be overcome.

Haiti's political history, too, was in part responsible for creating and perpetuating poverty and for encouraging a legacy of poor public management. In chapter 3 we examine this history.

3 POLITICAL HISTORY

One ignores Haitian history at a terrible peril to contemporary
policymaking.

—Anthony Maingot, a sociologist,
speaking in 1994, Florida International University, Miami

Haiti celebrated its 200th anniversary as the Western Hemisphere's
second oldest republic in 2004 (the name derives from the original inhabi-
tants' name for the island, Ayti) (see Pierre 2005; Heinl and Heinl 2005). In
1992 Haiti celebrated the 500th anniversary of the "discovery" by Christopher
Columbus of the island of Hispaniola. Haiti is the only slave colony to gain its
independence by overthrowing a European power in armed revolt. Virtually
from its colonization by Europeans to the present day, Haiti has been plagued
by political instability, violence, tyranny, corruption, and autocracy, not to
mention foreign and internal exploitation—including slavery—of its population and, not surprisingly, extreme poverty. A small aristocratic elite has
always controlled the country or, more accurately, its political leadership,
regardless of the political regime in power. Haiti exists to fulfill the needs of
this elite—the "predatory state" (Fatton 2003). The United States, too, has
been influential in Haitian affairs for much of the twentieth century—not
necessarily for the better.

Much of Haiti's history has been continuously revised, politicized, or rein-
terpreted, and perhaps romanticized to support various political interests in
Haiti and abroad; many, regardless of their politics, hold an idealized view of
Haiti's glorious past (a similar phenomenon exists in Miami among exiled
Cubans who look upon pre-Castro Cuba as a Golden Age—*La Cuba de Ayer*).
This makes it difficult, if not futile, to attempt to separate out fact, fiction, and
myth.[1] But regardless of one's perspective, no one disagrees with the propo-
sition that Haiti has always been unstable or repressive and that this affects its

development, its relations with the United States, and its engagement with the international community and vice versa.

Depending on how one classifies them, there have been fifty-five "presidents" of Haiti since 1804, when the country gained its independence (see appendix A).[2] Of these, three were assassinated or executed, seven died in office (one by suicide), and twenty-three were overthrown by the military or paramilitary groups. Two—Henri Namphy and Jean-Bertrand Aristide—were overthrown twice. Only nine completed full presidential terms. Thirty-one held office for two years or less. In 1946 and again in 1988, a military junta ruled without a president. Nearly all presidents either were military officers or were closely affiliated with the military. Throughout Haiti's history, many presidents have attempted to become rulers for life. Every president has exploited Haiti's impoverished people and its resources, for political gain or personal aggrandizement or both. There have been very few months in its history when Haiti went without a revolt, uprisings, riots, political murders, or mass killings. During the twentieth century, the United States compelled five presidents to leave office.

Haiti's Early History: 1492 to 1915

Christopher Columbus claimed the island of Hispaniola (present-day Haiti and Dominican Republic) for Spain in 1492. The French eventually forced the Spanish to cede the island to them in 1692. France exploited Hispaniola's climate and terrain to grow sugar (and produce rum), coffee, and cotton on large plantations. For the next century, France enslaved 500,000 people of western African origin. African slaves intermarried with Spanish and French colonists, creating a mixed race whose members eventually became the mulatto social stratum, an economic force that persists and dominates in Haiti to this day.[3] From 1791 to 1803, slave armies, led by Toussaint L'Ouverture—a former slave, then an officer under the Spanish, then the French—rebelled against the French, who were assisted by Spanish and British armies, and eventually emerged victorious (see Garrigus 2006). The whole island of Haiti was an independent entity. L'Ouverture, having been betrayed, died in exile in France in solitary confinement, after he was no longer of use to France, then ruled by Napoleon. L'Ouverture is reported as saying, "In overthrowing me, you have done no more than cut the trunk of the tree of black liberty in Saint Dominique (Haiti)—it will spring back from the roots, for they are numerous and deep" (Bell 1995).[4] During this time, slave states in America, closely watching events in Haiti, tried to pass legislation prohibiting future imports of slaves, fearing that they would revolt (Thomas 1999).

General Jean-Jacques Dessalines (1804–06), a general in L'Ouverture's slave army, became free Haiti's first ruler, then declared himself emperor. Dessalines was assassinated two years later, in 1806, apparently because he expelled white settlers, oppressed mulattoes, confiscated lands, and massacred thousands (Rotberg 1988b; Bell 2007). According to some historians, Dessalines faced a dilemma: he could abandon the slave plantation economy to create a free but poor peasant society that would remain underdeveloped, or he could forcibly keep ex-slaves on the land to produce wealth, at least for a few. Dessalines chose the latter route, possibly dooming the country's future development. Alexander Petion (1807–18), and then Jean Pierre Boyer (1818–40), building on Dessalines's approach, decided that subsistence farming represented Haiti's best interest as represented by the wealthy, so while other regional economies were advancing, Haiti began to lag behind. Boyer, a free mulatto, unified Haiti during his reign but excluded blacks from power. Many believe that Haiti's first rulers wanted to exploit the people rather than help them, and this would be the case for the next 200 years.

From 1807 to 1820 a civil war raged between the northern region, dominated by blacks, and the southern region, dominated by mulattoes. When Spanish Santo Domingo became independent in 1821, Boyer invaded their portion of Hispanola and unified the island under his rule. Racial tensions have simmered under the surface ever since. In the years following the war for Haitian independence, the United States under Thomas Jefferson, other great powers of the day, and even the Vatican embargoed Haiti.[5] The U.S. embargo lasted sixty years, although there is disagreement about how strictly it was enforced and what its impacts were. In 1838 France recognized Haitian independence but exacted a payment of about $22 billion (in 2007 dollars) as compensation for French property lost, confiscated, or destroyed. Successive Haitian governments actually paid off the indemnity, which they felt was a cost of doing business (Corbett 1994). In 1844 the Dominican Republic declared its independence from Haiti. From 1806 to 1879, sixty-nine revolts took place against the Haitian government. In 1852 President Faustin Soulouque crowned himself emperor. The United States withheld recognition, ostensibly because Southern slave owners feared a similar uprising in America. The United States, during the administration of Abraham Lincoln, finally recognized Haiti in 1862, and Lincoln appointed the abolitionist Frederick Douglass as the American consul general in Port-au-Prince.

Between 1876 and 1913, the United States dispatched the Navy on fifteen separate occasions to protect Americans in Haiti.[6] Between 1908 and 1915, Haitians rose up twenty times against the government. From 1843 to 1915, there were twenty-two Haitian heads of state, most of whom were violently deposed. Much of this period was characterized by intense racial conflict between whites, mulatto elites, and blacks. At a 1904 Independence Day speech, President Rosalvo Bobo told Haitians that he was "tired of our stupidities," referring to repression of Haitians by Haitians.[7]

At one time, Haiti produced 75 percent of the world's coffee, but no more. In the nineteenth century, Haiti's public revenues derived almost entirely from indirect taxes on coffee. Some believe that as the state became the major employer through taxing labor and capital associated with coffee, the country began to move to the current state of affairs that some have dubbed the "parasitic state."

The U.S. Occupation: 1915 to 1934

In 1915, following the brutal lynching of President Guillaume Sam by the opposition, the United States began a nineteen-year occupation of Haiti, justifying its incursion with an intention to teach the Huitians democratic governance. The United States feared the possibility of German intervention in Haiti during World War I, and President Woodrow Wilson asserted global democratization as a foreign policy goal. American business interests were always paramount. The U.S. Marine Corps maintained strict order.[8] U.S. technicians centrally administered the country. Some $500,000 was transferred from the Bank of Haiti to a U.S. bank to safeguard it from the Haitians. During the occupation, presidential elections were not held: the United States appointed presidents and administrators and disbanded noncompliant parliaments. The United States converted the Haitian army into a professional force ostensibly to help maintain order. It also created a gendarmerie to maintain order, but it was really a military force controlled by the U.S. Marine Corps. The United States invested heavily in Haiti's financial infrastructure, including banking, substantially contributing to its economic development. In 1916 the United States intervened in the Dominican Republic as well, consolidating power on the island. Franklin Roosevelt, then secretary of the Navy, drafted the Haitian constitution, then imposed it on Haiti in 1917. The new constitution allowed foreign ownership of land, which had been prohibited since Haiti's independence. The Haitian legislature tried to draft an "anti-American" constitution in response, but the Wilson administration was so outraged that it forced President Sudre Dartiguevave to dissolve parliament. It was not to convene again until 1929.

Many Haitians resented the occupation, reportedly because they were conscripted to work on development projects as laborers on construction crews. Many felt excluded from their own government because the United States employed few Haitians in the country's administration. The Haitian gendarmerie also antagonized people by imposing racial segregation, press censorship, and forced labor policies. A resistance group called Cacos, whose members often acted like bandits and were only occasionally represented as "freedom fighters," sprang up to fight the Americans. A widespread peasant revolt lasted from 1919 to 1920. U.S. Marines killed Charlemagne Peralt, a leader of a peasant revolt against the occupation. Marines also killed an estimated 3,000 other rebels and peasants in various confrontations. In 1929 Haitians began rioting on a regular basis, forcing the eventual U.S. withdrawal.

The United States abruptly left Haiti in 1934 without preparing it for self-government. At the time, Roosevelt promulgated the Good Neighbor Policy for Latin America, which stated, "No state has the right to intervene in the internal or external affairs of another" (Barry 2005). A presidential commission of 1930 had criticized the American occupation as "a brusque attempt to plant democracy by drill and harrow" and went on to point out that the United States had failed to train Haitians for self-governance, or even to understand their own country's problems.[9] Earlier, in 1921, a Senate committee investigating the U.S. presence in and abuse of Haiti had complained that the administration was not in fact preparing Haiti for self-government as it had claimed in justifying the 1915 invasion. Ironically, the United States retained control of Haiti's finances until 1947, even after it pulled out. Some saw all of this as a portent for the future.

After the U.S. Occupation: 1934 to 1957

Sternio Vincent served as president from 1930 to 1941. After the U.S. withdrawal Vincent followed in his predecessors' footsteps, suppressing the press, co-opting the judiciary, and encouraging arbitrary arrest. From 1941 to 1956, three presidents were overthrown, and another served only one year. From 1956 to 1957, Haiti had four "presidents." In 1937 the dictator of the Dominican Republic, Rafael Trujillo, expanded his influence over Haiti, massacring thousands of Haitians who lived along the border. Trujillo is believed by many historians to have supported one of the many revolts against the Haitian government in this period. In 1946 a military junta brought the army to power in Haiti, something not unusual, except that it governed as a coalition, called the Military Executive Committee. During this period, Haitians approved three new or revised constitutions, in 1935, 1939, and 1946. In 1947 the United Nations Education, Social and Cultural Organization (UNESCO) conducted its first experiment in raising the standard of living in a developing nation in the provincial city of Jacmel. General Paul Magloire emerged as dictator during this period, greatly expanding state exploitation to such an extent that he was forced out in 1956 (in 1954 Magloire, decked out in full eighteenth-century military regalia, made the cover of *Time* magazine). Eight months of chaos followed.

François ("Papa Doc") Duvalier: 1957 to 1971

In 1957, following a series of military juntas, François "Papa Doc" Duvalier, a black Haitian of humble origins, was elected president in what some analysts have dubbed a relatively "free and fair" election in which there were thirteen candidates. The United States officially financed his presidential campaign, believing him to be a reformer of sorts and knowing that he had been educated at the University of Michigan Medical School. The election was reported by *Time* magazine (October 7, 1957): "Two Caribbean nations noted for their political turbulence in recent years accomplished an amazing election day reversal. On the same day, both the banana-land of Honduras and the Negro republic of Haiti went to the polls for their freest and most peaceful elections in decades. To further the coincidence, a physician with liberal notions was swept to power in each country. For Haiti, the peaceful election ended a hectic ten months of intermittent rioting and revolt during which six governments tumbled and two election attempts failed." *Time*, which referred to "mild-mannered Dr. François Duvalier," apparently was taken in, just like others. In 1963 Papa Doc, following a precedent set by the last nine dictators, extended his term of office, then declared himself president for life. The Haitian constitution was rewritten to reflect this.

In an effort to quell the perpetual threat of military coups and control civil unrest and political opposition, Duvalier created a paramilitary force, the Tontons Macoutes (Creole for "bogeyman"), to help him retain power. The group, armed by Duvalier, was essentially a praetorian guard or domestic terrorist group; it employed wanton violence—steeped in the practice of voudou—to keep the populace in line.[10] The Tontons Macoutes numbered more than 10,000, and the Haitian army only 7,000 (Rotberg 1988a). Duvalier was so fearful of the Haitian army that he resisted American pressure to modernize it. In 1958 he fired the entire general staff, replacing them with younger, black officers loyal to him personally. He created a small elite force reporting to him outside the army's chain of command. Much of the army's arms and munitions were under direct control of Duvalier. Ironically, the paramilitary elevated many poor blacks in society for the first time in the nation's history (DeWind and Kinley 1988). Papa Doc disliked the mulatto aristocracy; he exploited them whenever he could and tried to keep them out of power. Thousands of Haitians were murdered, tortured, and unjustly imprisoned. Duvalier all but closed the country to reduce outside influences against him. He continued a movement, noirism, under his regime to promote a kind of "black is beautiful" culture, returning to things African and promoting power sharing among blacks (Corbett 1994). Papa Doc expelled many French Catholic priests to try to eliminate foreign influences, an act that got him excommunicated by the Vatican. Duvalier kept his followers loyal by distributing public money, jobs, and benefits to them at the expense of the country. (Graham Greene, whose *The Comedians* is set in Haiti in the 1960s under François Duvalier's repressive regime and has the distinction of being one of the few novelists to be personally attacked by a dictator for an unflattering novel, referred to this situation as the "nightmare republic.")

Duvalier was an avowed anti-communist. In Haiti, being a member of the Communist Party was a capital offense. So the United States, at the height of the cold war, tolerated Duvalier. A key vote on an Organization of American States (OAS) resolution by Duvalier in 1962 offered U.S. policymakers an excuse to embargo Cuba. Shortly thereafter, the United States constructed a $2.8 million airport in Port-au-Prince. Military assistance flowed to Haiti to beef up the army, which Duvalier then used to support military factions loyal to him.

As the country deteriorated, especially from 1968 to 1970, Duvalier repelled three separate invasions by exiled Haitian groups. In 1970 the Haitian Coast Guard mutinied. In the late 1970s, thousands of Haitians fled the country, many ending up in the United States, the Dominican Republic, and Canada.[11] Papa Doc died in office in 1971.

Jean-Claude ("Baby Doc") Duvalier: 1971 to 1986

In 1971 a constitutional amendment allowed power to be transferred to his son, Jean-Claude Duvalier, called "Baby Doc," who was only nineteen at the time. Baby Doc appeared to institute some reforms (DeWind and Kinley 1988, p. 22), including opening up the country to more foreign investment. In so doing he gained moderate support and recognition from the international community and, importantly, foreign assistance. In 1973 *Time* magazine, in a feature story, "Haiti: New Island in the Sun," appeared elated at the accession of Jean-Claude Duvalier to the position of president-for-life. *Time* proved to be quite wrong. Foreign investment, which went to underwrite cheap labor, particularly in assembly plants, increased under Baby Doc; Haiti boasted some 60,000 textile jobs at the time. But in spite of reforms, the country was still a repressive dictatorship. The Caribbean Community (Caricom) rejected Haiti's application for membership in 1974 (but did approve provisional membership in 1998; see Tardieu 1998). Pope John Paul II visited Haiti in 1983 and embarrassed the regime by publicly calling for major reforms.[12] During this period, Haiti acquired a reputation as being the source of the HIV/AIDs epidemic, an event that discouraged foreign investment and tourism, which in turn might have adversely affected foreign aid. Epidemiological research has recently demonstrated that HIV/AIDs was transmitted from Africa to Haiti in 1969, whence it eventually reached the United States.[13] From 1984 to 1985, Haitians repeatedly rioted and demonstrated against the government. The government killed 200 peasants demonstrating for land reform. The military gunned down four schoolchildren, an event that contributed greatly to Baby Doc's downfall. Baby Doc eventually became despised by the Tontons Macoutes, in part because of his marriage into the mulatto aristocracy. (Baby Doc changed the name of the things to the National Security Volunteers in an effort to give them more credibility. They were officially disbanded on Baby Doc Duvalier's departure.) In 1986 U.S. threats and civil unrest forced Baby Doc into exile in France. The Reagan administration saw temporarily appointing a military leader to head Haiti as the best alternative: there were no other candidates who would guarantee that Haiti would remain a cold war ally (DeWind and Kinley 1988). Ironically, the Reagan administration allowed Duvalier to name his successor as president from among the members of the military junta replacing him (Gros 1997).

When Baby Doc was expelled in 1986, much of the Haitian economy crashed from widespread unrest and government in disarray, as did the government itself. In 1984 there were 60,000 assembly workers in Haiti. One year later, layoffs reduced their ranks to 40,000. Haiti's assembly plants migrated to the Dominican Republic. Government capacity to govern was never fully restored, which affected Haiti for the two following decades.

Military Junta: 1987 to 1990

The military, anxious to regain its power after the fall of Baby Doc, hastily
created a National Governing Council. Army General Henri Namphy took
over the country, ostensibly to manage the transition to an elected civilian
government to replace Baby Doc. Namphy was associated with the Tontons
Macoutes. The United States, curiously, did not object to this power grab. In
March 1987 Haiti held a referendum to approve a new constitution, in what
has been judged by many to be a free and fair vote. The constitution explicitly prohibited Duvalierists from holding office, likely fueling their resentment. The military junta held elections in 1987, but thwarted them when it
appeared they could lose control of the government; because of violence they
closed down the polls within three hours of their opening. Opposition candidates were killed and intimidated, and thirty-four voters were murdered,
which discouraged turnout. The military massacred several hundred peasants
who had been demonstrating for agrarian reform. General Namphy eventually suspended the constitution, commenting, "Constitutions are not for
Haiti" (Rotberg 1988a, p. 93). Also during this period, youthful gangs, egged
on by Catholic priests and missionaries who disdained Duvalier's association
with voudou, killed hundreds of Tontons Macoutes in revenge for their reign
of terror.[14]

In February 1988, a civilian, Leslie Manigat, in a tightly controlled election,
became a figurehead president with General Namphy holding the reigns of
power. Opposition parties, to the delight of the junta, boycotted the election.
The Manigat government repulsed four separate military coups. Manigat,
having sensed an opportunity to fill a power vacuum among military factions perpetually in revolt, tried to stop the military from supporting itself
through trafficking in drugs and smuggling. For his efforts he was deposed by
the junta in June 1988 and replaced by General Namphy (Rotberg 1988a,
1988b). In September 1988, Prosper Avril, a military officer, successfully lead
a coup against Namphy. Avril stated that his goal was to establish "an irre-
versible democracy in Haiti" and to "enter history as the one who saved his
country from anarchy and dictatorship."[15] The military then attempted a
coup against Avril in April 1989, but it failed. Avril attempted some reforms—
primarily dismissing hundreds of corrupt military officials, especially those
with ties to the Tontons Macoutes. The military was unable or unwilling to
control free-lance Duvalierist paramilitary groups and gangs who perpetrated violence in the country, apparently seeing them as useful in some cases,
or as a minor irritant. During Avril's regime, the military became even more

involved in drug trafficking to the United States as a way to enrich themselves (in 1989, 2.5 metric tons of cocaine was seized in Haiti by Haitians, despite the fact that Avril had attempted to deliver on his promise to shut down drug trafficking). The military controlled the judicial and executive branches of government, including village and provincial officials, police, prosecutors, courts, and prisons; no legislative branch existed. Avril faced extensive opposition, not only from right-wing groups but also from Communist groups supported by Cuba's Fidel Castro.

In 1990, under pressure from the George H. W. Bush administration, Avril stepped down and Supreme Court Justice Ertha Pascal-Trouillot took over the interim government, as the constitution required. A U.S. federal court ordered General Avril to pay $41 million in restitution to victims of torture under his regime.[16] When U.S. Vice President Dan Quayle visited Haiti in August 1990, he warned the military to "stand down" in any future political activities or there would be repercussions from the United States. Haiti's military was neither impressed nor persuaded to loosen its stranglehold on the country.

Jean-Bertrand Aristide's First Term: 1991

In December 1990, Jean-Bertrand Aristide, head of the Lavalas political movement, was elected president after receiving nearly 70 percent of the vote.[17] A popular Aristide campaign slogan hailed the victory as "Haiti's second independence." An aide to Aristide, though, looking back from exile in 1995, summarized this period accurately when he said, "Aristide started to become president with seventy percent of the people and wanted to forget the other thirty percent. After a while, they rebelled." Aristide was a former priest—he had been expelled from the Salesian Order for his antigovernment activities—who vigorously protested the Duvalier and military regimes, even in the face of assassination attempts. Duvalierists burned down his church. Aristide espoused the liberation theology that had become popular in some quarters in Latin America, along with anticapitalism and anti-Americanism (Aristide 1990, 1993; Gutierrez 1988). At the time, the conservative mainstream Catholic Church supported the military regime, Aristide's avowed enemies. Many hailed Aristide as the Caribbean Nelson Mandela or the Creole Vaclav Havel. Marc Bazin, the preferred candidate of the Bush administration, came in a distant second in the election.[18]

Aristide—combining a popular appeal to Haiti's poor and reaching out to the emerging black petite bourgeoisie eager to wrest control of Haiti from the

Duvalierists, the military, and the aristocracy—won in a landslide. Aristide also appealed to a variety of leftist parties and factions, many of which were staunchly anti-American. Dr. Roger Lafontant, a leader of the pro-Duvalier Tontons Macoutes and a defense minister under the junta, organized a coup to prevent Aristide from taking office, but it failed. Aristide later took revenge on Lafontant when the latter was tried in a show trial and sentenced to life in prison. Aristide took office in February 1991, with René Préval as prime minister. In the first few months of his term, Aristide concentrated on consolidating power against pro-Duvalier forces, military factions, and economic elites. When parliamentary forces began to debate a "no confidence" vote to oust him, Aristide supporters invaded the National Palace and threatened elected delegates with weapons (Falcoff 1996). By most accounts, though, violence and human rights abuses substantially subsided under Aristide. Ironically, many Haitians, contrary to the evidence, believed that violence and human rights abuses were on the rise because Aristide called on his supporters to place tires around the necks of his enemies and set them on fire, a form of killing and torture (known in South Africa as "necklacing") in which a gasoline-soaked tire is placed over the victim's shoulders and ignited. In Haiti this was known as Père Lebrun, the name of a well-known tire retailer in Port-au-Prince who used to be seen placing a tire around his neck in television ads.

Aristide appointed close associates to key cabinet and ministry government positions. Many in the opposition believed them to be unqualified. Many of those who had helped him get elected were not appointed to office, causing resentment that would later translate into political opposition. For example, Aristide fired General Herard Abraham upon taking office; Abraham was the junta general who had forced his fellow soldiers to allow free and fair elections, which were won by Aristide. Although Abraham was not behind Aristide's ouster, letting him go proved a bad decision when several months later the military overthrew the regime. Aristide also reportedly replaced newly elected local officials, judges, and police with his own loyalists (Falcoff 1996). Aristide eliminated the jobs of many "zombie" civil servants—those getting paid but not showing up for work—to reduce government costs, a decision that created much hard feelings and perhaps more opposition.

Having had so short a tenure in office, Aristide was able to accomplish few of his populist reforms. Many also believe that Aristide was consumed by an issue with the Dominican Republic's President Joaquin Balaguer, who had "repatriated" 50,000 Haitian field hands in response to insults made by Aristide. Aristide's efforts to consolidate power failed. General Raoul Cédras successfully led a military coup against Aristide's government on September 29 and 30, 1991, while Aristide was out of the country, visiting the United Nations. In fact, the coup came just two days after Aristide addressed the UN General Assembly, where, ironically, he stated that the darkest days of dictatorship in Haiti were over. On October 3, Aristide addressed the UN Security Council and pleaded for international support for his return to Haiti. A high-level delegation from the Organization of American States accompanied Aristide to Haiti to attempt to mediate a compromise but were soon expelled by the junta. As marauding soldiers killed people in the streets and openly threatened Aristide, Venezuela's President Carlos Perez sent a plane to Port-au-Prince to rescue him. In spite of claims to the contrary and numerous conspiracy theories about the Central Intelligence Agency's involvement, there is no hard evidence of which we are aware that the United States supported the coup.

Following Aristide's departure, the international community embargoed the Cédras regime. What this meant in practice for the country and its economy was that its textile and assembly plants, representing three-fourths of Haiti's exports, shut down, tax collection and expenditure control systems collapsed, and maintenance of the country's economic and social infrastructure was abandoned (World Bank 2005a).[19] The Vatican was the only state to accord the Cédras regime diplomatic recognition.

Military Junta: 1991 to 1994

The military dictatorship ushered in state-sponsored terror and right-wing death squads, reminiscent of Papa Doc's tenure. Violence during the coup internally displaced thousands of Haitians, who fled to the countryside, to the Dominican Republic, or to the United States, many as "boat people." By some estimates, as many as 4,000 people were killed, nearly all in Haiti's urban areas. The Bush administration supported Aristide in principle, but decided not to intervene militarily because of various international agreements that prohibited military incursions in sovereign states. In September 1992, Canadian Prime Minister Brian Mulroney called for a complete blockade of Haiti. The United Nations, the Organization of American States, the United States, and the international community embargoed trade with the country ruled by the junta, but to no avail—the military simply ratcheted up drug trafficking and smuggling over the Dominican Republic border (there is some disagreement about the extent of this; see U.S. General Accounting Office 1994; Ninic 2006). In any case, the embargoes were voluntary and were not particularly effective in influencing the military, but they were very effective in destroying the economy and making the lives of poor people even worse (discussed further in chapter 5). The military cared little about the people and were content enriching themselves, as they continued the tradition of the Haitian "kleptocratic state." The embargo also had the effect of expanding the black market and creating a good environment for the launch of organized and unorganized criminal gangs.

In the United States, the Clinton administration, under pressure from the Black Caucus in Congress to resolve the Haitian crisis, in turn exerted pressure on Cédras and Aristide to sign the Governors Island Accord on July 3, 1993, which provided for Aristide to return to Haiti to resume the presidency on October 20, 1993. But Cédras reneged on the agreement, resulting in contemplation of a show of force by the American Navy.[20] Senator Bob Graham, after meeting General Cédras in 1993, stated, "The difference between the military and the mass of desperately poor is so great that it was hard to believe the elite would negotiate themselves into poverty, prison, exile or death."

In October 1993, the United States Navy sent the USS *Harlan County* with 200 lightly armed troops to Port-au-Prince to assist in the transition from Cédras to Aristide, but pro-regime protesters forced the ship to withdraw, embarrassing the Clinton administration. The Clinton administration had just weathered the Somalia affair, in which U.S. peacekeeping troops were slaughtered by insurgents in the streets of Mogadishu. Ironically, Clinton's secretary of defense, Les Aspin, had opposed any intervention in Haiti, the United States having suffered a setback in Somalia shortly before (Halberstam 2001). Cédras supporters proceeded to murder or execute Aristide supporters in the streets, including Aristide's minister of justice, Guy Malary. A prominent Catholic priest who was a strong Aristide supporter was assassinated by Cédras's followers. In April 1994, Clinton appointed a former congressman, William Gray, as special adviser on Haiti. Gray successfully advocated for much stronger action against Cédras, and in May 1994, Argentina, Canada, France, the Netherlands, and the United States imposed a naval blockade of Haiti.

On September 17, 1994, former President Jimmy Carter, Senator Sam Nunn, and General Colin Powell visited Cédras and convinced him to accept a deployment of U.S. troops, rather than an invasion force as had been planned.[21] On September 18, 1994, the United States, with authorization from the UN Security Council, occupied Haiti to restore Aristide; the 20,000-strong force included troops from twenty-eight nations. (It still stands as the only instance in which the UN Security Council has authorized the use of force to restore democracy in a member state.) Cédras quickly capitulated, negotiated a peaceful departure, and went into exile in Panama.

The U.S.- and UN-sanctioned intervention, Operation Uphold Democracy, was estimated to cost $2.3 billion (Dailey 2003a, 2003b). The Clinton administration tried to build support for Aristide's reinstatement by drawing attention to drug trafficking, urban violence, and the refugee problem (Millett 2001), but polls of Americans at the time consistently showed two-thirds against intervention in Haiti (Kohut and Toth 1994). Some observers felt that the invasion would not have been necessary had Aristide allowed the Haitian prime minister, Robert Malval, appointed by Aristide and confirmed in August 1993, to work with the military junta to get them to give up power. Aristide seemed to undercut these efforts. In September 1993 Cédras had gone so far as to condemn, rather than simply ignore, the Malval government, setting the stage for outside intervention. Malval resigned in November 1994.

Aristide and Préval: 1994 to 2000

In September 1994 Aristide from New York called for a special session of parliament to be convened so that it could pass legislation allowing the coup leaders to leave Haiti. In October 1994 Aristide resumed his presidency under the protection of the 20,000-man multinational force, and the UN lifted the sanctions and embargo the next day.[22] Because the constitution limited presidents to one five-year term and because Aristide had reluctantly promised the Clinton administration that he would not extend his term, he couldn't run in the presidential election in December 1995. Many Aristide supporters agitated, sometimes violently, for an extension of his interrupted five-year term. Had Aristide not stepped down, Haitian democracy would likely have come to an end. In March 1995, during Aristide's first term, his government apparently was complicit in the assassination of a well-known critic, an event that drew international condemnation (U.S. General Accounting Office 1997a). The FBI investigated this and other assassinations but no indictments were ever issued (Aristide's government reportedly thwarted the investigation; see Dobbins 2003). Aristide surprised many observers and called into question his commitment to democratic principles when he appointed numerous ex-military and Duvalierist officials who had human rights violations and drug-trafficking and corruption charges hanging over their heads (Fauriol 2000). These appointments also fueled opposition to Aristide's cause from his own supporters.

The Haitian constitution requires that Haiti have a standing army. The United States wanted Aristide to professionalize the army, but he balked and retired the officer corps en masse. Some claim that Aristide, fearing the army, thought he would have a better chance of enforcing his political will through a corrupt police force and militant pro-Aristide gangs called Chimères (literally, "ghosts"), along with the goodwill of the people. Some claim that Aristide did not originally intend to disband the military. Apparently, Aristide intended to appoint some officers who had human rights violations pending, and the United States thwarted this. Aristide then disbanded the army (Dobbins 2003) in March 1995 (but retained the forty-two-member army band so that technically the constitutional requirement was fulfilled).

A major issue for Aristide was privatization, which he basically was against but which the Clinton administration and the International Monetary Fund wanted. The government owned not only all public utilities but also manufacturing firms and other businesses. These public organizations barely delivered services, serving mostly as pass-throughs for public money to political cronies. Additionally, a large number of workers depended on employment in these firms and resisted all reforms. The prime minister, Smarck Michel, was forced to resign when he pressed for privatization (Dobbins 2003). This won Aristide political points with poor Haitians, but cost him support with the Clinton administration and multilateral donors, especially the International Monetary Fund.

René Préval, a close associate of Aristide and a past prime minister, was duly elected president in December 1995 and took office in February 1996. Aristide held back support for Préval until two days before the election. Some historians speculate that he did this in an effort to set up his own future reelection by undermining Préval, who had become a rival. Others think he intended to express his disdain for Préval's reform policies, many of which had been mandated by multilateral donors. Only 30 percent of eligible voters turned out to vote. The Clinton administration, the Organization of American States, and the UN accepted the electoral result as valid. Many in the opposition considered this a questionable decision, but to do otherwise would have embarrassed the Clinton administration, which had just placed Aristide back in power (Dupuy 2003). Significant numbers of Haitians, including many in the opposition, believed that Aristide remained in control even though Préval had become president (see Fatton 2003). Early on in the Préval administration, Aristide and Préval were so close that they jokingly referred to themselves as the twins. Préval attempted to privatize government enterprises, downsize the civil service, and impose an austerity plan on government spending—initiatives, approved by the Haitian Senate, that were necessary to secure funding from the International Monetary Fund. But they led to demonstrations against his regime, because people feared that privatized companies would be controlled by elites and foreign interests. Aristide was against privatization and civil service reform. Préval, privately, has suggested that Aristide tried to undo or thwart his efforts, one indication that the two had grown apart.

After Préval became president, Aristide intentionally fractured the political system to weaken the opposition. In January 1997, he formed a new party, Fanmi Lavalas (Lavalas Family), drawing on elements of the Lavalas Movement, which split off from the Organisation du Peuple en Lutte (Struggling People's Party), and planned to run as its candidate in the 2000 presidential elections. At this, his supporters split even more, and some formed separate parties or factions, leading to considerable political instability. In April 1997, elections were finally held for representatives in parliament and local governments after several postponements. The opposition—now including not only neo-Duvalierists, Communists, and other opposition groups but also former Fanmi Lavalas supporters—boycotted elections, and international observers uncovered a great deal of fraud in their execution. Prime Minister Rosny Smarth resigned, stating that it was unfair and unwise to accept fraudulent electoral results that would undermine the government's legitimacy. Indeed, election shenanigans, along with Aristide's association with a forced return to power in cooperation with the United States, greatly undermined Aristide's legitimacy (Coughlin 1999). The chair of the Provisional Electoral Council (Conseil électoral provisoire), Léon Manus, was forced by Chimères to flee for his life to the United States when he tried to correct problems affecting electoral results. Makeup elections were delayed several times. The opposition took delays in holding elections as an attempt by Lavalas and Préval to smooth the way for another Aristide victory in 2000.[23]

Préval attempted to appoint a prime minister on four separate occasions, but failed when parliament refused to confirm each one. Because the April 1997 elections did not yield a working parliamentary majority, Préval began ruling by decree, installed his own cabinet, and appointed a Provisional Electoral Council, all in an effort to control the government. The lack of a legitimate parliament meant that Haiti could not borrow money from multilateral donors, or enact laws, for that matter. As evidence of how bad things had become, 80 percent of prisoners held in jail were awaiting trial, rather than serving sentences. Only occasionally was there a quorum in parliament. Opposition parties refused to cooperate, because the prime minister controlled the

Provisional Electoral Council which in turn could determine electoral outcomes by scheduling elections, certifying parties and candidates, and tabulating votes. In July 1999, Préval, seeking an end to the impasse, annulled results of the April 1997 elections and scheduled a new round of elections for May 2000. This strategy was like pouring gasoline on the fire.

In the May 2000 parliamentary and municipal elections, intended to resolve the governance problems under Préval (Erikson 2004a, 2004b), Aristide's Fanmi Lavalas won eighteen of nineteen senate seats and seventy-two of eighty-two Chamber of Deputies seats, and the vast majority of municipal offices (Dailey 2003a). Although Aristide's party had been expected to win, observers could not believe that he had won with such a wide margin. In a subsequent investigation by the Organization for American States, analysts found that the Provisional Electoral Council, controlled by Aristide's party, had manipulated electoral results. The election results were denounced by the UN secretary general, Kofi Annan, and representatives of the Organization of American States, the European Union, the Clinton administration, and the governments of Canada, Venezuela, Argentina, and Chile. The United States and other donors suspended foreign assistance to Haiti. Most observers believed that election fraud was unnecessary for Aristide: Fanmi Lavalas would have easily won in any case.[24] Certainly the international community did not want to accept fraudulent elections that gave total control of all levels of government to one political faction.

Aristide won the presidential election held in November 2000. Opposition parties boycotted the election, which meant that Aristide was able to win, even though only a small percentage of voters participated; various sources estimated voter turnout from as low as 5 percent to as high as 60 percent. On December 27, 2000, Aristide wrote to President Clinton promising to undertake major political, economic, and judicial reforms, and to hold new elections and nullify those of May 2000 (Organization of American States 2001; see Hallward 2007 for an assessment of this period). Opposition parties never accepted the election as legitimate, but the George W. Bush administration, which came to power in January 2001, accepted the reforms promised by Aristide in his letter to Clinton, and Aristide took office in February 2001. Questions surrounding the election led to a long-standing governance crisis in Haiti.

During this period drug trafficking became a major issue for the Bush administration, as Haiti greatly scaled up cocaine trans-shipments to the United States via Colombia, by as much as 5 to 15 percent, according to some estimates.[25] Haiti's deputy minister of justice, Robert Manuel, asserted,

"Drugs are the main enemy of democracy. Drug money is our main enemy" (TransAfrica Forum 1998, p. 9). In spite of U.S. concerns, the Haitian government repeatedly failed to either sign or enforce formal agreements with the United States on narcotics control and law enforcement (Stromesen and Trincellito 2003).

Aristide's Second Term: 2000 to 2004

Given the questions surrounding the November 2000 elections, many opposition factions wanted to hold new elections. Aristide's response to these demands was to unleash widespread violence and human rights abuses by police and paramilitaries on the opposition and his critics. Aristide purposefully reignited class warfare, especially against the aristocracy, whom many poor Haitians blamed for their poverty. Like his predecessors Papa Doc and Baby Doc, Aristide encouraged paramilitary groups who were loyal to him to intimidate opponents, often violently. On occasion Aristide encouraged the Chimères publicly, but mostly he abetted them by failing to condemn the violence. Unlike Papa Doc, Aristide was careful to remain at arm's length from the Chimères, who were much less organized than the Tontons Macoutes and whose behavior was perhaps more random and uncontrollable. A failed assault on the National Palace by pro-Duvalierists led to retaliation against opposition officials and supporters by Aristide paramilitaries.[26] Aristide's government did nothing to prevent partisans from firebombing radio stations and murdering journalists, which prompted international condemnation by freedom-of-the-press groups. In 2002 and 2003 the police broke up peaceful, lawful rallies by opposition parties and civil society organizations. According to the National Coalition for Haitian Rights, a corrupt police force in the service of Aristide returned to "threats, illegal and arbitrary arrests, arbitrary detention, summary executions and police brutality as everyday events" (Dailey 2003a, p. 1; Dailey 2003b). Amnesty International, America's Watch, and other human rights groups roundly criticized Aristide (Amnesty International 2005). The Aristide government failed to bring lawbreakers to justice.

In 1996 Aristide resisted transforming Fanmi Lavalas into an organized political party (Dupuy 2003; Gros 1997). Rather, he treated the organization as a loosely affiliated collection of members with allegiances to him personally. To many observers in Haiti and in the United States, Canada and France, this mirrored the behavior of previous presidents who were intent on becoming dictators. As a result of the lack of a clear party hierarchy and structure, Lavalas members formed factions as power seekers began to compete against the charismatic leader and one another. Aristide unwittingly created a situation where he lacked the support of an organized party and unwittingly at the same time sewed the seeds of a powerful, determined opposition, many of them former supporters of his. Aristide may have thought that the support of the Haitian people and of his paramilitaries were enough to sustain him in power, but he had strengthened the opposition. This opposition formed a movement called Democratic Convergence, a broad coalition of "parties" all united against Aristide. Even though some of the political parties that formed Democratic Convergence were undemocratic and of dubious intent—including neo-Duvalierists, bourgeois middle-class neoliberals and reformists, social democrats, Communists, and disenchanted Lavalists (Fatton 1995)—the opposition Aristide fostered was attractive to the Bush administration and to the government of France, both of whom were looking for an alternative to Aristide. In September 2003, Amiot Métayer, the Cannibal Army gang leader and on-again, off-again Aristide supporter, was assassinated; his brother, Buteur, avenged him by joining forces with the ex-soldier paramilitaries to overthrow Aristide in February 2004 (see box 3-1).

Most explanations for Aristide's fall rely on the interplay of a complex set of forces all aligned against him.[27] The ex-military, Tontons Macoutes, and neo-Duvalierists were against him. The Democratic Convergence saw an opportunity to take over the country. Many Chimères had become disenchanted with Aristide. The economic elite believed their privileged status was in jeopardy. The United States feared another extreme undemocratic, left-wing government and lost patience with inept attempts to interdict drug traffic. The French government, too, disliked Aristide's politics.

Questions have also been raised about the actual strength of popular support for Aristide among the poor. Even though he promised the poor a better life and in the end delivered nothing, they still supported him in large numbers. But many Aristide cronies visibly enriched themselves, rising from meager circumstances to great wealth. They became part of a new elite paralleling the old that they once opposed.[28] One union organizer commented (Coughlin 1999, p. 1) in 1999 that the U.S. invasion and restoration of Aristide had as its purpose "to preserve the old social order, impose neoliberal order, and block popular demands for the fundamental transformation of Haiti." The extensive construction of mansions just above the slums where the poor lived in Port-au-Prince cannot have improved their view of Aristide. By some estimates the rebel army that ousted Aristide consisted of only 200 insurgents, which if true is an indication of how far Aristide's popularity had fallen.[29] An October 2005 survey of Haitians found they considered Baby Doc

Box 3-1. *The Murder of Amiot "Cubain" Métayer*

Amiot Métayer is an example of a person caught up in entangled alliances between Haitian leaders. An early Aristide supporter turned "megathug" who eventually was murdered, he started out as an anti-Duvalicrist and supported Aristide in his bid to become president of Haiti. He organized demonstrations against the military dictatorship and became a major player in pro-Aristide activism in northern Haiti. After Aristide was elected president, Métayer remained in the north, continuing to support him. After Aristide's removal via military coup in 1994, Métayer set up shop in Raboteau, a small community west of Gonaïves, his hometown, which had been the site of the infamous "Raboteau Massacre" the preceding April (see box 3-2 on page 44). Métayer became the leader of the "Cannibal Army," a group of Aristide supporters who used street violence and intimidation to quash opposition forces during Aristide's second presidency in 2000. Popular support for Aristide gradually decreased, and Métayer turned to the Cannibal Army to enforce his authority. Aristide, responding to public intolerance of such behavior, had Métayer arrested and thrown in jail for arson after the Cannibal Army burned several opposition-party buildings. Métayer's supporters were outraged and ran a bulldozer into the jail to free him shortly after his imprisonment. Months followed where Métayer took to the streets, flanked by his bodyguards and now publicly criticizing Aristide and calling for his resignation. In September of 2003, his body turned up on a roadside in Gonaïves. Métayer's supporters blamed Aristide for his murder, and vicious protests began in the city, led by his brother, Buteur Métayer, who had taken control of the Cannibal Army. They drove police from the city and eventually combined forces with several military groups to force Aristide into exile in February 2004.

to be the best president since 1987; apparently, Baby Doc, in exile in France, awaits the call from his supporters to come back to Haiti.[30]

The OAS and Caricom made several attempts to resolve the crisis between Aristide and the Democratic Convergence opposition factions, but to no avail. Aristide to his credit had agreed to Democratic Convergence demands, but the Democratic Convergence nonetheless sent the process into gridlock, sensing it was possible to oust him. In January 2004, with the expiration of the parliamentary term, Aristide began ruling by decree. Growing civil unrest, followed by an armed rebellion in February 2004 that took over Gonaïves, a city in the northern half of the country (it was the home of Amiot Métayer), led to Aristide's resignation. The United States took no action to stop the coup, and neither did Canada nor France; all had apparently tired of Aristide.[31]

The Bush administration flew Aristide to exile in the Central African Republic. Préval remained in Haiti as a private citizen. Aristide later claimed that he had been kidnapped by the United States (see Robinson 2007), but there is no evidence to support this, although conspiracy theories abound even today. UN Security Council Resolution 1529 recognized Aristide's resignation and the swearing in of a new president, Supreme Court Justice Boniface Alexandre (as provided for by the constitution), to preside over the formation of a new government. Public- and private-sector damage attributed to the uprising amounted to 5.5 percent of GDP, or $100 million to $300 million. Haiti by then had become what some called a "pariah state."[32]

Transition Government: 2004 to 2006

Following Aristide's ouster a transition government was put in place. In January 2004, Caricom had tried to mediate differences among stakeholders but failed. On March 17, 2004, under the auspices of the UN Security Council, a seven-member "Council of Wise Men," including representatives from Aristide's Fanmi Lavalas, the civil opposition, and the international community, chose an interim prime minister, Gerald Latortue, to form a government. The cabinet was made up of "technocrats" representing neither Lavalas nor the Democratic Convergence. As a condition of appointment cabinet members agreed not to seek elective office. Caricom considered Aristide to be the rightful president of Haiti and declined to recognize the Transition Government (nor reject it, for that matter) even though they had worked at the margins to form it, causing strained relations between the United States and Caribbean countries. Haiti had become an orphan democracy.[33]

On February 29, 2004, the UN Security Council voted unanimously to authorize a multinational U.S.-led force to restore order and remain in Haiti for not more than three months. On April 30, 2004, a UN Stabilization Mission in Haiti, a peacekeeping operation consisting of 6,700 troops and 1,600 civilians, replaced the multinational force. The UN force, intended to provide security and stability through its military and police presence, was led by Brazil, which was not especially popular among Brazilians. In May 2004, in a show of support for Aristide, members of the Congressional Black Caucus refused to meet with Prime Minister Latortue when he visited the United States.

The Transition Government immediately began working with donors to craft a plan, called the Interim Cooperation Framework, to finance Haiti's recovery (discussed in greater detail in chapter 4). Some elements of the plan had already been developed under the Aristide government, as part of a Poverty Reduction Strategy Paper prepared for the World Bank in 2003 (Erikson 2004a, 2004b). In January 2005, the Haitian government paid off $52 million in overdue debt-service payments to the World Bank, which made it eligible for more loans and grants.

The Transition Government, having represented itself as a departure from politics as usual, nonetheless engaged in dubious practices not unlike those of its predecessors. In February and March 2004, armed gangs burned down and ransacked local prisons (not to mention other government facilities) and freed over 4,000 prisoners and returned them to the streets. The government granted amnesty to other prisoners, further adding to the chaos. Aristide supporters continued to violently agitate for his return, and in October riots broke out in support of Aristide. In a provocative act, Aristide visited Jamaica, possibly to heighten tensions in Haiti. Many believe that Aristide directed the violence from South Africa and was plotting a return, which did not occur.

The government launched an investigation of Aristide's finances and found that he had embezzled millions from the country, which he denied. In November 2005, the Transition Government filed charges against Aristide accusing him of embezzlement.[34] The Transition Government jailed pro-Aristide factions, most notably Yvon Neptune, Aristide's former prime minister, for the massacre of fifty people in St. Marc. After waiting sixteen months before being charged, Neptune went on a much-publicized hunger strike to protest his innocence.[35] Thousands of ex-soldiers in the army Aristide had disbanded now demanded "severance pay" for their service (Republic of Haiti, 2004b). Ex-soldiers, gangsters, and rebels demanded formal positions in the new government and the reconstitution of the army. Transition Government officials openly praised rebel leaders as freedom fighters, while failing to bring them to trial for human rights violations and violence associated with Aristide's ouster.[36]

The Transition Government did not have full control of the country, nor even of Port-au-Prince. In January 2005, gangs controlled upscale shopping districts such as that on Rue Pave, a stone's throw from the National Palace (Kolbe and Hutson 2006). In July 2005, UN peacekeeping troops conducted a raid on a massive slum district of 200,000 people in Cité Soleil controlled by gangs—some pro-Aristide and others not—and killed dozens.[37] In August 2005, a soccer match in a Port-au-Prince slum, "Play for Peace," sponsored by the Haitian Transition Initiative and International Organization for Migration, with U.S. Agency for International Development funding, turned into a bloodbath when hooded gangs, some of whom might have been police, attacked the crowd with machetes and killed eight people, while the UN peacekeeping force and Haitian police stood by just outside the stadium.[38] The chief of the national police, Mario Andresol, stated, "Too much blood has been spilled by police. If this country does not have an honest police force that also respects human rights, we will never reach true democracy."[39] From March 2005 to December 2005, about 1,900 people, including twenty-eight Americans, were kidnapped on the streets of Port-au-Prince (Buckley 2005a; World Bank 2006a), and about 300 homicides occurred during this period. On January 9, 2006, businesses called a general strike to protest the continuing kidnappings that have hurt commerce. Businesses attributed the kidnappings to Aristide supporters in the slums. On January 27, 2006, gangs kidnapped an eighty-four-year-old nun.[40]

To compound the political problems, some 4,500 Haitians were killed in flooding in May and September 2004. In August 2005, the Dominican Republic began rounding up thousands of Haitians and deporting them back to Haiti (Haitians in the Dominican Republic have been periodically abused or deported; discussed further in chapter 7).[41]

Presidential elections were originally scheduled for fall 2005 (see Erikson and Minson 2005 on preparations for elections), but they were postponed four times: voter ID cards were not available on time; more than 8,000 polling places had yet to be set up; candidate lists were not prepared; ballots were not available; poll workers had not been selected or trained; and violence was still all too prevalent.[42]

The real point of the process seemed to be uncertainty (the UN asked donors for an additional $16 million to offset the costs of election delays). Parties and candidates profited or were penalized unevenly when delays occurred, and voters lost interest. This led inevitably to claims of illegitimacy—something endemic to Haitian democracy.[43] The Haitian human rights organization Reseau National des Droits de l'Homme, for example, complained that the Provisional Electoral Council had "ruined the credibility of its members and displayed its inability correctly to organize elections." Amnesty International also questioned the legitimacy of the process on its website.

The elections were finally held on February 7, 2006. Sixty-seven political parties registered with the Provisional Electoral Council, of which 45 were certified. There were fifty-four candidates for president, among them former prime minister René Préval; Marc Bazin, Aristide's opponent in 1990, who had served as prime minister under the Cédras junta (June 1992 to June 1993) and then was a member of Fanmi Lavalas; and Lesli Manigat, who had served as president under the military junta from February 1988 to June 1988. Meanwhile, throughout the presidential campaign of 2005 and 2006, speculation as to whether the newly elected president would allow or encourage Aristide to return to the country raged in every quarter.

Préval: 2006 to 2008

On February 7, 2006, Haitians elected René Préval president with a turnout of 60 to 65 percent of the eligible voters. As has occurred so many times in the past, the election was marred by charges of fraud, accompanied by mass demonstrations and violence.[44]

In the first few days after the vote, election returns showed Préval winning handily with 51 percent of the vote, enough for him to be declared president outright without a runoff election. As more votes were tallied, however, Préval's percentage began to fall, eventually stabilizing below 50 percent, mandating a presidential runoff. Préval supporters took to the streets, rioting and blockading traffic. Protesters even invaded the Hotel Montana, a luxury hotel housing the Provisional Electoral Council, the UN headquarters, and the press. Although they likely terrified those staying at the hotel, jumping into the hotel swimming pool was the protesters' most audacious act. But the chaos did force the Nobel laureate Desmond Tutu to be evacuated by helicopter after he had urged for calm.

Préval claimed to be the victim of electoral fraud, which raised tensions. Ballots with Préval's name marked on them were found in a garbage heap, local polling places lost tally sheets with certified election results, and the Provisional Electoral Council allowed 85,000 blank ballots to be counted—which dropped Préval's count below 50 percent. The international community pressured other presidential contenders to drop out or transfer their votes to Préval, but they refused. Finally, with prodding from the international community, the Provisional Electoral Council apportioned blank ballots across candidates—the so-called Belgium model—and this allowed Préval to be declared the winner.[45] Jacques Bernard, the director-general of the Provisional Electoral Council, fled Haiti when opponents threatened him and ransacked his farm. Préval was duly inaugurated in May 2006. The original March 2006 inauguration had to be postponed because of problems with the elections being held at that time.

Some would have preferred it if Préval had taken the high road, allowing diplomacy to work on his behalf—which it eventually did—rather than claiming fraud and refusing to call off mob actions terrorizing the country. As

---

Box 3-2. *The Raboteau Massacre, April 18–22, 1994*

Raboteau is a small shanty town west of Gonaïves in northern Haiti. It gained a reputation in 1985 as a pro-democracy community when it was the scene of protests against "Baby Doc" Duvalier that eventually led to his downfall. When Aristide was removed from power in 1991, the citizens of Raboteau protested and condemned the Haitian military. In 1994 the military junta, bothered by the still-fierce opposition to their government in Raboteau, undertook a military operation to quell the resistance. They began assaults on April 18, chasing people through the streets and shooting at them. The major firefight took place on April 22, but it was hardly a two-sided battle. The military surrounded the small village and attacked from all sides, ransacking homes, beating residents, and eventually killing an estimated twenty people. Thousands of people were forced from their homes, and many were tortured in broad daylight. In 2000, after Aristide returned to office, many of the perpetrators of the massacre were brought to trial and convicted. Many of the defendants were tried in absentia, however, which in Haiti means that they may later request a retrial in person. This led many to decry the trials and convictions as meaningless.

---

has been true in Haiti all too often, the 2006 elections started off the new regime amid controversy, violence, and the taint of illegitimacy.[46] Haiti is clearly at yet another crossroads.[47] In an expression of confidence in Préval, the Caricom nations voted to extend Haiti full membership in the organization in June 2006.

As of May 2008, Préval is completing his first two years in office (see chapter 9 for an assessment of this pivotal period).

The Black Man's Burden—Racism

Works dealing with Haiti's history appear to be characterized by both subtle and not-so-subtle racist attitudes, beginning with Haiti's slave rebellion against the French and continuing through today.[48] In the nineteenth century, the world shunned Haiti, fearing that its example as a free country of former slaves would inspire other revolts, especially in colonies controlled by European powers and in the United States (see Fischer 2004). At one time, the fear of black rule in Haiti meant that the country could not find any printer in the world to print its currency. The best illustration of how Haitians were perceived by the outside is illustrated by the book cover for John Craige's *Black Bagdad* (1933), a memoir of his experiences during the 1915 occupation.[49] No further explanation is necessary.

Figure 3-1. *Black Bagdad's Book Jacket*

In the twentieth century, racism evolved from fear of rebellion to the idea that blacks were simply incompetent, childlike creatures who could not govern themselves. Haiti's problems—poor governance and poverty—were seen to be largely of the country's own doing and likely a result of the nature of the people. The international community had two preferred solutions: leave them alone without support or take them over as a colony or protectorate. Occasionally, columnists have debated the second alternative at length.[50] We believe that both of these views are extreme and are a throwback to a time that is no longer appropriate in the twenty-first century. Haitians need help, not a leash.

It is tempting to isolate racism to the Haiti experience, but this view of blacks was (and probably remains) quite common in some sectors of the international community. Herbert Morrison, a British Labour Party official in the 1950s, when commenting on the desirability of granting British colonies in Africa their independence, opined that it would be "like giving a child a latch-key, a bank account and a shot-gun" (Meredith 2005, p. 11). Attitudes probably have not changed very much, and such views may well play a part in debates about the effectiveness of foreign assistance.

Summing Up

Papa Doc, perhaps Haiti's most notorious tyrant, summed up governance best in 1957, shortly after taking office as president (Gingras 1967, pp. 105–06):

> Our governments never cared about the national inheritance and never attempted to stop social grievances. They talked a lot about liberty, only to fool the free world instead of using it fairly as a domestic policy. The Country is split into two groups: the exploiters—restless and foolhardy minority—monopolize the administrative power and paralyze the progress of the masses; the exploited—the great majority—[are] victims of a wrongful and cruel system.

Papa Doc managed to surpass even the low standards for governance established by previous tyrants throughout Haiti's history.

Haiti's history suggests four important themes relevant to aid effectiveness in the country.

1. Haiti has always lacked political leadership willing to deal with poverty in the country. Rather, political leadership has obsessed over pursuing political power, retribution, and personal aggrandizement. In many ways, poor people were just in the way. Economic elites do not have the interests of the country at heart. Living in a culture of corruption, they use their power over the political leadership to get tax breaks and various concessions. Without committed leadership, aid likely will not succeed. Richard Millett (2001, p. 1) describes this situation as a "nation occupied by a state," where the government's main preoccupation is extorting taxes from the poor and enriching itself.

2. Poor people in Haiti are not the problem, and should not be the targets of blame. They have nothing to do with causing the situation in that country. If any people can claim to be victims of tyranny, it is Haiti's poor. The fact is that the political system in Haiti has impoverished its people for hundreds of years. Haiti's elites and aspiring elites bear responsibility for this.

3. Haiti has been considered by many to be a dysfunctional "black republic." There is a decided element of racism toward Haiti, according to which some people believe that the country's problems are self-inflicted. Therefore, Haiti should just be left alone or recolonized. Some advocates for Haiti believe this "colors" the country's aid prospects even at present.

4. Haiti has always been a shuttlecock in a larger global diplomatic game (see chapter 5). Haiti's destiny has never been really quite its own.

4 | FOREIGN ASSISTANCE

U.S. interests in Haiti include promoting sustainable democracy and respect for human rights, stemming the flow of undocumented migrants and illegal drugs, fighting hunger and HIV/AIDS, encouraging economic development, and effective cooperation with the UN.
— U.S. Department of State, Budget Request, FY2006

Since 1944, Haiti has relied heavily upon on-again, off-again foreign assistance from the United States and the international community. Before 1990 assistance was meager, by today's standards. In 1980 aid was about $131 million. In 1983 the UN Development Program estimated foreign assistance to Haiti to be at least $167 million, and the U.S. Agency for International Development (USAID) placed it more at $200 million. From 1990 to 2003, though, Haiti received allotments of more than $4 billion in foreign assistance from bilateral and multilateral sources. The World Bank has estimated that between 1969 and 2004 Haiti received $8.3 billion in assistance in 2004 dollars (Eberstadt 2006). The level of assistance rose another $1.3 billion in 2005 and 2006, with even more to follow. Figure 4-1 shows Haitian estimates of foreign assistance from all sources over the past decade. The figure shows the precipitous decline in assistance over the decade as donors withdrew all but humanitarian assistance to Aristide's regime. Sadly, a great deal of aid allocated was never expended, or it was delayed.

USAID offered a more detailed breakdown of major foreign assistance flows, by source, for the period from 1990 through 2003 (see table 4-1).

In this chapter we provide an overview of foreign assistance investments from 1990 through 2006, the time period under study, along with projections of assistance commitments for 2007 (see table 4-2).

As is the case with most developing countries, it is complicated to calculate aid flows to Haiti. When aid is suspended it does not stop altogether. Humanitarian assistance continues, and funds to some projects already in

Figure 4-1. *External Assistance to Haiti, 1994–2005*

U.S.$ million

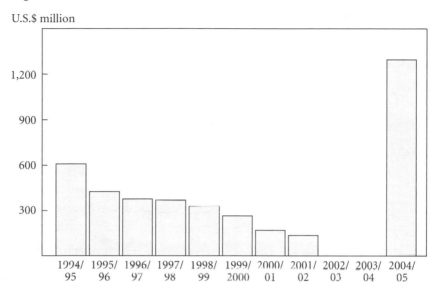

Source: Republic of Haiti (2004a), Summary Report, p. 3.

the pipeline flow as well. Further complicating accounting, aid allocated may never be spent, or it may not be spent on time, or it may simply disappear in the system without a public trace—an annoyance to ambassadors, who would like to know what is going on in the countries where they are posted. Also, different donors and agencies compute aid flows differently.[1] Some include U.S. Coast Guard refugee interdiction, refugee support, anti-drug-trafficking initiatives, disaster relief, and military assistance as aid—some or all of which are debatable. Some consider debt relief on past borrowing as aid, and others do not (see Klein and Hartford 2005). Charitable, nongovernmental, and private donations are not usually reported. Often, publicly available data on aid omit such details, making unclear what the figures really mean. So poor are these data on foreign aid, even for the U.S. government, that Senator Tom Coburn (R-Okla.) has been on a personal crusade to make the aid numbers "transparent" so that agencies can be held accountable.[2]

Our position in this analysis is that given the massive amount of aid invested in Haiti—by any tally—it is not especially useful for our purposes to spend time trying to sort out the nuances in the numbers. Rather, the question is, how effective were these contributions in assisting Haiti?

Table 4-1. *Sources of Development Assistance to Haiti, 1990–2003*
U.S.$million[a]

Donor	1990	1991	1992	1993	1994	1995	1996	1997	1998	1999	2000	2001	2002	2003
Canada	10.4	12.8	9.4	14.6	14.9	18.4	24.4	31.1	22.4	25.8	19.7	13.1	10.2	15.8
France	31.8	37.1	16.6	16.5	14.9	31.1	29.6	24.8	18.3	14.3	10.9	13.7	17.2	19.5
United States	50.0	66.0	38.0	57.0	541.0	382.0	67.0	88.0	82.9	91.7	91.0	81.1	69.9	94.7
Other nations	117.5	140.9	77.6	96.8	598.1	510.2	151.4	176.6	250.9	157.5	154.0	136.2	126.0	153.5
European Commission	10.5	12.9	12.6	10.0	13.6	85.8	67.4	42.2	47.5	35.4	11.2	15.8	15.4	10.0
Inter-American Development Bank	11.7	6.7	0.5	0.0	-15.5	67.4	36.2	44.2	56.2	49.2	26.4	0.3	3.8	25.8
World Food Program	1.7	0.6	3.3	3.7	2.1	4.6	0.2	4.0	2.8	3.4	6.1	5.0	3.6	6.0
International Development Assocation	12.0	8.0	0.2	-0.0	…	39.4	62.9	35.1	34.2	8.2	1.5	0.7	-0.1	…
Multilateral organizations	51.2	39.7	24.9	26.4	4.0	215.8	218.8	148.8	156.2	105.7	54.4	34.7	30.0	46.4
Total	168.7	180.6	102.5	123.2	602.1	726.0	370.2	325.4	407.1	263.1	208.4	170.9	156.0	199.9

Source: USAID, *Latin America and the Caribbean: Selected Economic and Social Data—2004* (www.dec.org/pdf_docs/PNADB700.pdf).
a. Total does not include transition initiative ($4.57 million), narcotics control ($17.5 million), or HIV/AIDs funding ($47.3 million).

Table 4-2. *U.S. Foreign Assistance to Haiti, Fiscal Years 1990–2007*
U.S.$ million

Fiscal year	Develop- ment assistance and children's health	Economic Support Fund	U.S. Food Program	Peace Corps	Foreign military	Inter- national military education and training	Totals
1990	40.2	1.5	16.0	0.7	0.0	0.1	58.5
1991	38.5	12.3	29.1	1.0	0.0	0.3	81.2
1992	26.6	4.5	19.6	0.3	0.0	0.0	51.0
1993	23.3	24.0	41.3	0.1	0.0	0.0	88.7
1994	26.0	36.7	42.7	0.0	0.0	0.0	105.4
1995	56.6	56.0	44.0	0.0	3.0	0.0	159.6
1996	14.1	45.3	39.2	0.5	0.0	0.2	99.3
1997	24.4	53.5	22.5	0.9	0.0	0.3	101.6
1998	0.9	65.1	34.9	1.1	0.0	0.3	102.3
1999	0.0	65.1	27.0	1.4	0.3	0.2	94.0
2000	0.0	52.5	25.1	1.4	0.0	0.3	80.0
2001	0.0	46.9	25.1	1.3	0.0	0.3	73.6
2002	0.9	30.0	23.1	1.5	0.3	0.0	55.9
2003	33.2	0.0	36.6	1.7	0.4	0.1	71.9
2004	31.7	55.0	30.5	1.4	0.3	0.2	119.1
2005	45.0	39.7	37.7	1.4	0.3	0.2	124.3
2006	49.5	47.5	36.0	0.2	0.9	0.2	134.3[a]
2007 (est.)	32.8	63.4	34.5	0.0	0.0	0.2	130.9[a]
Total	443.7	699.0	564.9	14.9	5.5	2.9	1,731.6

Source: Taft-Morales (2007a); U.S. State Department, Congressional Budget Justifications, various years. See www.state.gov/s/d/rm/rls/perfrpt.

a. Total does not include transition initiative ($4.57 million), narcotics control ($17.5 million), or HIV/AIDs funding ($47.3 million).

Contributions from the United States

The United States is, and has always been, the largest contributor of foreign assistance to Haiti. But the composition of that assistance has varied greatly, depending on U.S. foreign policy concerns, the nature of the current Haitian government, and the humanitarian needs of the Haitian people. From 1973 to 1982, the United States provided about $214 million to Haiti in food aid and economic assistance (U.S. General Accounting Office 1982, p. 5). From 1990 to 2005, the United States obligated at least $1.47 billion in assistance to Haiti under the State Department (U.S. General Accounting Office 1993).

From 2004 to March 2007, the United States contributed $640 million in assistance. Funding flowed to development assistance projects and child survival and health programs, economic support funding and food assistance. Peace Corps and military spending were minor. This portfolio is similar to aid provided to other fragile states: U.S. policymakers try to spread funding across all line items in the budget.

HUMANITARIAN AID, HIV/AIDS, AND DISASTERS

The United States has steadfastly provided humanitarian assistance to Haiti, regardless of the regime in power or U.S. interests in the country. Periodically, devastation resulting from hurricanes and natural disasters draws additional funding for Haitians as needed.

The Peace Corps was accepted in Haiti in 1983, but was expelled in 1988 and 1989 under the military junta, only to return under Aristide. In 2004 the Peace Corps reduced its presence in Haiti again because of political instability.

In 2004 the United States began pouring funding into HIV/AIDs prevention and treatment through President Bush's Emergency Plan for AIDs Relief, under the U.S. Global HIV/AIDs Initiative. That year about $13 million was allocated; in 2005, $39.4 million; and in 2006, $47 million. In FY2007–08 the United States invested $76 million in HIV/AIDS prevention, care, treatment, and reporting. Simultaneously, the Global Aid Fund invested $65 million of U.S. funds and $50 million from other donors in Haiti over the next two years.

JUDICIAL REFORMS

Until the election of President Aristide in 1990, following the collapse of the most recent in a long line of military juntas, the judicial system (the courts, police, and prisons) was controlled entirely by the military. Aristide, although not in the military, controlled the justice system much as his predecessors had done.

Donors have tried to assist the Haitians in reforming their judicial system. Its shortcomings are serious and legion. The 1987 constitution calls for an independent judiciary, yet the executive branch under both the military and Aristide has controlled the appointment of judges, budgets, training, evaluation, and removal of judges from office. The government has failed to support the investigation and prosecution of major crimes, including drug trafficking, murders and assassinations, political violence, and corruption. The system relies on outdated legal codes and time-consuming, complex procedures. Court buildings have no windows, running water, bathrooms, or electricity, not to mention legal texts, office supplies, and telephones. There are severe personnel shortages in the judicial system. Proceedings are conducted in French, yet the lion's share of the population speaks only Creole, and many who appear before the court are illiterate. Judges receive no training after graduating from law school. Many judges are not current in Haitian law. Judges are frequently intimidated by members of gangs, the military, the police, and politicians. Many thrive on bribes in a corrupt system. Communication is sparse between the courts, police, and prosecutors (National Center for State Courts 2005; U.S. General Accounting Office 2000a, 2000b; R&RS 1996).

From 1995 to 2000 the United States spent about $27 million on judicial reforms in Haiti, including courts, prisons, and police (U.S. General Accounting Office 2000a, 2000b). Since Aristide's overthrow, the United States has begun heavily investing in the system once again.

ELECTIONS

In 1995 the United States expended $18.8 million to support Haitian elections. Some $9.1 million went to a UN trust fund for technical assistance and budget support, $6 million to nongovernmental organizations, and $3.7 million to the Organization of American States, for election observers (U.S. General Accounting Office 1996b, p. 2).

In 2005, under the Transition Government, the United States spent a total of $30 million on the fall 2005 elections (which were postponed to spring 2006) for electoral administration, registration, observation, and monitoring, and for civil society and political party development (Franco 2005a, 2005b). The European Union donated $25 million, and Canada $22 million.

MILITARY AID

Haiti's army has always been a key component in the U.S. Caribbean strategy, especially as a counterbalance to Castro's Cuba. Haiti's army was not expected to be able to defeat the Cubans, or even slow them down, in the event of an attack, but rather to give the United States a reason to come to the aid of an ally perceived or stated to be under attack. From 1950 to 1977, though, the United States spent only $3.4 million on military assistance to the country. In addition to Department of State foreign assistance funding, the Department of Defense spent $1.6 billion removing the military junta from power in 1994 so that President Aristide could return to Haiti (U.S. General Accounting Office 1996a, p. 2; U.S. General Accounting Office 1996b, p. 6; U.S. General Accounting Office 1997b, p. 3;). Funds were used to support the multinational force and UN peacekeeping mission. Of this amount, $292 million went to support various subsequent UN peacekeeping operations:[3]

—UN Mission in Haiti: 1993–96

—UN Support Mission in Haiti: 1996–97

—UN Transition Mission in Haiti: 1997

—UN Civilian Police Mission in Haiti: 1997–2000 (from 1995 to 2000, the United States spent about $70 million on the Haitian National Police [U.S. General Accounting Office 2000a, 2000b])

—UN Stabilization Mission in Haiti: 2004–08

Over the first fourteen months of its deployment, donors budgeted $428 million for the UN Stabilization Mission in Haiti (MINUSTAH), of which the United States contributed $116 million (U.S. Government Accountability Office 2006, 2007b). As of March 2005, MINUSTAH had disbursed about $382 million. In 2005 and 2006 the UN budgeted $516.4 million, then in 2006 and 2007, $490.6 million.

ERADICATION OF DRUG TRAFFICKING

Haiti is reputed to be one of several major transfer points for drug trafficking to the United States and other Central American countries. U.S. policy intends to eliminate drug trafficking. This policy has met with only limited success.[4]

REFUGEES

Just in the two years 1991 and 1992, the U.S. Coast Guard incurred costs of about $24.5 million to intercept about 41,000 Haitian refugees. In 2004 the Coast Guard intercepted the most refugees since the record-setting numbers during the military junta (1991–94; see Corral 2005). Although regime change may have caused some Haitians to flee for political reasons, the vast majority fled for the same reasons they have always done so: economic reasons. In January 2007, Haitian advocates in Congress called for temporary protected status for refugees, but the bill failed.[5]

ECONOMIC ASSISTANCE

U.S. assistance flows through an Economic Support Fund and Development Assistance Fund designed to generate sustainable increased income for the poor, improve human capacity, foster inclusive democratic governance, slow environmental degradation, and encourage healthier families of desired size.[6] Other agencies also contribute: the Overseas Private Investment Corporation has offered political stability insurance and financing to U.S. companies investing in Haiti since at least 1973.

REMITTANCES

Remittances are monies sent home by Haitians living abroad, primarily in the United States and Canada.[7] An estimated 90 percent of the Haitian diaspora sends money home. Although not regarded by some as foreign assistance, remittance amounts are so significant that this source of funding must be considered in understanding Haiti's economy and the politics of aid; the amount of remittances continues to grow annually (though it must be borne in mind that Haitian financial management systems are unable to track remittance amounts reliably). The size and extent of remittances have also been related to remediation of natural disasters, such as hurricanes (see Fagen 2006). In 1999 Haiti received $720 million in remittances, amounting to about 17 percent of GDP. By 2004, remittances to Haiti were estimated to be 25 percent of GDP, or about $1 billion annually, a figure that dwarfs foreign assistance to Haiti (USAID 2005b, p. 5). In 2006 remittances rose to $1.65 billion, according to the Inter-American Development Bank (2007b).

Some donors are attempting to link remittances and foreign aid. As an example, the Pan American Development Foundation (PADF, an affiliate of the Organization of American States) worked with a USAID project, "Building Capacity of Immigrants to Serve as Development Actors in Latin America and the Caribbean," and the D.C.-based National Organization for the Advancement of Haitians.[8] The project involved working with local farm cooperatives and the Haiti chapter of PADF to develop fruit tree grafting and seedling projects. PADF also developed a business model with Unibank, an important Haitian financial services institution, which makes a financial contribution per remittance transfer from the New York City area toward select development activities. USAID–Haiti provided matching funds for a pilot project focusing on the reconstruction of rural schools in Haiti.

FINANCIAL OUTFLOWS

Although remittances and aid are a major source of revenue for Haiti, funds flow out in equally large amounts because of corruption and disinvestment (that is, moving business capital overseas). In countries such as Haiti, financial outflows as a result of corruption probably dwarf inflows of aid. Likewise, wealthy people in Haiti tend to send their money abroad to foreign banks or invest in foreign ventures and real estate to protect their assets, especially to avoid taxes.

Contributions from Canada

Since 1968 the Canadian International Development Agency (CIDA) has provided more than $700 million in assistance to Haiti. Canadians invested $27.5 million in Haiti in 2003 and 2004 alone, not counting either military expenditures or police support, which the Canadians also fund. In 2005 the Canadian Ministry of International Cooperation committed another $180 million, to be spent over the next decade in Haiti. Since 1994, Canada has concentrated on promoting human rights and providing for basic human needs, democratization, and good governance. Canada also has contributed a great deal to policing and elections.

CIDA's aid and development programming in Haiti aims to reflect the priorities of the Interim Cooperation Framework (see box 4-1). CIDA's disbursements from April 1, 2004, to March 31, 2006, were for the following projects:[9]

—Political governance and national dialogue: security, justice, policing and disarmament, penitentiaries and human rights, the electoral process, and national dialogue ($45 million, including $30 million for the elections)

—Economic governance: institutional capacity building and local development ($12 million)

—Economic recovery: electric power, rapid job creation and microfinance, and environmental protection and renewal ($9 million)

—Access to basic services: water and sanitation, health and nutrition, and education ($74 million)

Canada also contributed to the re-engagement of certain international financial institutions by paying a portion of Haiti's arrears to the World Bank, Haiti's membership cost to the Caribbean Development Bank, and a portion of Haiti's debt to the Inter-American Development Bank (these initiatives cost $37 million). Finally, Canada supported MINUSTAH through the deployment of 100 police officers ($20 million).

Other Bilateral Donors

In 2001 and 2002 top bilateral donors to Haiti included France, $16 million; Japan, $9 million; Netherlands, $4 million; and Germany, $4 million. Taiwan also has supported Haiti in the past few years with modest amounts of aid.

Multilateral Donors

The World Bank, Inter-American Development Bank, UN Development Program, and European Community all are active in financing development in Haiti.

Box 4-1. *Updated Interim Cooperation Framework (ICF)*

The Haitian government's main development priorities are detailed in the Updated Interim Cooperation Framework Document presented at the July 25, 2006, Donors' Conference hosted by the Haitian government in Port-au-Prince: to rebuild the state while creating and distributing wealth through private investment, mainly in the agriculture and tourism sectors. This program represents a continuation of the strategic objectives of the 2004 ICF, with an increased emphasis on a national development approach including all of Haiti's departments and communes and interventions aimed at meeting pressing social and economic needs in disadvantaged and conflict-prone areas. Also, based on the lessons learned in the implementation of the 2004 ICF, the government emphasized the importance of aid harmonization according to the principles of the 2005 Paris Declaration on aid harmonization, in particular the alignment of international aid with the country's priorities.

The government's program as detailed in the 2006 updated ICF is organized around four main pillars:

1. Strengthening political governance and promoting dialogue and reconciliation
2. Improving economic governance and modernizing the State, both at the central and at the decentralized levels
3. Promoting economic growth
4. Improving access to quality basic services, particularly for the most vulnerable groups

For the period June 2006 to September 2007, the total financing requirement identified by the government was US$1.8 billion, of which more than two thirds are already covered by both domestic and external funding, leaving a gap of US$544 million.

This program received strong endorsement from the donor community and representatives from the Haitian society, including the parliament. More than thirty delegations from international organizations and foreign governments attended, as well as a large representation from the parliament. The conference was broadcast in its entirety on the national radio and TV and was open to the media. At the conference, the donors pledged about US$750 million for the period July 2006 to September 2007 (in excess of the requested financing of US$544 million), to support the implementation of the government's updated ICF.

Source: See www.imf.org/external/np/dm/2006/072506.htm.

WORLD BANK

The World Bank is a major provider of assistance to Haiti. In 1953 Haiti became a member of the World Bank and thus able to take advantage of the bank's IBRD (International Bank for Reconstruction and Development) loan programs for middle-income and marginally creditworthy countries. In 1956 the World Bank lent Haiti $2.6 million for highway maintenance. In 1961 Haiti joined the International Development Association (IDA), which issues interest-free credit, and received $400,000 for highway improvements. From 1970 to 1991, IDA lent $452.6 million to Haiti for infrastructure projects. From 1987 to 1991, IDA lent $142 million for infrastructure, fiscal and trade reform, and health care. Aid was suspended from 1991 to 1994, but after Aristide's return, IDA lent $174 million between 1994 and 1997. The World Bank opened its first office in Port-au-Prince in 1997. In 2001 all IDA loans were suspended, and the country office closed, not to be reopened until February 2004, on Aristide's departure. In 2003, after an evaluation of its investments, the bank approved $2.5 million investment from its Post-Conflict Fund for health and another $1 million grant for Community Driven Development (CDD). In 2005 IDA allocated $150 million to Haiti.

The CDD project builds upon a pilot project, executed in 2004 by the Pan-American Development Foundation and financed by the World Bank's Post-Conflict Fund. The project seeks to improve basic economic, social, and infrastructure services while building social inclusion, participation, transparency, trust, and public-private partnerships at the local level. The project transfers $38 million in funding to local community organizations to improve their access to basic social and economic infrastructure and income-generating activities such as the following:[10]

—*Community Subproject Funds, Management, and Support.* This component will finance approximately 1,300 small-scale investments in fifty-five to sixty-five targeted municipalities of rural and suburban Haiti. The investments are identified by community organizations and prioritized in project development councils.

—*Capacity Building and Technical Assistance.* This component will finance the training of trainers in basic management, administration, accounting and financial management, and will facilitate the sharing of experiences and knowledge between municipal and regional representatives and local councils.

—*Project Administration, Supervision, Monitoring, and Evaluation.* This component will finance incremental costs associated with project implementation and operate under the oversight of the Ministry of Planning and External Cooperation.

The World Bank summarized its current commitments to Haiti (World Bank 2006e, p. 3):

> The IDA envelope for FY2007 totals $68 million. The IDA envelope for FY2007 includes a rural water and sanitation project ($5 million), a Development Policy Grant (DPG) to support the second phase of the Government's economic governance reform program (Economic Governance Reform Operation, EGRO 11, $23 million), a $25 million project supporting the implementation of the Education for All (EFA) initiative in Haiti, and a $9 million Catastrophic Risk Insurance Project. An Electricity Loss Reduction Project was delivered in early FY2007 by using IDA allocations carried over from FY2006. For FY2008, Haiti's IDA allocation will be structured in line with performance, as per the usual performance-based allocation process of IDA. Actual allocations will depend on: (1) the country's performance in the *Country Policy and Institutional Assessment* (CPIA); (2) its performance relative to that of other IDA countries; (3) the amount of overall resources available to IDA; (4) changes in the list of active IDA-eligible countries; and (5) the terms of financial assistance provided. On a preliminary basis, Haiti could be eligible for additional $12.9 million at today's rate in IDA funds, which could be used to scale up LICUS/Post Conflict–funded operations with IDA resources with a focus on urban slum areas.

INTER-AMERICAN DEVELOPMENT BANK

From 1961 to 2004, the Inter-American Development Bank (IADB) made fifty loans totaling $984.3 million to Haiti, and disbursements during the period totaled $661 million. Since 1994, IADB has invested mostly in poverty reduction, private sector development, and strengthening government. In 1997 IADB made only one loan; in 1998 it made three. In 2000 Haiti's parliament ratified four large projects worth $146.5 million, but disbursements were suspended in 2001. In 2004 IADB approved no new loans to Haiti. In 2005 IADB allocated $260 million.

CARICOM

In July 2006, the Caribbean Development Bank contributed $17 million toward Haiti's social and economic recovery, in keeping with Caricom's commitment to assisting Haiti in its reconstruction.

UNITED NATIONS

Virtually the entire UN system was represented in Haiti. Since Aristide's return in 1994, the UN has invested $128 million in the country. The UN Development Program has been the largest UN donor, at $54 million.

EUROPEAN COMMISSION

The objective of European policy is to reinforce the democratic process and good governance in order to meet necessary conditions for economic development and reduction of poverty. To achieve this objective, cooperative programs focus on reinforcement of rule of law, human and social development, and economic environment. The European Commission maintains its presence in the country, while working toward a solution of the political crisis, through programs oriented directly to the Haitian population, civil society, private sector, and process of democratization and reinforcement of the rule of law. Under the Interim Cooperative Framework, the European Commission pledged $325 million in assistance to Haiti.[11]

Charitable and Nongovernmental Organizations

Tracking charitable contributions to Haiti is difficult, as it is elsewhere. NGOs do not report amounts expended, nor are "in-kind" contributions reported as cash equivalents. USAID has estimated that from 1981 to 1983, some 300 nongovernmental organizations annually contributed about $65 million to Haiti (U.S. General Accounting Office 1985). Many more NGOs are now in place, although no accurate count seems available. The latest figures are that upon Aristide's restoration, the UN Development Program estimated that charitable organizations contributed $3 million, $8.5 million, and $7.8 million in assistance for 1995, 1996, and 1997, respectively. In April 2004, the International Committee of the Red Cross (ICRC) called on donors to contribute $3.5 million to support emergency medical care. The ICRC has about 40 health care workers in Haiti. Worldwide, charitable contributions run about 11 percent of total aid provided; this seems a reasonable approximation for the percentage in Haiti.

Three projects illustrate the work of charities and NGOs.

PAN AMERICAN DEVELOPMENT FUND

In two local communities along the Haitian side of the border with the Dominican Republic, PADF is implementing a World Bank–funded pilot program, adapted from a Brazilian model, that provides small grants through democratically elected community councils for small infrastructure, social, and productive projects.[12] The local councils were formed to choose, prioritize, and monitor projects proposed and managed by the community. In 2004 over 100 community associations received training in project design and implementation, and some forty-four productive, infrastructure, and social activities were selected that benefited close to 40,000 people and empowered local residents. Projects included the rehabilitation of irrigation and potable water systems, road and bridge repair, grain mill installation, fishing fleet improvement, fruit and produce transformation and marketing, small loans, and municipal clean-up. This program promotes decentralized governance and strengthens local civil society—building blocks of a budding democracy. The pilot program's success has led the Haitian government to make plans to expand the program throughout the country over the coming years.

In 2004 PADF began an important new initiative along the Haiti–Dominican Republic border designed to bolster ties between the two countries and improve living conditions on both sides of this traditional conflict zone. Through a five-year USAID grant, the Frontyè Nou–Nuestra Frontera ("Our Border") program is building institutional capacities of 110 Haitian and Dominican nongovernmental organizations to deliver vital community services in health, education, human rights, agriculture, natural resource management, women's development, and disaster assistance. An initial round of small community grants was awarded to support computer literacy through the construction of cybercafés; expand local fishing, beekeeping, and 4-H goat-raising associations; strengthen cross-border disaster assistance capabilities of local Red Cross chapters; and provide language training for national park guides hosting the first binational eco-fair. Organizational strengthening includes training in finance, administration, leadership, strategic planning, fund-raising, project design, monitoring and evaluation, and technical skills in the targeted sectors. The Our Border program has also created a virtual computer network, sponsored bi-national workshops on issues such as HIV/AIDS, human rights, and trafficking in children, and conducted studies on attitudes and perceptions of border residents. Longer-term regional goals include tapping planning skills possessed by network members, identifying common strategic goals, strengthening links to public- and private-sector planning efforts, and building a sense of common purpose within and across sectors, communities, and borders. An ultimate goal of the Our Border program is to facilitate adoption of broader strategic plans for the frontier area that will attract further investments to promote the region's social and economic development.[13]

CARE

The humanitarian organization CARE began working in Haiti in 1954 to provide relief assistance after Hurricane Hazel. CARE shifted to development programming in 1959, with a focus on maternal and child nutrition. In 1966 CARE launched community development activities in the country's impoverished Northwest region. In the 1970s, CARE broadened its focus to include health care for preschool children, safe drinking water, and income-generating activities. By the 1980s CARE's programming in Haiti included agriculture and natural resources, preschool education, water and sanitation, primary health care, and small enterprise projects. Following the coup d'état in 1991 and subsequent embargo, CARE concentrated on humanitarian feeding and rehabilitation projects. Today CARE's work in Haiti reflects an integrated approach, with projects in HIV/AIDS, reproductive health, maternal and child health, education, food security, and water and sanitation.[14]

THE INTERIM POVERTY REDUCTION STRATEGY PAPER AND THE INTERIM COOPERATION FRAMEWORK

Since 1986, successive Haitian governments have made it a major priority to declare war on poverty (Inter-American Development Bank 2007a). In 2000 Haiti under Aristide participated in the UN Millennium Development Goal program, whereby countries set antipoverty targets they wish to attain. Haiti had attained none of its goals as of 2007, and may have even lapsed on some. In 2003 Aristide's government participated in the Integrated Program to Respond to the Urgent Needs of Vulnerable Communities and Populations (PIR), a UN program to assist nations in implementing targeted responses to poverty reduction. In Haiti PIR came to naught.

Also in 2003, the Haitian government began preparation of its Interim Poverty Reduction Strategy Paper (I-PRSP), an innocuous sounding document that will serve as the blueprint for reducing poverty and for securing funding from the World Bank and other bilateral and multilateral donors. The I-PRSP methodology requires extensive production of needs data, consultation with and participation by wide segments of society, and considerable planning and management. I-PRSP failed when Aristide's government fell in 2003 and 2004 (Inter-American Development Bank 2007a). Key groups in society boycotted the planning process as a protest against Aristide's politics. Groups that did participate were ignored or were just provided information about the process. Too many groups were invited to participate, which bogged down the process. There was no sense of proper roles for various groups, nor was there a vision to guide their work. Required data were never produced. Management of the entire process was faulty.

In 2004 the international community and the Haitian government embarked on a new partnership to address the country's urgent and medium-term needs. In May and June 2004, the Transition Government, with assistance from the international community, national and international experts, and civil society organizations, prepared a needs assessment, the Interim Cooperation Framework (see UN Economic and Social Council 2006a, 2006b).[15] The ICF identified priority interventions and related financing needs to support the country's economic, social, and political recovery over the next two years. The Transition Government presented results of the ICF to the International Donors Conference on Haiti on July 19 and 20, 2004. The four institutions coordinating the international community's support of Haiti—the World Bank, the Inter-American Development Bank, the UN, and the European Commission—hosted the conference. (Caricom, having refused to recognize the Transition Government, played only a minor role in ICF.) The ICF plan noted, "The quality of the debates and the enthusiasm demonstrated at the presentation of the ICF, as well as its acceptance by most of the sectors and the open voicing of different perspectives by other, indicate that we are on the right track and a new era has begun in Haiti."[16]

The ICF needs assessment estimated that over the next two years—that is, in 2005 and 2006—Haiti would require at least $1.3 billion to meet its social, political, and economic needs. Existing commitments of funding of $440 million would be supplemented with an additional $924 million from donors. As of July 2005, ICF had dispersed approximately $500 million. Donor expenses for the 2006 elections were $76 million, with an estimated $16 million additional funding to cover delays.

In 2005 the Transition Government revisited the I-PRSP in recognition of its importance in securing aid for Haiti, especially in obtaining funds from the Poverty Reduction and Growth Facility (PRGF) program and the IMF's low-interest lending program, and qualifying for the Highly Indebted Poor Country (HIPC) program of the International Monetary Fund and World Bank intended to reduce the debt burden of poor countries (IMF 2006b). The Transition Government presented the I-PRSP (IMF 2006b, p. 8) to the Préval government in March 2006. The strategy included the following directives:

—Give priority to investment projects with social and human benefits.

—Ensure that programs are distributed equitably among regions.

Table 4-3. *Haiti: Donor Pledges, 2006–07*
U.S.$million

Donor support[a]	707.3
Bilateral	390.7
Canada	107.2
France	28.8
United States	192.5
Spain	25.3
Other	37.0
Multilateral[b]	316.6
European Union	58.1
International Development Bank	150.0
World Bank	61.0
International Monetary Fund	23.0
Other	24.5

Source: International Monetary Fund (2006b), p. 31.
a. Excluding humanitarian relief and financing of the United Nations contingent in Haiti.
b. Pledged at the July 2006 donor conference in Port-au-Prince.

—Set clear and realistic objectives that take into account available resources and the capacity to absorb foreign assistance.

—Insist on the accountability of various participants whose performance will be evaluated against pre-established indicators.

—Establish an effective partnership with grassroots organizations, the private sector, and the international community.

—Ensure consistency and coordination of programs, especially among NGOs and international financing agencies.

The I-PRSP deals with most of the major drivers of failure of foreign assistance provision to help Haiti in the past (discussed in more detail in chapter 6). Now it remains to be seen whether new aid flowing from this new strategy will be an improvement.

In July 2006 the strategy was presented to the International Conference on the Economic and Social Development of Haiti in Port-au-Prince. Haitians requested aid for the period July 2006 to September 2007. Donors pledged $707.3 million in new funding for Haiti, $316.6 million from multilateral organizations and $390.7 on a bilateral basis. The United States pledged the largest amount, $192.5 million (table 4-3). Haitians also produced a budget for FY2007 and 2008. The final PRSP was due in July 2007, to be implemented starting in October 2007.

Figure 4-2. *Haiti: Value of Loans and Disbursements, 1998–2007*

U.S.$ million

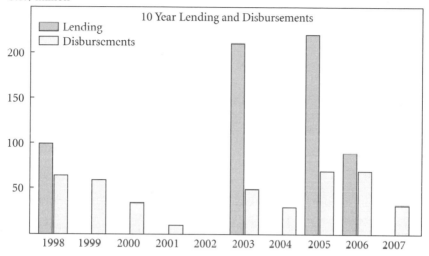

Source: Ministry of Finance, Republic of Haiti.

Capacity to Spend Aid

Although large amounts of aid have always flowed to Haiti, albeit in fits and starts, substantial amounts of money have never been dispersed or have not been spent in a timely fashion (see figure 4-2). In evaluating its lending experience in Haiti through 2006, the IADB decried the inability of a succession of Haitian governments to actually use the money made available to them. Since the IADB's creation, in 1959, Haiti has been eligible for loans and it has received over $1 billion in loans, but over this entire period Haiti has been unable to use its IADB funding (Inter-American Development Bank 2007a, p. 11):

> Haiti was allocated $205 million for 1990–93, but given the embargo to the military authorities only 33% was used. During 1994–97 $314 million out of $544 million (58%) was approved, and during 1998–99 only 60% of the approved $161 million was utilized. During 2000-2001 Haiti did not use any of the $281 million that was allocated, which led to a reallocation of 25% of that amount to other countries. For the period 2002-2003, $177 million was allocated, $200 million was used and $116 million was carried over to 2004.

Table 4-4. *Haiti's External Debt at the End of 2005*
Units as indicated

	US$ million	Percentage of total
Total	1,336.3	100.0
Multilateral	1,097.8	82.2
International Development Bank	507.1	37.9
International Development Bank	533.9	40.0
Group		4.2
Bilateral	238.5	17.9

Source: International Monetary Fund (2006b), p. 20 (Haitian Authorities and Staff Estimates).

Haiti's Debts

In the past several years, many advocates—prominent among them the rock star Bono—have called for forgiving the debt of extremely poor countries, arguing that they could never succeed economically if perpetually saddled with loan repayments.

In 2003 Haiti cleared its debt payments, paying $30.9 million it owed to the Inter-American Development Bank; in 2004, $1 million to the International Fund for Agricultural Development; and in 2005, $52.3 million to the World Bank's International Development Association program. This allowed Haiti to borrow again.

At the end of 2005 Haiti had a $1.3 billion debt, of which $1.1 billion was owed to multilaterals, primarily the IADB and World Bank, and $239 million to individual nations, mostly debts held by Italy, France, and Spain (see table 4-4).

In 2007 Haiti became eligible for HIPC (Highly Indebted Poor Country) funds. In November 2006, the International Monetary Fund determined that Haiti would qualify for debt relief.[17] Under the HIPC arrangement, Haiti will receive debt relief from creditors and be eligible to participate in the Multilateral Debt Relief Initiative (MDRI), a program in which 100 percent of debt is canceled by IDA and the IMF once countries qualify for enhanced HIPC status. Some features of Haiti's debt profile as of 2006 (International Monetary Fund 2006a, 2006b):

—Haiti's public and publicly guaranteed external debt was estimated at $1.3 billion as of September 2005.

—Debt relief under the enhanced HIPC Initiative will be approximately $140.3 million in net present value (NPV) terms, equivalent to a 15.1 percent reduction of its debt after traditional debt relief mechanisms. Over time, this will reduce Haiti's debt service payments by about $212.9 million annually.

—IDA's share of enhanced HIPC assistance to Haiti amounts to $52.8 million in NPV terms, including $33.1 million already provided through an arrears clearance operation undertaken in early 2005. Immediately following the approval of the decision point by the boards of IDA and the IMF, IDA will begin to provide the remaining assistance ($19.7 million). The IMF will provide assistance of $3.1 million in NPV terms. Under the enhanced HIPC Initiative's burden-sharing approach, other creditors of Haiti will provide the remainder of the initiative's debt relief.

—MDRI debt relief from IDA could amount to $243.3 million in NPV terms or approximately $464.4 million over time, assuming that Haiti reaches its completion point by the end of September 2008. Haiti is not expected to have any IMF debt eligible for MDRI relief.

Implications of Haiti's Financial Profile for Aid Effectiveness

By most standards, donors have given Haiti lots of financial aid. The figures are even more astonishing when one considers that for large portions of the period from 1990 to 2007, donors suspended, delayed, reduced, or reprogrammed aid, and the Haitian government was unable to absorb and spend some aid that was available. So to understand the actual situation vis-a-vis aid to Haiti, it is misleading to look just at the total amount of aid contributed and on this basis to assess whether this amount was insufficient to address Haiti's problems, or was excessive. Rather, one must examine the exact flow and suspension of aid and what aid actually funded, as well as the implications of allocated aid not disbursed. We contend that it is unlikely that any amount spent would have yielded better results. Chapter 5 lays out this case in the foreign policy context. In chapter 7 we argue that fragile states deserve debt relief because in many instances they failed to achieve their aims because they were following the advice or dictates of the donors who controlled the purse strings.

5

FOREIGN AID AND FOREIGN POLICY

Aid policy is . . . a sophisticated instrument of control.
—Stephen Weisman, "Rice to Group Foreign Aid in One Office
in State Department," *New York Times,* January 19, 2006

Haiti is strategically important to the United States. Lying just 600 miles off the U.S. coast, and a stone's throw from Cuba, Haiti must remain a viable, stable, and strategic partner of the United States in the Caribbean. Its location as a drug transfer point for Latin America and the Caribbean to the United States is of concern. From a humanitarian perspective, Haiti's extreme poverty remains an embarrassment to both Latin Americans and North Americans. Some observers lament the periodic influxes of Haitian refugees and migrants who flee repressive governments or seek economic opportunity. The sizable Haitian community in the United States, about 2 million, is concerned about the welfare of relatives and friends left behind, as well as business relationships and opportunities. Haiti has the potential to be a significant trading partner, as it was prior to 1987. Last but not least, Haiti carries important historical symbolism: few want to see a former slave republic that defeated European colonial powers to establish its independence fail to realize its potential. To be sure, there are those who for the very same reason may not want Haiti to succeed.

Virtually throughout Haiti's history, the country's politics has tended to run afoul of U.S. foreign policy interests, even under sympathetic U.S. administrations. The United States has felt compelled to embargo Haiti, to restrict its own assistance, and also to influence assistance offered by other entities: other nations, multilateral organizations, and, to some extent, charitable organizations. Haitian politics has also precipitated cleavages within the U.S. Congress, political parties, advocacy groups, ideologues on the right and left, and Haitian expatriate communities, as these factions have supported or criticized the official U.S. position.

Haitians have always taken cues from American political wrangling as guides to their own course of action; simultaneously, Haitian politics has influenced U.S. policy and assistance. But the United States speaks with contradictory and often ambiguous voices, which compounds the complexity of the situation on the ground in Haiti. U.S. policy toward Haiti has always been intertwined with the politics of assistance, a fact that helps explain the trajectory of assistance.

Foreign Assistance Ups and Downs

Many observers, too numerous to mention individually, have pointed out that every American president since Woodrow Wilson (with the exception of Gerald Ford, who was not in office for a full term) have had issues with Haiti (see figure 5-1).

TAFT TO REAGAN

In 1910 President William Howard Taft (1909–13) authorized a large loan to Haiti to pay off its international debts, with the intent of lessening the influence of foreign powers in the hemisphere. The loan failed as an effective instrument of foreign policy because Haitians were unable to meet the loan's terms, and the United States lost its leverage. Under Woodrow Wilson (1913–21), in 1915, the United States began an occupation of Haiti that was to last until 1934; it invested heavily in the country's infrastructure and developed a professional army. The purpose of the occupation was to keep the people under control. In 1944, under the Roosevelt administration, the United States helped Haiti to improve agricultural production. In 1949, under Truman, aid was expanded to include rural education, public health, public works, and public management. In 1955 the Eisenhower administration, through the Food for Peace program created under Title II of the Agricultural Trade Development and Assistance Act of 1954 (Public Law 480), offered food relief in response to humanitarian concerns following Hurricane Hazel. In 1958 the United States began providing food security support under P. L. 480.

The Kennedy administration (1961–63) discontinued direct aid in 1963, when Duvalier declared himself president for life, began stepping up repression in Haiti, and became aggressive in trying to manipulate the United States. U.S. embassy dispatches at the time noted that in 1960 Duvalier had

Figure 5-1. *Timeline of Foreign Assistance to Haiti*

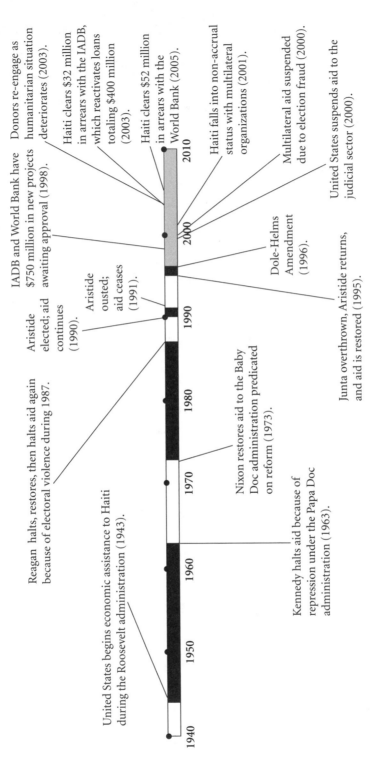

Donors re-engage as humanitarian situation deteriorates (2003).

Haiti clears $32 million in arrears with the IADB, which reactivates loans totaling $400 million (2003).

Haiti clears $52 million in arrears with the World Bank (2005).

IADB and World Bank have $750 million in new projects awaiting approval (1998).

Haiti falls into non-accrual status with multilateral organizations (2001).

Multilateral aid suspended due to election fraud (2000).

United States suspends aid to the judicial sector (2000).

Aristide ousted; aid ceases (1991).

Aristide elected; aid continues (1990).

Dole-Helms Amendment (1996).

Junta overthrown, Aristide returns, and aid is restored (1995).

Reagan halts, restores, then halts aid again because of electoral violence during 1987.

Nixon restores aid to the Baby Doc administration predicated on reform (1973).

United States begins economic assistance to Haiti during the Roosevelt administration (1943).

Kennedy halts aid because of repression under the Papa Doc administration (1963).

1940 1950 1960 1970 1980 1990 2000 2010

Source: Authors.

brought development progress to a halt by insisting that he have unilateral hiring and firing authority over USAID aid workers and control over their projects (U.S. State Department, Bureau of Public Affairs 2005). U.S. officials at the time estimated that 80 percent of aid was not reaching poor people because of mismanagement and corruption (DeWind and Kinley 1988). As a consequence, Haiti did not participate in the Kennedy administration's Alliance for Progress initiative, the largest foreign assistance program since the Marshall Plan after World War II. The Kennedy administration did fund humanitarian efforts in Haiti indirectly through NGOs, however. The Johnson administration (1963–69), following Kennedy's lead, also withheld assistance; among other things, it could not abide Duvalier's insistence on having total control over aid. Duvalier appears to have felt that he had nothing to lose by being tough on the United States (U.S. State Department, Bureau of Public Affairs 2005). In October 1966, things had deteriorated between Duvalier and the Johnson administration to such an extent that the CIA, the State Department, and the Defense Department were drawing up contingency plans for yet another intervention in Haiti.

The Nixon administration (1969–74) officially restored military and economic assistance to the Baby Doc Duvalier government in 1973, an action predicated in part on reforms Baby Doc had or appeared to have undertaken in the country, but more on the necessity to watch out for American interests in the cold war. Nixon wanted allies in the Caribbean to counterbalance Fidel Castro's growing influence. Assistance continued under Gerald Ford (1974–77), Jimmy Carter (1977–81), and Ronald Reagan (1981–89), on through Baby Doc's ouster in 1986. The 1975 International Food and Development Assistance Act directed assistance toward improving the standard of living of poor Haitians. Reagan, like Nixon, supported Duvalier as an anti-Communist presence in the Caribbean. Humanitarian aid continued to Haiti under Reagan. In 1983 the Reagan administration substantially boosted the Haitian economy in a trade benefits package. The Reagan administration suspended, restored, then suspended aid once again in 1987, in response to the electoral violence in the military-sponsored November 1987 elections.[1]

THE GEORGE H. W. BUSH YEARS: 1988 TO 1992

Aristide came to power in 1990 as a populist, supported in part by leftist organizations. This attracted the American left,[2] eager to see a progressive rise to power in the Caribbean. Aristide initially sought their support, then after his overthrow became a cause célèbre, especially among some high-visibility Hollywood figures. In his first seven months in office before the coup, Aristide had an unprecedented opportunity to attract aid from multilateral donors eager to support his democratic, antipoverty agenda. Yet his government was unable convert his campaign rhetoric into concrete proposals and projects, so aid did not flow as it should or where it should. Then it was too late—the coup occurred (Dupuy 2007).

The George H. W. Bush administration (1989–93), in response to Aristide's ouster, suspended all but humanitarian assistance to Haiti. The Bush administration embargoed Haiti, froze government assets, stopped arms shipments, and suspended American business activity in Haiti (apparently on a case-by-case basis). The advocacy group TransAfrica Forum and the Congressional Black Caucus claimed these interventions were only halfheartedly pursued, because Bush, like previous presidents, found Haitian nondemocratic governments useful. The Bush administration stated in its defense that these critics were forgetting that the European Union had refused to go along with the sanctions, greatly weakening the U.S. initiative. In any case, Secretary of State James Baker seemed unequivocal: at a 1991 emergency meeting of the OAS convened to discuss Haiti he said, "It is imperative that we agree for the sake of Haitian democracy, and the cause of democracy throughout the hemisphere, to act collectively to defend the legitimate government of President Aristide."[3]

While in exile in the United States from 1991 to 1994, the years of the military junta, Aristide tried to get the Bush administration to assist him in his effort to be reinstated as president, but to no avail. Bush initially backed Aristide's return, but then he reneged. Bush was respectful of the various international agreements prohibiting military interventions. And the thirty-four-nation OAS refused to even consider endorsing an armed invasion to restore Aristide. Bush was sensitive to the checkered history of the United States in Haiti and the Western Hemisphere—recall the recent invasions of Panama and Grenada, not to mention that of the Dominican Republic in 1965.[4] Bush also became increasingly suspicious of Aristide's antidemocratic, anti-American, and liberation theological leanings.

In 1992, in an agreement mediated by the OAS between Aristide and Haitian parliamentarians, the Haitian parliament recognized Aristide as head of state (because so many Aristide parliamentarians had fled, Haitians referred to this as the *faux* parliament). Aristide then appointed the leader of the Haitian Communist Party, René Théodore, as prime minister, furthering his reputation as a polarizing figure. Théodore was attacked by gangs supporting Cédras. The United States condemned the assault. Aristide was successful in lobbying for an embargo of Haiti, and for a suspension of aid, in order to weaken and bring down the military junta. During the military junta years, the Bush administration began blocking Haitian "boat people" from reaching the shores of the United States; some were attempting to flee the repressive military regime, but many more were likely economic refugees searching for job opportunities not plentiful on the island. The mass migration may have been precipitated by the Immigration and Naturalization Service's reluctance to turn back a boatload of partisans of Bazin (who was the U.S.-backed candidate for president).

The blockade did serious damage to Haiti's economy and people, but didn't seem to hurt the junta.[5] Some 140,000 private-sector jobs were lost, many permanently. In 1989 there were 40,000 jobs in Haiti's textile industry; by 1994, there were none. Smuggling and trafficking across the shared border with the Dominican Republic exploded. Unable to obtain fuel, Haitians cut down more and more trees, accelerating deforestation and exacerbating the ecological disaster already under way. Many Haitian refugees who tried and failed to flee the regime were forcibly returned to the island, where arrest, torture, and murder awaited them and these crimes shot up. The health of the population deteriorated substantially. Because electric power was scarce, vaccines and medicines could not be preserved for use. By most accounts, the embargo made life much worse for the poor, those it had been intended to help.[6]

THE BILL CLINTON YEARS: 1993–2001

Critics of Clinton's Haiti policy explain its shifting direction mostly as a reaction to domestic politics, rather than as arising out of foreign policy concerns for Haiti.[7] One of Bill Clinton's campaign pledges in his 1992 run for president was to reverse the Bush administration's policies on Haitian refugees and Aristide's return. After Clinton took office in 1993, the administration reversed itself and continued the Bush policy on refugees and resisted pressure to invade Haiti to restore Aristide's presidency. During this period, the Clinton administration interred thousands of Haitian "boat people" in the U.S. base at Guantánamo Bay, Cuba, where they were detained for the duration of the crisis.

The Clinton administration kept the embargo and aid suspensions in place, imposed additional bans on commercial flights to and from Haiti, and stopped international financial transactions, including credit card business and wire transfers.[8] These measures put a stranglehold on remittances to Haiti, much of the money intended for poor people. Clinton convinced President Joaquín Balaguer of the Dominican Republic to close the border with Haiti in order to further tighten the blockade. Balaguer, having agreed to border enforcement, nonetheless complied only halfheartedly—smuggling across the Haitian-Dominican border was very lucrative for the Dominican Republic (Dobbins 2003).

In 1994 Clinton began to warm to the idea of ratcheting up pressure on the junta to step down and, failing that, invading Haiti to restore Aristide to his rightful place as president. Aristide helped his own case for an invasion. From his home in the Georgetown neighborhood of Washington, D.C., Aristide moderated his anti-American rhetoric, hired well-connected lobbyists, and worked closely with African American leaders, the Congressional Black Caucus (including Jesse Jackson), the advocacy group TransAfrica Forum, former President Jimmy Carter, influential Democrats, and others to mount a campaign in support of an invasion (Gros 1997, p. 103).[9] In May 1994, Randall Robinson, founder of TransAfrica Forum, went on a much-publicized hunger strike, stating, "The president is responsible for what constitutes a disaster in Haiti. The longer he waits, the more people die" (McCarthy 1994, p. 1).

Many believe, however, that in addition to appeasing Aristide supporters on Haiti, Clinton considered an invasion the only way to solve the refugee, urban violence, and drug-trafficking problems (Dobbins 2003; Palmer 2006). A report suggesting that the international blockade of Haiti had dramatically increased infant mortality and that food riots likely helped push Clinton toward an invasion.

The Clinton administration, in addition to its political reasons for intervention, believed that eventually an intervention would be necessary and that doing so earlier would be cheaper and more effective than later. Deputy Secretary of State Strobe Talbott argued this point before the Senate Foreign Relations Committee in March 1995 in justifying the invasion in hindsight.

Congressional Republicans were dead set against the invasion, as was the Central Intelligence Agency.[10] Clinton's own secretary of defense also opposed it. Interestingly, the Senate voted 100 to 0 to require Clinton to seek congressional approval for the invasion. In 1994, over frustration with the Immigration and Nationalization Service's efforts in Port-au-Prince to manage Haitian refugees, the Congressional Black Caucus lobbied for a scheme to use boats docked in Jamaica to transport migrants out of Haiti.

Following the invasion, Clinton restored aid to Haiti in 1995. In 1996, under the Development Assistance Program, P.L. 480 Title II programs were expanded to include health, nutrition, agriculture, natural resources, education, and microcredit (discussed in detail in chapter 8).

In an August 2005 interview, Aristide claimed that in 1994 the Clinton administration's major demand in exchange for his return was an agreement to privatize firms owned by the Haitian state.[11] Aristide agreed, then did everything he could to block privatization (as described in chapter 3). Aristide stated that the Clinton administration no longer trusted him, although it continued to support him. The George W. Bush administration, aware of Clinton's concerns over Aristide's trustworthiness, became much less generous in its support for Haiti.

Jimmy Carter became disenchanted with Haiti in 1995, when his offer to help Aristide promote democracy was rebuffed. Carter and his staff claimed to have witnessed massive fraud in the 1995 elections. Carter was poorly treated by Haitians protesting in the streets when he visited the country. Haitians resented Carter for his willingness to negotiate with Cédras in 1994. André Bouchard, an election consultant with the Canadian International Development Agency, has said he witnessed poll workers discard truckloads of ballots they were too overwhelmed by to count.[12]

The Clinton administration, having restored Aristide to power, actively supported him.[13] In 1995 Vice President Al Gore visited Haiti to celebrate the anniversary of Aristide's return to power.[14] Clinton began trumpeting Haiti as a "successful" foreign policy outcome in anticipation of the 1996 presidential elections.[15] Somalia and Rwanda were not so successful, so the administration was looking for some good publicity.

Aristide and Haiti became pawns in a battle between Clinton and Congress. Although Clinton was reelected in 1996, Republicans took control of the House and Senate. Just prior to the Aristide affair, Republicans, in an attempt to thwart the administration, blocked Clinton's move to send U.S. ground troops to Bosnia, leaving the administration to fight an air war that increased the likely risk of failure. Republicans also roundly criticized Clinton on Somalia and Rwanda. Republicans responded to Clinton's Haiti initiative with the Dole-Helms Amendment, which required Aristide to reform or risk loosing aid. Republicans also tried to launch an investigation into murders of Aristide's opponents and accused the Clinton administration of withholding damaging intelligence about him. Republicans suspended aid for police reform in retaliation against Aristide. Republicans also had concerns about documents confiscated by the Marines from Aristide's home but kept secret by the Clinton administration. (These papers had to do with Aristide's alleged mental instability; we know of no research that has resolved the question of Aristide's mental state.) Another motivation of Republicans for their opposition to Aristide's restoration was that Democrats had continually criticized Reagan and Bush for supporting "right-wing death squads" in several Latin American countries, including El Salvador and Nicaragua. They figured that

Aristide's Chimères were now fair game, because Clinton supported Aristide (Dobbins 2003).

Haiti's 1997 elections were a disaster, for both Haiti and the Clinton administration: the turnout was extremely low and a constitutional crisis led to the suspension of foreign assistance. In 1997 and again in 1998, Secretary of State Madeleine Albright visited Haiti to try to resolve conflict and stalemate surrounding the elections. On her return to the United States, inexplicably to her critics and some supporters, she announced that Haiti had a functioning democratic system and that U.S. assistance had led to success (Mobekk 2001). In Albright's memoir she claims Haiti as a foreign policy success, as does Clinton in his.[16] Clinton detractors argue that in ignoring realities in Haiti, the United States may have fueled further protests and instability, because political opposition and the citizenry came to believe that elections just didn't matter.

The Clinton administration also appeared ambivalent on drug policy, which many critics thought the president had downplayed for political reasons. In 2000 the State Department decertified Haiti for failing the annual policy cooperation review on drugs but protected it from U.S. sanctions through a White House waiver stating concerns of national interest (Fauriol 2000). The White House should have reduced aid to Haiti after it was decertified, but did not.

In 1998 the Inter-American Development Bank and World Bank had $570 million in new projects awaiting approval by the Haitian parliament. Aristide's government referred to the blockages as "economic terrorism."[17] In 2000 the World Bank, the European Union, the Inter-American Development Bank, Canada, the United States, France, and the Netherlands suspended assistance as a result of widespread election fraud. From 1997 to 2000, under pressure from the Clinton administration, the World Bank International Development Association and the Inter-American Development Bank suspended aid, because Haiti had no legitimate parliament to approve loans and grants. In July 2000, the United States suspended assistance to the Haitian judicial sector (U.S. General Accounting Office 2000a, 2000b). The International Criminal Investigative Assistance Program terminated assistance to police over congressional concerns about the May 2000 Haitian and local elections. USAID terminated assistance to the judicial sector, having been unable to negotiate an agreement for assistance with the Haitian government. Multilateral organizations, lacking funding to remain in the country, withdrew their office staff.

Haiti became a presidential campaign issue for Al Gore and George W. Bush in 2000. Some critics blamed the Clinton administration for the failure of anticorruption efforts, claiming that Aristide's letter of commitment to Clinton to undertake government reform, accepted by Clinton, was so non-committal that it apparently gave the nod to continued abuses by Aristide's government.[18]

In 2001 Haiti fell into non-accrual status with multilateral organizations, meaning that the country could not borrow. In 2001 the UN Development Program ceased funding its projects in Haiti involving police reform.

Some news commentators suggested that one lesson to be learned from Haiti in 1995 was, "Define your goals so minimally that it will be easy to meet them, declare victory and go home."[19] There also is a compelling case to be made that other foreign policy hotspots—Somalia and Bosnia—were legacies of the cold war, hence attention was given to them and not to Haiti, which is solely in the U.S. sphere of influence.

THE GEORGE W. BUSH YEARS: 2001 TO 2008

Unlike the Clinton administration, the George W. Bush administration policy toward Haiti was more foreign policy–oriented. Members of the administration (2001-09), spurred on by neoconservatives, made no bones about their visceral dislike for Aristide (see Morrell 2003 for an overview of the Bush policy toward Haiti). They believed Aristide to be antidemocratic, intent on extending his presidency indefinitely and consolidating his power around a single party, Family Lavalas. They resented Aristide's government for not fully assisting the United States in its drug interdiction efforts. In 1999, for example, an estimated sixty-seven tons of cocaine passed through Haiti without a single arrest by Haitian authorities: they had only twenty-four staff assigned to interdiction efforts.[20] In 1998 Miami customs agents seized 600 pounds of cocaine (Robinson 2000). They disliked Aristide's anti-American attitude, his toleration of violence, and his liberation theology, all publicly displayed in speeches widely covered in the media (though some Aristide supporters dismiss these actions as those of an inexperienced politician). They were annoyed at his flirtations with Fidel Castro, who was supporting Haiti with hundreds of Cuban physicians and advisers. Mostly, though, Aristide's government and politics in Haiti flew in the face of Bush's commitment to global democracy.

But some supporters of Aristide felt that the Bush administration was sending mixed messages to Aristide. Roger Noriega, then U.S. ambassador to the Organization of American States, indicated that U.S. policy supported democratic elections as the best way to resolve political crisis but then charged Aristide with becoming the illegitimate head of a pariah state when he won the election (Dupuy 2003, 2007). Events in Haiti also coincided with the election of two leftist presidents in Latin America, Hugo Chavez in Venezuela and Lulu da Silva in Brazil. Chavez seemed to be openly flirting with the Cuban dictator, Fidel Castro. The Bush administration was clearly attempting to halt a dangerous socialist movement in the Hemisphere.

The U.S. ambassador to Haiti, Brian Curran, seemed to confirm that there was a problem of mixed messages coming from the Bush administration.[21] Curran, a career foreign service officer who had originally been appointed by the Clinton administration, tried to get Aristide and the opposition to compromise in an effort to avoid greater political instability and possible revolt over the 2000 elections—to preserve the democratic process that brought Aristide into office. The International Republican Institute (IRI), a nonprofit, nonpartisan organization whose mission is to support democracy, Curran asserted, was actively promoting the opposition and encouraging it not to compromise by claiming that Aristide would soon be out. (Later, some critics even claimed that IRI helped rebel groups oust Aristide in February 2004, something IRI has vigorously denied.) Luigi Einaudi, an OAS representative, shared Curran's view that the United States was working at cross purposes.[22]

As the political impasse in Haiti resulting from the 1997 elections continued under the Bush administration, the administration continued the suspension of U.S. aid and blocked other multilateral donors from providing aid already approved. The Bush administration also came to believe that government delays in holding makeup elections had been intended to penalize opposition parties, which would favor Aristide and his party, Fammi Lavalas.[23] The World Bank, Inter-American Development Bank, and the UN still had no offices in the country. In 2004 the Bush administration reimposed a blockade against entering Haitian migrants (Wasem 2005). Aristide did not help his own case for aid: in 2001 the government reportedly built four hillside mansions for senior officials at a cost of $7 million.[24]

In 2004 the Bush administration decided not to save Aristide's presidency and leaned on him to step down, which he did. Some sources report that the OAS had brokered a meeting between Aristide and Haitian rebels in the Dominican Republic but that the U.S. embassy stopped the meeting, allowing the rebellion to overwhelm Aristide.[25] What was surprising was that a handful of rebels were able to overthrow the government and the population failed to support Aristide. The Bush administration's dilemma in Haiti was to try to use democratization as a foreign policy tool while withholding support from an undemocratic, anti-American Aristide regime that enjoyed good relations with Latin American and Caribbean states and regional organizations and simultaneously aiding Haitian undemocratic, anti-American opposition forces not enjoying Latin and Caribbean state and regional organizational support.[26]

The Bush administration's actions have reactivated interest in Haiti among congressional Democrats, some in the Congressional Black Caucus, who have been longtime Aristide supporters. Congresswoman Maxine Waters is the most visible and vocal Aristide supporter in Congress. Congresswoman Waters assisted Aristide in marketing his claim that the United States kidnapped him from Haiti in February 2004. She takes credit for securing Aristide's release from exile in the Central African Republic to Jamaica to keep pressure on the Transition Government. She led the boycott by the Congressional Black Caucus of the 2005 visit of Haitian Prime Minister Latortue to the United States. She was an outspoken critic of the Transition Government and the Bush administration.[27] She continues to introduce legislation supporting foreign assistance expenditures and preferences for Haiti.

Following Aristide's ouster, the Bush administration offered humanitarian aid during the unstable political situation. It also launched an antiviolence program in conflict zones across the country, called the Haitian Transition Initiative (discussed in more detail in chapter 6 and appendix B).

In February 2006, the Transition Government held presidential elections. René Préval, who had been Aristide's prime minister in 1990 and president from 1995 to 2000, was the leading candidate.

Donors again reengaged in 2003 as the humanitarian situation continued to worsen without any signs of a turnaround. In 2003 Haiti cleared its $32 million debt with the IADB. In 2005 Haiti cleared its $52 million debt with the World Bank. The IADB immediately updated and reactivated loans totaling $400 million. The European Community (EC), though, finding that Haiti had violated provisions of the Cotonou Agreement—a pact to end poverty between poor countries seeking aid and the European Commission—partially suspended assistance in January 2001 and offered no direct budget assistance to the government through 2004.

In 2004 foreign assistance began to flow yet again. Secretary of State Condoleezza Rice visited Haiti in September 2005 and encouraged Haitians to vote. In January 2006, Secretary Rice and five foreign ministries of the OAS "Core Group"—Argentina, Brazil, Canada, Chile and France—reaffirmed their commitment to Haiti (OAS 2006). This augured a new commitment on the part of the Bush administration to Haiti's Transition Government and to its new president, René Préval.

Préval was elected president of Haiti in February 2006, in yet another flawed, somewhat violent election that was resolved in the end by the international community.

Bush Administration Priorities

One way to get a handle on Bush administration policy priorities is to analyze different budget requests, such as annual Congressional Budget Justifications, submitted by the State Department to the congressional appropriations committees. Table 5-1 draws on these documents for the years 2002 to 2007 to show that the U.S. State Department made budget requests that did not emphasize decentralization, privatization, prisons, and anticorruption. A major focus was security—especially the Haitian Coast Guard—and police reform. Civil service reform, justice reform, and private-sector development are priorities in some years but not in others. It is not clear from the Congressional Budget Justifications whether these priorities are part of strategic thinking about Haiti or reflect on-again, off-again interest in an issue or are a budgeting compliance exercise.

The testimony of representatives of USAID before the House Committee on International Relations on U.S. policy for the Caribbean is more instructive (Franco 2005a, 2005b). Democratization is a central issue. In Haiti, USAID emphasizes building local government capacity as a way to promote stability. USAID continues to promote civil society as essential in monitoring government actions, advocating policy, and providing quality services. USAID is supporting Haiti's Provisional Electoral Council directly and through the OAS and UN Development Program, including voter registration, election oversight, voter education, journalist training, party strengthening, and public relations. USAID is helping improve agriculture, especially among small holders, as well as funding microcredit, seed banks, and improved access to markets.[28] A program to ease tensions along the Dominican Republic–Haiti border is under way, as is an HIV/AIDS prevention initiative. USAID is undertaking a major disaster mitigation and preparedness program in Haiti. Arms shipments to Haiti resumed in October 2006 in support of its security needs and in recognition of its stability.

Another way to look at Bush administration priorities is to examine budget objectives (see table 5-2). The Bush administration increased its budget request for Haiti from $205.5 million in FY2006 to $222.9 million in FY2008. The peace and security budget line overall showed a slight decrease of about $2 million, but for security-specific projects budgets fell significantly, from $23.2 million to $15.5 million. Governing justly and democratically remained about the same over the three fiscal years. Funding to support political competition fell by about $4 million, and spending to support the rule of law and improved governance increased. Funding to encourage the development of institutions of civil society remained about the same over the three-year period.

Over the decade from 1998 to 2008, Haiti has been a low priority within the context of U.S. foreign policy overall. USAID issued a policy framework for dealing with fragile nations, *Fragile States Strategy* (2005a), but Haiti is not mentioned at all in the document, even though the agency has poured millions of dollars into Haiti. Yet this emphasis, or lack of it, is not all that surprising, given U.S. demands in Iraq and Afghanistan, not to mention the Middle East generally. But the latest budget allocations for fiscal year 2008 to Haiti from USAID show a much more thoughtful approach to that country's needs. Perhaps this is a new era for Haiti.

Congressional Priorities

Congress is and always has been a major foreign policy actor with respect to Haiti.[29] When one party controlled the presidency and the other controlled Congress, Congress tended to thwart presidential initiatives when policy disagreements occurred, as was the case for George H. W. Bush and Bill Clinton. George Bush, in partnership with the Republican-controlled Congress, had nothing but support from Congress on Haiti policy, but there was a vocal Democratic opposition. Furthermore, congressional parties in the minority often submitted bills, resolutions, or sense-of-Congress statements in support of Haiti, even though they would not be passed, to embarrass the administration or majority party into action, or to maintain support from their political base. In general, though, Congress has always been suspicious of Haiti's leadership, regardless of which party was in the majority. Every Congress compelled the president to monitor aid expenditures and report back to congressional committees. Occasionally, Congress imposed conditionality on aid to Haiti to force compliance. Congress tended to add another set of mixed voices regarding Haiti policy to the mixed chorus coming from every administration and the donor community.

Table 5-1. *State Department Budget Priorities for Haiti, 2002–06*[a]

Sector	2002	2003
Civil service reform		
Decentralization		
Privatization of government enterprises		
Private-sector development		ESF will focus on generating sustained increased income for the poor
Rule of law		
Justice		
Police	Support to the Haitian National Police through IMET and FMF was curtailed by Congress	FMF aid to the Haitian National Police
Prisons		
Corruption		
Security	Legislation may permit EDA grants	EDA helps the Haitian Coast Guard patrol the coast and aid the United States in interdiction and counternarcotics functions

Source: Congressional Budget Justifications, 2002-2006, see www.state.gov/s/d/rm/rls/perfrpt/
DA= development assistance; EDA = excess defense articles; ESF = economic support fund;
FMF = foreign military financing; IMET = international military education and training
a. The absence of text in cells indicates that a sector was to receive no emphasis in that year.

2004	2005	2006
Following the leadership change in February 2004, the United States set up a reconstruction program to address the transitional needs of the Haitian government	Planned support includes provision of commodities to technical assistance for ministries and building rehabilitation at the Ministry of Justice	ESF funds provide technical assistance to the newly elected parliament and government ministries after November 2005 elections
	DA will broaden the availability of credit to small and micro-entrepreneurs	ESF funds help the government foster private-sector growth and long term job creation
DA fosters institutionalized inclusive democratic governance		
Initiated a training program for judges and prosecutors	DA supports justice reform through aid	ESF funds expand training programs for judicial personnel
IMET and FMF aid the Haitian National Police	IMET will enhance police professionalism in counternarcotics operations; FMF	ESF funds provide support to reform the Haitian National Police into an apolitical security service
	Aiding government ministries and agencies by making available technical assistance and funding to the Ministry of Finance to assist with creating an anti-corruption unit	
EDA helps the Haitian Coast Guard patrol the coast and aid the United States in interdiction and counternarcotics functions	FMF supports the Haitian Coast Guard maritime interdiction and interoperability and provides spare parts and maintenance for vehicles; Haiti is eligible for EDA on a grant basis	ESF funds support reforms of the Haitian National Police; enhance operational and logistics skills of the Haitian Coast Guard through FMF and EDA programs

Table 5-2. *U.S. Department of State Funding for Haiti, 2006 and 2008*
U.S.$ thousand

Objective	FY2006 actual	FY2008 requested
Peace and security	46,270	44,174
Security	23,201	15,544
Governing justly and democratically	24,747	23,173
Rule of law	5,650	7,073
Good governance	10,702	12,000
Political competition	5,250	1,100
Civil society	3,145	3,000
Investing in people	103,759	122,941
Economic growth	30,270	32,112
Humanitarian assistance	480	500
Total	205,526	222,900

Source: U.S. State Department, *Congressional Budget Justification FY2008*, pp. 651–55.

In addition to prompting policy differences, Haiti has been and continues to be a vehicle for partisan sniping. For example, in January 2007 Representative Barbara Lee (D-Calif.), in an effort to embarrass the Bush administration, submitted a bill to Congress calling for the establishment of an independent commission to investigate the "2004 Coup d'Etat in the Republic of Haiti."[30] During the Clinton administration, congressional Republicans took the same tack. But Congress has come together on the very divisive, thorny issue of trade preferences—eliminating tariffs and quotas—for Haiti, possibly signaling a new era of U.S.-Haiti relations (discussed further in chapter 9).

Impact of Shifting Policies on Aid

The jury is still out—and may remain so—concerning the effectiveness of the embargo, military intervention, and aid suspension as foreign policy decisions. There should be little disagreement, however, on the proposition that these foreign policy decisions greatly reduced the chances that aid would succeed in developing Haiti. The embargo substantially worsened the economy and the plight of the people, making the problem of development all the more severe. Many observers are of the opinion that it was a near death blow for the country and its citizens. The military intervention precipitated considerable opposition and ushered in an illegitimate government, which exacerbated already poor governance and a dysfunctional political culture. Divisions across U.S. administrations and with and between political parties in Congress likely resulted in some Haitians' hanging on to power as they waited to see whether their supporters in the United States would prevail (Millett 2001).[31] Aid suspensions not only reversed any positive benefits programs might have had but also have precipitated a host of negative unintended consequences. Some detractors say that the United States destroyed Haiti to save it—a sentiment reminiscent of assessments of the Vietnam War.[32]

One might ask whether any donor country could offer foreign assistance that is not subject to the vicissitudes of that country's foreign policy. In democratic donor countries, where power can change hands quickly, foreign assistance is always vulnerable to changing foreign policy priorities, and there is no way to eliminate this risk. Could multilateral donors, then, offer more stability in the provision of aid? The answer, again, is no. The nations that provide funds to multilateral organizations continue to exercise control. Donor countries occupy leadership positions (the president of the World Bank is an American), they offer aid with strings attached or with restricted use, they delay funding transfers, and they threaten multilateral organizations that do not do their bidding. Most important, though, is that those working for multilateral organizations do not vary all that much in their views of how aid should be distributed. It is likely that aid flows will be interrupted in spite of best efforts of donor agencies not to do so.

Given the history of aid suspensions, interventions, and embargoes, it is no wonder that there has also been a history of aid failures in Haiti. This is the subject of chapter 6.

6 FOREIGN ASSISTANCE FAILURES

> The outcome of [World Bank] assistance programs [for Haiti] is rated
> unsatisfactory (if not highly so), the institutional development impact,
> negligible, and the sustainability of the few benefits that have accrued,
> unlikely.
>
> —Manager Alice Galenson
> World Bank, Operations Evaluation Department (2002)

There is strong consensus among various aid donors—Canada, France, the United States; multilateral organizations such as the World Bank, the Inter-American Development Bank, the European Commission, and UN; and regional organizations such as the Organization of American States and Caricom (Caribbean Community)—that foreign assistance to Haiti has failed to achieve its goals and is likely to continue to do so long into the future unless certain drivers of failure are eliminated. The reasons for failure stem in part from bilateral and multilateral foreign assistance policy and implementation, and of course the embargo and military intervention also have set the stage for failure. The international community has been remarkably candid about its collective failure to develop or reconstruct Haiti. In this chapter we summarize some of these conclusions. We describe the aid context for Haiti, discuss the failures of Haitian governance, and then analyze donor failures.

Development Context

The Canadian International Development Agency (2003) summed up the context in which donors work in Haiti as one very similar to that of the least-developed, most fragile countries in sub-Saharan Africa with the following characteristics:

   —A society profoundly divided between a traditional culture and an elite, ex-military, and petite-bourgeoisie class, each seeking or clinging to power

—An unstable government and a weak public institutional capacity

—A seriously deteriorated economic and social infrastructure

—An absence of capacity for law and order, allowing continued violent insurgencies and rioting, perpetrated by paramilitaries and gangs

—An uncontrollable influx of migrants from rural areas into the slums of the capital, Port-au-Prince

—A concentration of wealth in the hands of a few traditional families and new mafia-like groups

—An inadequate and constantly deteriorating natural environment

Assessments by various international organizations all confirm the Canadian diagnosis.[1]

The World Bank's Operations Evaluation Department (2002), in its 2002 evaluation of foreign assistance efforts since 1996, concluded, "Haiti is an extreme case of a country caught in a vicious circle in which unemployment, inequality, and poor education feed into lawlessness and violence, making it difficult for the economy to grow and create jobs, thus perpetuating unemployment and inequality" (p. 3). The Aristide government, in its formal response included in an appendix to the assessment, agreed with this statement.

In an earlier country assessment, in 1998, the OED commented, "Haiti has never had a tradition of governance aimed at providing services to the population or creating an environment conducive to sustainable growth. Instead, a tight economic elite has supported a 'predatory state' that makes only negligible investments in human resources and basic infrastructure. Pervasive repression through army, police and paramilitary groups has created deep-seated distrust between civil society and the state. The absence of a culture of democratic decision-making and peaceful consensus building has generated tensions and hampered Haiti's rehabilitation effort" (World Bank, Operations Evaluation Department 2002, p. 3).[2]

In 1996 Haiti joined the Multilateral Investment Guarantee Agency (MIGA)—an important tool for attracting private investment to distressed economies. "MIGA has not issued any guarantees nor provided any technical assistance. The general lack of investor interest stems from the political instability and violence, anti-business inclinations of government, lack of a cohesive economic reform program and prolonged economic stagnation" (World Bank, Operations Evaluation Department 2002, p. 13).

The Inter-American Development Bank (2003a) stated in its 2003 assessment: "Haiti has been characterized as having very poor governance: the Haitian State is weak and barely functional, it has had very little institutional development; society is fragmented and the political discourse has been extremely fractious, with very low capacity for compromise, reflected, historically, in pronounced government and social instability" (p. iii).

The Organization for Economic Cooperation and Development (OECD) created a special task force under its Development Assistance Committee to develop aid policies for fragile nations. OECD rates countries using five matrices having two dimensions each: initial conditions and development; initial conditions and security; capacity and resilience; capacity and development; and resilience and security, with a high or low rating on each dimension. Of fifty-three countries ranked, Haiti was the only one scoring "low" and "unfavorable" on each paired dimension:

—Low development and Unfavorable initial conditions
—Unfavorable initial conditions and Low security
—Low capacity and Low resilience
—Low capacity and Low development
—Low security and Low resilience

OECD concluded that Haiti is one of two or three fragile states representing the greatest development challenge.

The failure of assistance programs to help Haiti is not a new phenomenon. The U.S. General Accounting Office (1982), in assessing the U.S. Agency for International Development effort in Haiti from 1973 to 1981, found that "the United States has provided Haiti about $218 million in food aid and economic assistance. After 8 years of operating in Haiti, USAID is still having difficulty implementing its projects.... Past projects, designed to improve Haitian government institutions, have had only limited impact" (p. i). A follow-on assessment in 1985 concluded much the same (U.S. General Accounting Office 1985).[3]

The Failures of Haitian Governance

Arguably, Haitian governments, influenced by the dominant economic elite, seem to have failed the country throughout its history, and in the past two decades appear to have accomplished very little in reducing poverty, promoting development, or securing the peace.

The World Bank's 2002 *Haiti: Country Assistance Evaluation* concluded (World Bank, Operations Evaluation Department 2002, p. 17; see also Hassan 2004), "The development impact of World Bank assistance to the country since 1986 has been negligible, as the critical constraints to development—governance and public sector capacity and accountability—have not diminished.... Without improved governance and institutional reforms, the World

Bank and other donors will be able to accomplish very little. . . . The single overarching constraint to satisfactory implementation, outcome and sustainability of development assistance to Haiti has been the continuous political turmoil and governance problems in the country. In project after project, the reason for delayed implementation or cancellation, is a coup, civil unrest, or the inevitable results of these events, such as lack of ownership by a frequently changing government and aid staff turnover. Despite efforts on the part of the World Bank and other donors, it has been all but impossible to carry on a coherent lending program."

Without exception, donors agree with this sweeping indictment.

The four major drivers of failure are the following:

—Government incapacity generally and poor aid administration

—Lack of government support for or "ownership" of programs funded by foreign assistance

—Aid dependency

—Dissension between president and parliament

Haitian governments and elites have seemed more consumed by politics than by ambitions to attain good governance. Foreign assistance programs have not comported with governing elites' desire to acquire power and aggrandize themselves. Haitian governments have abdicated responsibility for meeting the needs of the citizens and have left this responsibility to bilateral and multilateral donors, through aid, and the Haitian diaspora, through remittances. No shared vision or consensus has developed as to where the country should be headed and who should lead it.

The four drivers of failure are causally related. The proximal cause of government failure is the inability to govern generally and to administer aid specifically. Because the government had little to do with administering programs intended to assist Haiti, the government cared little about owning them. The four immediate drivers operate against a historical backdrop of the political instability endemic in Haiti since its founding. Successive governments have been unable or unwilling to provide for the people, and so Haiti has become aid-dependent. The first priority, then, is to create a stable government that can independently manage the country's affairs with decreasing need for outside assistance.

Lack of General Government Capacity

The Préval government, in presenting its Interim Poverty Reduction Strategy Paper in September 2006, recognized that management capacity for development had been sorely lacking in efforts in the recent and distant past (Republic of Haiti 2006, p. 5). The report's introduction states,

> Since 1986, successive Haitian governments have on several occasions declared the reduction of poverty to be a priority. However, poverty reduction has never been the subject of a systematic policy or of a coherent program with precisely defined measures and objectives. In 2000, the government subscribed to the Millennium Challenge Goals (MDGs). In 2003, the government backed the Integrated Program to Respond to the Urgent Needs of Vulnerable Communities and Populations (PIR) launched by the United Nations. The goal of this program was to provide coordinated, rapid and targeted responses to urgent needs of a growing portion of the population. However, despite all of these initiatives, no realistic path leading to attainment of the MDGs has yet opened up.

Since 2000, successive Haitian governments have failed to advance much on any of the 18 quantifiable targets and 48 indicators representing MDGs so important to its people. Thus, "Haiti stands no chance, with the public policies adopted thus far, of reaching the MDGs by 2015" (p. 13). And the government even speculates that things will worsen in Haiti on some indicators.

Poor Aid Administration

According to the World Bank, since 1995, there was a "total mismatch between levels of foreign aid and government capacity to absorb it."[4] USAID's Mission in Haiti echoed the sentiment in its *Resource Review—1998:* "Most of Haiti's public institutions were too weak and ineffective to provide the level of partnership needed with USAID or other donors to promote development. These institutions are characterized by lack of trained personnel; no performance based incentive system; no accepted hiring, firing and promotion procedures; heavy top down management; and a decided lack of direction" (U.S. Agency for International Development 1998, p. 2). Incapacity still exists a decade later. To be effective, the Haitian government at a minimum would have needed to articulate its needs to and marshal support from the donor community; coordinate, harmonize, and align the myriad of bilateral, multilateral, and charitable contributions coming into the country; and allocate funding, spend it, and deliver services, all of which would have needed to be accomplished with strict financial controls, transparency, and accountability mechanisms in place.

The UN Ad Hoc Advisory Group on Haiti concluded in 1999 (UN Economic and Social Council 1999, pp. 15, 18) during the recurring electoral crises that government capacity was at issue:

> Unfortunately, capacity building within those national institutions that have a mandate for aid coordination is being hampered by the political stalemate which has made it difficult to approve new technical cooperation projects, some of which would have strengthened managerial and coordination capacity.... The long-term development program of support for Haiti address[es] the issues of capacity building of governmental institutions, especially in areas such as governance, the promotion of human rights, the administration of justice, the electoral system, law enforcement, police training, and other areas of social and economic development, which are critical for enabling the Haitian government to adequately and effectively coordinate, manage, absorb and utilize international assistance and development aid."

The Haitian government in 1996 tried to create greater capacity for aid administration. Policymakers assigned aid coordination to separate ministries, each with responsibility for a sector. Within each ministry, one office dealt with administration while another focused on programs. A World Bank Consultative Group assessment in 1997 found that ministries faced major problems communicating with donors, negotiating government administrative procedures, negotiating donor-imposed administrative procedures, and acquiring information on projects (World Bank 1997). The government of Haiti, in 1997, also determined that it had a serious aid management problem (Republic of Haiti 1997). The reason for incapacity was the near complete collapse of government, first under the 1987 junta, then under the 1991 junta, leaving little capacity for Aristide to work with, assuming that he wanted to improve governance.

The transitional nature of national government also posed problems for Haiti. Successive governments were slow to seek "consultative" meetings with donors, which effectively delayed foreign assistance flows or relegated administration to donors or their agents. In March 1999, for example, a UN study concluded, "The implications, once again, are that all long-term policy dialogue between the Haitian authorities and its major development partners will have to wait until governmental institutions are renewed through the upcoming elections" (UN Economic and Social Council 1999, p. 12).

The International Development Association (IDA) is the lending arm of the World Bank for the poorest nations. Its loans are really credits, in that IDA does not charge interest. IDA's eighty-two eligible borrowers have very significant needs for loans, but funds available for lending—a fixed pool whose size is determined by donors' pledges of contributions—is well below developing countries' needs. IDA therefore allocates scarce resources among eligible borrowing countries on the basis of a developing country's policy performance and institutional capacity to concentrate resources where they are likely to be most helpful in reducing poverty.

Beginning in 2005, IDA began making its country performance ratings public (IDA 2007b). In 2006 Haiti was ranked sixty-ninth of eighty-five countries eligible for IDA funding, meaning that sixty-eight countries had better scores, and thus a better chance of receiving IDA funds, than Haiti. Haiti is below average on three major indexes, and has an average score on portfolio management.

Resource allocation index: Average = 3.3; Haiti = 2.9

Portfolio rating: Average = 3.5; Haiti = 3.5

Governance rating: Average = 3.0; Haiti = 2.4

IDA performance rating: Average = 2.9; Haiti = 1.7

To put the performance of past Aristide and Préval regimes in perspective, it must be noted that capacity issues have always plagued Haiti. For instance, in 1981, under Baby Doc, the U.S. General Accounting Office (1982) reported that poor governance produced generally unsatisfactory performance such as the following problems: "project delays resulting in large amounts of unexpended funds, projects which were never implemented, projects accomplishing less than originally expected, and a variety of other implementation problems" (p. 6). A 1985 USGAO (1985) report found much the same situation, as did Josh DeWind and David H. Kinley (1988) in their study in the late 1980s, in which they reviewed many USAID reports. Between 1976 and 1979, only 65 percent of bilateral and multilateral aid to Haiti was actually spent (English 1984).

FINANCIAL MANAGEMENT

Lack of capacity went considerably beyond poor aid administration. For all intents and purposes, Haiti had dysfunctional budgetary, financial, or procurement systems, making it difficult to financially manage the country, let alone administer foreign assistance (World Bank 2005b). A budget reform law enacted in 1985 was never fully implemented. Offices were not created and personnel remained unassigned. Budget procedures and policies were not in place, data for the budget were unavailable. From 1997 through 2001 there was no approved national budget. Internal and external audits were weak. No external audits were conducted for years. Not even parliament had access to or approved the budget. Public procurement procedures were never fully implemented. Procurement was decentralized without controls or accountability. Government used sole source contracts and unadvertised bidding. Government was unwilling or unable to pay vendors for services in a timely fashion. Budget reductions and low salaries drove away most finance professionals. One-half of government expenses were non-recurrent or discretionary, making it virtually impossible to identify fund use, beneficiaries, or impact (World Bank, Operations Evaluation Department 2002, p. 4). Government has one of the lowest tax raising capacities of any country (Inter-American Development Bank 2007a). Donors view poor financial management practices as a breeding ground for corruption, and have always been nervous about giving government control of financing.[5]

TAX REVENUES

As discussed below, Haiti's government is heavily subsidized by foreign assistance transfers. Not only is foreign aid necessary because government has failed to control spending, it also is required because government has proved ineffective in gathering taxes. According to the State Department's Bureau of Economic and Business Affairs (2002, p. 4), tax revenues are a problem because:

> Haiti's tax collection system is inefficient. Direct taxes on salary and wages represent only about 25 percent of receipts. Moreover, tax evasion is widespread. Not surprisingly, the government has made improved revenue collection a top priority. The DGI has organized a large taxpayers' unit which focuses on identifying and collecting the tax liabilities of the 200 largest corporate and individual taxpayers in the Port-au-Prince area, which are estimated to represent over 80 percent of potential income tax revenue. In mid-1999, the Haitian government created a State Secretary for Revenue to coordinate and oversee both Customs and DGI operations with a view toward increasing receipts from each. Efforts were also made to identify and register all taxpayers through the issuance of a citizen taxpayer ID card. In addition, the Value Added Tax has been extended to include sectors previously exempt (banking services, agribusiness, and the supply of water and electricity). Collection remains sporadic and inefficient, even though the tax authorities are under increasing pressure to raise tax revenues and have announced new measures to do so.

But inefficiency is only part of the problem. The other is that the vast majority of Haitians work in the informal economy and pay no taxes. It is unlikely that taxes could ever be collected from this sector. (See chapter 8 for a discussion of converting the informal economy into a formal one.)

CIVIL SERVICE

The civil service has been a perpetual problem in Haitian government as well. U.S. assessments revealed that about 30 percent of the civil service consisted of "phantom" employees, who accounted for about half of the public wage bill. Aristide had a similar concern when he took office in 1991: Namely, that the government was paying people who were not really working. One ministry had 10,000 employees, only about half of whom were ever at work. Further, about 93 percent of the Haitian state budget went to salaries (U.S. Agency for International Development 1996a, pp. 1–2; U.S. Agency for International Development 1996b). An IMF assessment of Haiti's civil service in 1998 reached the following conclusions: (1) the civil service has played a very limited role in providing social services; (2) the small size and very limited capacity of the government contrast with the massive development challenge facing the country; (3) the public sector is far smaller than in other developing countries; (4) the public-sector wage bill in Haiti is very low; (5) the public wage bill takes up a significant portion of the government budget in Haiti; and (6) public-sector wages are not comparable to private-sector wages. The IMF had strong doubts about Haiti's ability to deliver services, attract quality civil servants, and avoid corruption (International Monetary Fund 1998).

As a consequence, not only were Haitians unable to manage aid—not to mention government generally—but they had no funds either to contribute to the country's development or to maintain the programs that had been funded earlier.

Lack of Government "Ownership" of Programs

"Ownership" means taking responsibility for implementing the projects funded and then following through to ensure effectiveness, continued improvement, and success.

The World Bank's 2002 *Haiti: Country Assistance Evaluation* (World Bank, Operations Evaluation Department 2002) found that the government of Haiti was not playing the "ownership" role that donors expect a recipient government to play: "The government did not exhibit ownership by taking the initiative for formulating and implementing [its] assistance program, encouraging a consensus among key ministries and decision makers, or adopting timely action to support the program" (p. 19). The Interim Cooperation Framework issued by the Transition Government echoes this assessment: "The preceding governments lacked the political will and the means to make the necessary changes in key areas, particularly justice, police, administrative reform and decentralization" (Republic of Haiti 2004a, p. 6).

In a 2004 assessment of its foreign assistance efforts in Haiti since 1994, the Canadian International Development Agency (2004) concluded: "Considering the resources invested, scattered Canadian projects do not seem to provide a critical mass of results, do not foster efficiency and effectiveness of the action taken, and make it difficult to achieve sustainable results in view of the surrounding high-risk environment" (p. 7). The Canadian agency discussed rule-of-law initiatives (targeting improvements in the justice and police systems) as an example: "Many obstacles have been and continue to be faced in coordination with the Government of Haiti. The government's objectives are often hazy and subject to change. Plans and policies are not approved or implemented. Its actions are often diametrically opposed to the projects carried out" (Canadian International Development Agency 2003, p. 12). Often, no one was in charge (which is understandable when one recalls that from 1994 to 2004 there were ten ministers of justice): "This type of project has admittedly been the one to yield the most disappointing results for Canada and other donors. The main reasons for this being the Haitian government's lack of political will to reform the public sector as a whole and improve all forms of governance and the government's flagrant lack of cooperation. Canada has had to terminate most of its support to public institutions, especially in the area of security and justice" (p. 9). Rule of law is the underpinning of democratic society. These programs target the justice system, so that Haitians can count on their courts to function and deliver justice to all citizens.

The U.S. effort to promote rule-of-law initiatives yielded similarly disappointing results.[6] From 1995 to 2000, the United States spent nearly $100 million on rule-of-law programs in Haiti. Yet a July 1997 poll showed that only 24 percent of Haitians believed the justice system to be fair (U.S. Agency for International Development 1998, p. 7). One might assume that the Haitian government would be a willing participant in programs to reform two highly troubled institutions, the judiciary and the police. Yet U.S. General Accounting Office reviews (2000a, 2000b) of the programs concluded:

The Haitian government's lack of a clear commitment to addressing the major problems of its police and judicial institutions has been the key factor affecting the success of the U.S. assistance provided to these institutions. U.S. assistance to the police has been impeded because the Haitian government has not acted, for example, to (1) strengthen the police organization by filling currently vacant key leadership positions, such as the Inspector General and the heads of many field units; (2) provide the human and physical resources needed to develop an effective police force; (3) support vigorously police investigations of serious crimes; and (4) keep the police force out of politics. U.S. assistance to the judicial sector has been undercut because the Haitian government has not, for instance, (1) followed through the broad reform of the judicial sector needed to address its major problems, (2) assumed ownership of many of the improvements made possible by U.S. assistance, and (3) provided the physical and human resources needed to operate the sector effectively.[7]

In its reports the General Accounting Office did not speculate as to why government might not be cooperating, but Alex Dupuy (2003) theorizes that Aristide, like his predecessors, used the judicial system for several purposes, none consistent with rule of law or democratic principles. Traditionally, in Haiti, the courts and police have been used to intimidate the opposition and to exact revenge for past offenses. Additionally, Aristide used the system to offer patronage positions to loyal supporters, particularly members of the Chimères, who did the government's dirty work. Aristide took over the courts and police simply by ignoring parliament and the constitution. Even if one is reluctant to accept this characterization of Aristide, the fact remains that the Haitian government invested virtually nothing in judicial reform and failed to support donor initiatives through policy, legislation, or funding.

The failure to implement programs was widespread in Haiti's ministries. In recognition of Haiti's environmental disasters, the Environmental Secretariat was elevated to ministry status. In 1999 a National Environmental Action Plan was approved after extensive citizen participation, but it was never implemented (Inter-American Development Bank 2004a, p. 12). The Ministry of Education approved a National Education Plan, but never presented it to parliament for approval. The Ministry of Health was unable to establish norms and standards for health programs and could not implement a decentralization program. The Ministry of Justice balked at implementing many reforms.

A similar lack of will to implement programs occurred in the justice system (see International Crisis Group 2007a). Haiti's judges are poorly educated: many do not have law degrees, few have adequate experience in judicial process, and some have been found to be illiterate. The 1990 constitution, in recognition of this perpetual problem, required the establishment of a National Magistrate's School. Haitians failed to establish the school until 1995. After graduating only three classes, it was allowed to terminate in 2004.

Another Inter-American Development Bank initiative concerns sustainable development. The IADB invested heavily in infrastructure projects. The Haitian government failed to provide maintenance funds for most projects, especially roads, irrigation, water, sanitation, education, and health. The national government also failed to develop any revenue-generating capacity in poor communities outside Port-au-Prince, leaving them unable to maintain the infrastructure funded earlier by donors (Inter-American Development Bank 2003b). Haiti's infrastructure is in ruins, in spite of the expenditure of millions to develop it.

Lack of Haitian "ownership" of aid is not new (see DeWind and Kinley 1988). A U.S. General Accounting Office assessment of assistance to Haiti in 1981 reported that assistance over the long term was ineffective because USAID funded initial development, but was unable to get the government to pay either for continuing operating or maintenance costs (U.S. General Accounting Office 1985). A 1982 General Accounting Office report on USAID's efforts in Haiti concluded that "poor Government of Haiti participation/involvement has been the major reason that the AID projects had problems. . . . Lack of commitment to the development process is a root cause of Haiti's poor performance" (U.S. General Accounting Office 1982, p. 9).

Aid Dependency

Haiti has become dependent on foreign assistance and remittances to sustain itself, as have many other developing countries. The per capita value of remittances to Haiti was $50 in 1996 and $19 in 2002. In 2003 per capita aid rose to $23.70, as compared to an average of $9.90 for Latin American and Caribbean nations. Haiti depends more heavily on foreign assistance than the average Caribbean nations, measured as a percentage of GNI (gross national income): 12.4 percent in 1996 and 4.5 percent in 2002, compared to 6.2 percent (1996) and 3.9 percent (2002) for the Caribbean. In 2003 Haiti's foreign assistance as a percentage of GDP, 6.8 percent, was much higher than for developing countries generally on average, 3.0 percent, but not for least-developed countries,

Table 6-1. *Aid Dependency of Haiti and Developing Countries*
Unit as indicated

Region	Official development assistance per capita (U.S.$) 2004	Official development assistance as percentage of GDP 1990	Official development assistance as percentage of GDP 2004	Debt service as percentage of GDP 1990	Debt service as percentage of GDP 2004
Developing countries	10.5	2.7	0.5	3.5	4.9
Least-developed countries	33.4	13.0	9.6	2.8	2.6
Arab states	5.9	6.8	0.6	4.1	—
East Asia and Pacific	3.3	1.0	0.2	3.0	—
Latin America and Caribbean	10.	1.3	0.3	4.0	7.8
South Asia	4.5	1.6	0.5	2.6	2.6
Sub-Saharan Africa	33.0	12.0	0.5	3.8	—
Haiti	28.9	5.9	6.9	1.2	3.8

Source: United Nations (2006).

18.7 percent (United Nations 2005a). In 1999 the UN found that 86 percent of development investments came from external sources.

The most telling figures for 2005 showed central government revenues at 9 percent of GDP, as compared to 18 percent for other developing countries, but central government expenditures varied from 9 to 16 percent of GDP over recent years, evidencing the uncertainty of aid flows. Meanwhile, only 18 percent of government revenues derived from taxes.

Table 6-1 shows not only Haiti's aid dependency, but the effects of aid suspensions and reductions, which if not applied to Haiti would have substantially increased its aid dependency and indebtedness, at least compared to other developing countries.

Aid dependency has negative consequences for developing countries, especially those like Haiti.[8] Aid dependency undermines institutional quality by weakening accountability, encouraging rent seeking, facilitating corruption, fomenting conflict over control and distribution of funding, siphoning off scarce resources from the civil service, and alleviating pressures to reform from the government (Knack 2000; see also Klein and Hartford 2005).

Remittances also can have deleterious effects on developing countries when they become the largest source of outside revenue (see Uribe and Buss 2007). Governments have no need to provide public services because they know relatives in other countries will sustain much of the population. But some poor people, those who do not receive remittances, are severely disadvantaged because they have few channels of support. Often this is tied to race. In Cuba, for example, the black population is poor and tends to have many fewer relatives remitting to them from abroad than does the white population. This is because waves of exiles leaving Cuba in the 1980s under the repressive Castro regime were white and were much better off and able to do well economically, primarily in Miami. Black Cubans, still a small minority of all Cubans, have benefited from the Castro regime. In the case of Haiti, many wealthy elites in the country, including many mulattoes, also have extensive economic interests in Miami.

Aid and remittance dependency also relieves government of its responsibility to fund development through taxation and other government revenues. This means the government has no need to present itself to the electorate who would ordinarily reject government policy through tax revolts, political action, and elections.

Some critics of Aristide say that he expected donors to contribute aid so that the government could do with it what it wanted, whereas donors bore responsibility for meeting needs of the country (Falcoff 2004). Others argue that Aristide, having precipitated the crisis in Haiti for political reasons, exhorted donors to do something about poverty. In any case, to many observers, the Haitian government under Aristide seemed to have little concern for nation building, institution building, or postconflict reconstruction; in many ways, it seemed to be uninterested in governance at all.

Dissension between President and Parliament

Because Haiti has a weak presidential system (see chapter 2), donors must work with both president and parliament to develop strategies and approve aid funding (Inter-American Development Bank 2003a). Unlike the case in many developing countries, donors found it much more difficult to promote "country ownership" for their initiatives, because there was likely to be much more divergence of opinion on what should be done and considerably more political gamesmanship. Small factions were able to veto decisions of others, or thwart them by denying decisionmakers a legislative quorum. The constitutional impasse over the 1997 elections is an extreme example of intragovernmental conflict that negatively affected foreign assistance. The IADB (2003a) has stated that it "was unable to foresee that the lack of coordination between the executive and legislative branches of government would become a strong obstacle to the delivery of its program" (pp. iii; see also Inter-American Development Bank 2001).

The impact on Haiti of the lack of cooperation among the branches of government and political factions is hard to overestimate (U.S. Agency for International Development 1998, pp. 2–3). Under Préval's first presidency, only two bills were "passed" in parliament. No budget was submitted to parliament for approval. Then there was the decentralization issue in 1997 and 1998: the 1987 constitution mandated a decentralization or devolution of state authority back to local governments, but it was never implemented. No ministry was able to implement any devolution program. The Decentralization Framework Law, Law on the Commune, and Law on Municipal Development and Management, among others designed to define guidelines for national and local financing, were not passed.[9]

Failures on the Part of Donors

Haitians should not be blamed exclusively for the failures of foreign assistance in their country. Bilateral, multilateral, regional, and charitable organizations all failed to some extent to effectively help Haiti. Aid shortcomings likely originated in the collective failure of donors to grasp that issues of Haitian politics and governance were *the* important drivers of success—or failure, from which everything else would follow. Having failed to assign to politics and governance the highest priority, donors adopted an assistance model more appropriate to Latin America than to Haiti, which was more like a nation of sub-Saharan Africa. The initial ineffectiveness was magnified by aid suspensions and cutbacks; inappropriate conditionality; unclear policy focus and program design; poor alignment and harmonization; inadequate accountability; ineffective capacity building; faulty implementation; lack of coordination; and delusions about what constituted program success. No donor stepped forward to lead the rest. These issues, perpetually in play, may have caused donor fatigue, so that ultimately aid organizations tired of trying to help Haiti (see Ortiz 2003).

FAULTY AID PRIORITIES

In recent years, there has been increasing recognition that "failure to give highest priority to resolving the political and governance problems that undermined economic development" nullified attempts by the donor community to improve conditions in Haiti (World Bank, Operations Evaluation Department 2002). Mark Schacter (2000), in an analysis of World Bank programs, concluded, "Only recently have Bank-supported activities paid systematic attention to deeper rooted institutional issues at the root of the dysfunctional patrimonial state—issues related to leadership, incentives, and human capacity deficits. Yet the hallmarks of patrimonialism—corruption, cronyism, and critically ineffective service delivery—remain embedded in the fabric of government" (p. 5). Donors tended to focus on macroeconomic policy, security, military demobilization, health, and infrastructure—all critically important, to be sure. A review of donor projects since 1994 shows increasingly more attention to politics and governance, especially projects funded by the United States, Canada, the World Bank, the UN Development Program, and the Inter-American Development Bank. Yet Haiti continued to flounder. It is likely that governance projects either failed outright or made only dents in the problem, while other factors overwhelmed even what few gains may have been realized.

INEFFECTIVE DONOR ASSISTANCE STRATEGIES

The World Bank's Country Assistance Evaluation concluded that donors had erred in offering traditional assistance programs on the Latin American model when governance and political barriers were likely insurmountable in that framework (World Bank, Operations Evaluation Department 2002; see also World Bank 1991, 1996, 1997, 1998). The Latin American model assumes a stable democratic political system, a supportive government with capacity to partner and then implement in a well-functioning economy, buttressed by peace and security. For Haiti, decisionmakers should have assumed they needed to use a sub-Saharan Africa model, such as would be appropriate for countries like Sierra Leone, Liberia, Somalia, Congo, Uganda, Zaire, and Zimbabwe, to name a few (World Bank, Operations Evaluation Department 1998). These countries received assistance, but expectations were low. It may also be the case that in the mid-1990s the donor community was just beginning to struggle with the notion of fragile states and postconflict reconstruction as special cases for development. Methods of the past simply were inappropriate for Haiti, as they were in several other fragile states.

TIMING

Timing is crucial in aid provision (UN Economic and Social Council 1999, p. 10). Given the difficulty donors had switching back and forth between emergency relief, reconstruction, and normalization assistance during the Aristide years, it has become apparent to many experts that engagement of the donor community in Haiti should have occurred immediately after the fall of Baby Doc's regime in 1986, when it may well have been possible to promote equitable growth and democratic change (World Bank, Operations Evaluation Department 1998, p. 220). The military junta, having virtually no popular support, could have been easily displaced and aid could have flowed to set the stage for Aristide or other democratic candidates.

Even under the Transition Government, it was difficult for policymakers to figure out how to proceed. The IADB (2004a), when putting together its Transition Strategy for Haiti in November 2004, concluded: "The interim government is struggling to reestablish political and social stability; however, the political situation and stability outlook remain uncertain: full deployment of the UN stabilization force has yet to materialize, the government's authority throughout the country is not fully restored, the former ruling political party—Lavalas—refuses to participate in the election process and the framework for national elections in 2005 has yet to be established" (pp. 2–3). Finding the best timing and method for providing aid is at best an art, certainly not a science.

MISREADINGS OF THE HAITIAN CONTEXT

Donors may have seriously misread the situation in Haiti at various points. The Clinton administration, along with other donors, suspended or greatly reduced aid after the 1997 election debacle and its aftermath. Why? Democratization had effectively collapsed; some say it had never existed. Although the U.S. State Department in its budget requests for FY2002 through FY2004 comments on the turn away from democracy and drift toward instability, the FY2004 report also states, "U.S. engagement in Haiti is transitioning from the crisis-driven activism of the 1990s to a more normal and long-term approach aimed at building an evolving inclusive democracy." The U.S. Agency of International Development in its Strategic Plan, 1999–2004, echoes the State Department's conclusion. Yet 2004 produced another Haitian revolution—in fact, all of the features of democracy were absent in Haiti, yet democratization was seen to be going well. Some donors wanted normalization of relations so badly that they were willing to see progress in Haiti when it did not exist. Others believed that donors may simply have been out of touch with country dynamics in which they offered assistance. Still others wanted to declare victory and withdraw. And some were trying to put a good face on the situation to assist country leadership, or to please U.S. policymakers. None of these were likely good justifications for continuing aid that wasn't working. At the same time, aid suspensions and disbursement delays played havoc with assistance programs.

AID SUSPENSIONS

Foreign assistance to Haiti has waxed and waned as donors, usually acting collectively—certainly under U.S. pressure—responded to political situations in Haiti they did not like. In 1990 and 1991 donors flooded the newly elected

Aristide government with aid, then shortly thereafter, from 1992 to 1994, instituted an embargo under the military regime. Aid dropped from $174 million per annum to $112 million on average and shifted to humanitarian programs. From 1995 to 2000 donors revived aid, an average of $383 million annually over the period, only to suspend it over the disputed elections of 2000 and 2004 to about $195 million annually.

Haitian political leadership in the executive and in parliament made Haiti an "aid orphan"—this is the insider term for a country that has great needs but is so dysfunctional that donors do not want to invest resources in it, especially if there are better or more deserving candidates. Aid, after all, is scarce, and competition for it is intensifying. Aid suspensions have been widely acknowledged as contributing to ineffective aid policies. Programs that were in place suddenly terminated when aid stopped, unraveling many positive benefits they may have produced in country. Once assistance started up again, programs had to regain what was lost before they could move forward. This was disastrous because many development projects, even in the best of circumstances, take years to mature and produce results. It was difficult, time-consuming, and expensive to re-create capacity and programs when aid to Haiti was restored. An additional problem was that capacity created in government or among NGOs also dissipated. At the same time, the Haitian government was unwilling or unable to continue programs on its own. As discussed earlier, the Haitian government rarely funded maintenance of its infrastructure or ongoing operations.

To complicate matters, Aristide, after being deposed, from exile in the United States called for aid suspensions and embargoes as a punishment of those who had deposed him. In the eyes of his critics this meant that the president of Haiti was willing to sacrifice aid to his people to secure his return to power. Donors were conflicted about whether to support Aristide and put pressure on Cédras, using aid as leverage. Much the same quandary occurred in the international community in connection with Nelson Mandela in South Africa, or with Miami's Cuban community and the Castro regime.

USAID's decentralization project illustrates the confounding effects of aid suspensions. The project was to decentralize or devolve state authority back to local governments, as was mandated by the 1987 constitution but was never implemented (ARD Inc. 2000; World Bank 2006a). The project was authorized in May 1991, then suspended in September 1991, because of the coup d'état. The project was reworked so that some civil society components could be activated, something the military junta approved. Then, in October 1994, Aristide returned to Haiti. The new government did not sign an agreement to start up the project again until September 1995. Perhaps the government faced more pressing demands. But so much time had elapsed by then that USAID had to go through a new round of bids from NGOs for carrying out the project before it could be relaunched. When it was once again in place, a deadlock occurred between President Préval and parliament over the resolution of the 1997 fraudulent elections, which the president finally resolved by ruling by decree. The decentralization project was affected because there were no local officials in place from January 1999 to September 2000. The project accomplished very little.

Another initiative suffered a similar fate. After 1994 the Inter-American Development Bank invested in loans and technical assistance for poverty reduction, private-sector development, and institution building (Inter-American Development Bank 2003b). In 1997 and 1998 IADB suspended its loan programs as a result of electoral turmoil—it continued to pursue projects already in the pipeline but did not fund any new projects. Programs of the IADB, World Bank, UN Development Program, and other donors were left with huge holes in them that are only now, a decade later, beginning to be filled. The impacts on bilateral donors' programs were less severe because these donors tended not to fund comprehensive development strategies but rather individual projects.

Aid suspensions also made it difficult for donors to move funding around in the short term, even when readily available. Because Haiti's military regime, in power from 1991 to 1994, impoverished Haitians even further, foreign assistance concentrated on projects supporting humanitarian efforts. Once Aristide returned to power, donors were slow to recognize the need for capacity building as a centerpiece in the foreign aid strategy and were slow to reprogram funding into capacity building. Donors also had difficulty determining when to shift from emergency relief to reconstruction assistance, something critical to aid's success. Just as they did so, of course, aid was once again suspended in 1997 over faulty elections.

Finally, some donors, even though aid had been suspended, nonetheless undertook projects that typically are long-term initiatives, and appeared to waste money in the process. From 1991 to 1994, the United States and others embargoed all but humanitarian aid to Haiti. But USAID decided that rather than just fund short-term humanitarian programs having no sustainability, they would launch the Job Creation program whereby poor Haitians were paid to work on infrastructure projects. But these investments were not maintained by the Haitian government, so their efforts were for naught (U.S. Agency for International Development 1999). Some claim that USAID created a short-term income transfer program disguised as job generation, while diverting funding away from more productive uses, particularly in agriculture, where investments might have yielded more benefits. There seemed to be a tendency to spend money even when it made little sense. This contributed to failures.

The suspension of projects that had already started up may have created false hopes and unrealistic expectations among the people. When projects failed to deliver, this may have damaged the reputation of donors who were already held in suspicion. Numerous NGOs undertook projects to build civil society in Haiti at the grassroots level, ranging from unionization through citizens associations to political party building. In their final project reports NGOs claimed to have reached thousands of citizens and hundreds of organizations. But each time Haitian groups organized, their NGO advisers were pulled back, leaving them without support or encouragement. This cannot have been good for democratization.

A 2003 United Nations system report (United Nations 2003, p. 5) summed up the situation:

> The reform programs that were implemented in 1995 and 1996, particularly the civil service, are basically at a standstill, and only a few activities involving preparations or support for the reforms and financed by external aid are operational. Any progress that has been made in strengthening administration of justice and respect for human rights appears to be threatened. In the meantime, the capabilities of the public sector fall short of needs, corruption continues, and inadequate public policies have not been changed.

Some analysts noted a possible further unintended consequence of aid suspensions. They claim the Aristide government, starved for aid funding and lacking any other public revenues, turned to drug trafficking as a way to sustain its operations.[10] Rumors perpetually had it that major drug charges were about to be forthcoming against Aristide after he fled Haiti. Money laundering and corruption indictments were already in place.

DISBURSEMENT DELAYS

Donors may delay disbursement of aid to countries either because they want to see what's going on in the country before transferring money, or donor bureaucracies may delay fund transfers through inefficiency or indifference. Although not as devastating as full aid suspensions, aid delays can have negative consequences.[11]

In June 2006, Haiti unveiled its Social Appeasement Program, designed to urgently help impoverished areas in conflict-prone zones in the country. The rationale for the initiative was to demonstrate government commitment to poor people trapped in ghettos in Haiti's urban areas, where gang violence, lack of public services, and hopelessness prevail. Donors—including the United States, Belgium, Brazil, and Canada—approved the program at one of their conferences on aid to Haiti in 2004 and agreed to funding of $50 million over five years. As of April 2007, however, little of the money pledged to the program actually had reached the government, which threw the initiative into disarray.

Earlier, Spain in 2005 threatened to pull its 200 troops out of the UN Stabilization Mission in Haiti (MINUSTAH) if donors did not fulfill their pledges to Haiti. At the time, only $300 million of the $700 million pledged had arrived in Haiti. Spain made good on its threat in 2006, announcing that it was pulling out of Haiti. It was still concerned that only half of the $1 billion allocated to Haiti had arrived.

Not all donors agreed with Spain's assessment, however. Some complained that Préval's government kept changing its priorities: first children's needs, then infrastructure, and finally security (see Taft-Morales 2007a, p. 18).

In fairness to the government and donors, it should be pointed out that the disbursement problem plagues even advanced countries when they are faced with the challenge of distributing large amounts of funding, especially during a crisis. In Hurricane Katrina's aftermath, countries around the world made donations to help Americans, but much of the aid was not distributed (U.S. Government Accountability Office 2005c). The American Red Cross was unable to spend millions in donations in a timely fashion, and even had major problems with accountability and fraud internally and externally. The U.S. Small Business Administration took months to approve billions in disaster loans to home owners whose properties were damaged during the storm. Many charitable organizations, such as the Congressional Black Caucus Foundation, also reported delays in disbursing their funds.

CONDITIONALITY

Donors set conditions on the recipients of aid in several ways. They may offer programs targeted at a specific issue or problem, and if the country wants aid, then it must accept the program. Donors may attach goal attainment criteria on countries such that if they do not meet donor expectations, targets, or goals, aid will be reduced or terminated. Donors will withhold or redirect funds if countries do not resolve an issue or problem. Bilateral donors often practice "aid tying": requiring countries to purchase goods and services from the donor using aid funding. Some observers have noted that conditionality in the Haitian case may have been counterproductive, confrontational, or misguided, thereby increasing the likelihood that aid would fail (Canadian International Development Agency 2004). Though such assessments are highly subjective, there are a lot of cases where many might agree. Examples of conditionality gone awry are easy to find. Note that programs selected for funding may be good ones, but they may not be viewed that way by some Haitians.

Some multilateral and bilateral donors believe that conditionality likely has little or no influence on the success of foreign aid. The World Bank concluded (2004b, p. 6): "The Bank has been unable to leverage—[through] conditionality, delayed program/project funding, overall levels of funding—in support of the implementation of important reforms, particularly in governance and public sector management and in sound economic policies; political pressures of other stakeholders and the fragility of the whole situation were simply too great to allow the Bank to operate as it would have in a more normal setting." The Canadian International Development Agency (2004, p. 11) has stated:

> Haiti exemplifies some of the negative consequences of conditionality for both recipient and donor. The years 1994 to 1997 were marked by donor-driven reform agendas and conditionality-based financing in Haiti. Results from this period are unsurprising. Donor-driven agendas contributed to poor commitment and ineffective implementation on the part of the government of Haiti and to frustration and Haiti fatigue for the donor community. This in turn contributed to the withdrawal of some donor agencies. Following the 2000 disputed elections, strict conditionality was imposed to promote transparency of governance, solid macroeconomic policies, and fiscal responsibility. Once again, it is highly questionable how constructive this set of conditionality was given that the system did not reform.

DONOR-DRIVEN PROJECTS

Donor politics, methods, and foreign policy goals led donors to impose aid programs on Haiti, even though it might have been premature to do so. For example, the United States and other donors focused on elections as a major goal in democratizing Haiti (Falcoff 2004; Mobekk 2001). In 1995 the United States spent $18.8 million in election assistance following Aristide's return. Elections were equated with democracy. And in 1995, democracy restored was equated with Aristide's return (Falcoff 2004; Dobbins 2003). Few equated elections and Aristide's return with regime legitimacy, a much larger and more important question (Orr 2002). Even fewer equated democracy with the need for broad opportunities for grassroots citizen participation, not just the right to vote. Few observed that there actually was no democracy in Haiti to restore (Dobbins 2003).

Haitian commentators in the press warned that elections were not enough (Mobekk 2001). Each election since 1990 has been perceived by many as unfair and fraudulent, opposition parties have been intimidated and have engaged in boycotts, and voter turnout has been low. Further, Aristide, elected twice, has been ousted twice from power. The same pattern repeated itself in elections under the Transition Government, but to a lesser extent.

Haiti never had a culture of democracy in place, so elections merely became, in the view of many, another political tool of whichever faction was in power. To complicate matters, the international community accepted electoral results as fair on some occasions, but not on others, drawing into question the legitimacy of the whole process. So, the argument goes, elections may be a necessary condition for democracy, but not a sufficient one. Eventually the Haitian people will tire of the pretense of participating in a "democratic" society—if they have not already done so. Funding elections raised questions of intent for some Haitians: Were elections a way for the international community to declare victory and disengage, that is, "Vote and run"? (Fauriol 2005). Aristide's prime minister, Rosny Smart, remarked in retrospect that the focus mainly on elections was a mistake, because elections made no difference in people's lives (Mobekk 2000, p. 8).

Conditionality was also a factor in funding of civil service reform. Donors and the World Bank had a policy goal of downsizing and reforming the civil service, for several reasons. Particularly in Haiti, the civil service represented enormous patronage opportunities for the political faction controlling the country. A bloated civil service not only drained public resources into unproductive uses but also became corrupt and inefficient. Often the civil service had its own agenda—rent seeking, manipulating governance for private gain. The World Bank's 1996 Country Assistance Strategy for Haiti (World Bank, Operations Evaluation Department 2002) called for public-sector reform, but it noted that a "brain drain has decimated the ranks of both professional and technical skills, and a poorly designed civil service reform during 1998–1999 led to loss of many well qualified people" (p. 4). Civil service reform appeared ill-timed. Aristide had resisted civil service reform in 1994 and 1995, then blocked Préval from executing reforms as well. Yet donors continued to fund these programs, even though there was little government support for them.

Some observers believed that what should have occurred was civil service reconstruction—rebuilding capacity for administration of aid and for governance generally. In this way, even in a bloated bureaucracy, assistance could be managed. Reconstruction would likely have encountered relatively little resistance from the government. Reform could have begun once the delivery of services was stabilized (Mukherjee 2003).

Another area where conditionality was counterproductive was in programs to "build civil society." Some people and entities believe that civil society organizations (CSOs) are the backbone of democracy. From the World Bank's perspective, "participation of CSOs in government development projects and programs can enhance their operational performance by contributing local knowledge, providing technical expertise, and leveraging social capital. Further, CSOs can bring innovative ideas and solutions, as well as participatory approaches, to solving local problems."[12] But in nations dominated by one party—Haiti arguably fell in this category, being dominated by Lavalas—supporting CSOs either meant siding with the party in power or opposing it. The International Republican Institute (IRI), an NGO created in 1983 and funded by the U.S. National Endowment for Democracy, since 1993 has been working on projects that include party building, civil society action, and polling. Perhaps because much of IRI's work was done during Aristide's first and second administrations, some observers, especially on the left, have suggested that IRI is a tool of anti-Aristide forces, implying that the U.S. government is covertly funding the overthrow of Aristide, while appearing to support democracy (see Maguire 2004). One critic of IRI has remarked, "Undemocratic agendas may be pursued under the guise of 'democracy promotion' because the U.S. aid passes only through nongovernmental organizations, some of which are aligned with the anti-Aristide opposition."[13] A report (ARD Inc. 2000) on a USAID project on Haitian CSOs states, "The Government rarely meets with CSOs to solicit their input or to negotiate policies directly reflecting their sector. Moreover, Lavalas popular organization attacks on civil society meetings and members of the press indicate that the Government sees civil society critics of government policy as the enemy and in partnership with the political opposition that is seeking to bring down the Aristide regime" (p. 3).

Other donors tried to build a rudimentary competitive political party system. In July 2005, the UN Development Program supported the Transition

Government in organizing a workshop for all political parties planning to compete in the 2005 elections in which they could meet with informed representatives about a host of national issues, including the national budget and the Interim Cooperative Framework. Although this project appeared laudable in many ways, critics pointed out that most parties were not viable or credible, and by bringing them into a forum, the government and the UN tended to legitimize them—giving them all equal or elevated status. For critics, information dissemination was one thing, and legitimizing opposition forces another.

Anticorruption initiatives also were a high priority for donors, especially the World Bank (2006e). In 2004 Haiti created an anticorruption unit with donor funding and in 2006 a diagnostic survey of corruption. Both were criticized as odd funding choices. Anticorruption units assemble investigative and prosecutorial functions under an independent body to focus resources on all aspects of corruption. Although there are numerous such units in developing countries, only a handful have actually been successful in reducing corruption, according to numerous evaluations completed. Why? When donors bypass the traditional judicial system, this retards its reform and development, leading to the operation of parallel systems. Past experience suggests that these units will be used by those in power to persecute the opposition. Thus, consolidating judicial power in the hands of a few—whether this is done by donor projects or by the government itself—typically leads to the very abuses such units are created to eliminate, and anticorruption units themselves become corrupt.

The diagnostic survey is a survey of citizens and others to find out their perceptions of the extent of corruption in a country. This establishes a baseline against which to compare progress in reducing corruption. But critics questioned the reliability of perceptions, which are deemed by some to be inaccurate and unstable. Both initiatives were criticized as being a poor use of funds, given the country's problems.

World Bank analysts reviewing judicial reform programs through 2006 concluded (World Bank 2006b, pp. 75–76): "Assistance programs focused largely on providing training, some equipment and infrastructure, and reorganizing courtroom processing of cases. These programs have not proved very effective in improving performance even in less problematic settings, and where they have had any impact, have required far more time and resources as well as a fuller menu of complementary activities than provided to Haiti."

ACCOUNTABILITY

Since David Osborne, with his book *Reinventing Government*, practically single-handedly launched the reinventing government movement in 1992, governments around the world have been holding themselves accountable in part by setting goals, objectives, baselines, and benchmarks, then measuring their performance and reporting to the public.[14] Foreign aid programs are now heavily infused with accountability and performance,[15] but this movement has created a number of problems for developing countries such as Haiti.

1. Data gathering and reporting requirements are burdensome for developing countries. If they do not have the capacity to administer aid, they likely will struggle to demonstrate that aid produced the intended results. The UN System, in its 2003 report on an Integrated Emergency Response Program for Haiti, observed that assistance was hampered by the inability of Haitians to gather data, then provide them to donors to promote accountability. World Bank loan documents for projects in 2005 echoed this conclusion. To make matters worse, research shows that for developing countries, a lack of budget and finance data is directly correlated with high deficits (Wallack 2004).

2. Even if performance data had been available in Haiti, the fits and starts of aid programs would have thwarted assessment efforts. Most accountability efforts require baselines and benchmarks against which to compare ongoing performance—for example, Millennium Challenge Goals. But baselines in Haiti could never really be established, because programs were so frequently suspended or revised because of reduced funding and refocusing. The decentralization project was reworked several times, making performance measurement highly problematic.

3. Most important, donors may mandate accountability and performance, but history of aid provision in Haiti suggests they will continue to award aid even in the most problematic of cases. Such inconsistency is not unusual: North Korea and Palestine, in 2006 and 2007, continued to receive aid even though North Korea developed and tested nuclear weapons and Palestine refused to retract its calls for the destruction of Israel.[16] In Haiti itself, democratization programs, especially elections, continued to receive funding even though fraud, opposition boycotts, and low participation were endemic to them. So accountability provisos, rather than spurring Haiti to better performance, probably would make little difference.

Even though performance-based loans are difficult to execute, they remain the mainstay of multilateral lending. For example, the Inter-American

Development Bank loan for Basic Economic Infrastructure Rehabilitation offered Haitians loan payments in three tranches, each with clearly specified performance targets (Inter-American Development Bank 2004b).

Conditions imposed by the U.S. Congress on aid provision to Haiti have both helped and hurt that country (Taft-Morales 2007a).[17] Congress required USAID to pass aid through NGOs, but for decades this was considered state-of-the-art in service delivery in developing countries. And Congress occasionally indirectly delayed aid by asking USAID to provide it with information before releasing funds, a tactic that postpones funding availability without overtly appearing to do so (U.S. Agency for International Development 1996a, p. 2; 1996b). Even when conditionality seemed appropriate, the United States tended to avoid it. In its October 2000 assessment of USAID's foreign assistance to the Haitian justice system, the General Accounting Office recommended that any further assistance be linked to "performance-related conditions" (U.S. General Accounting Office 2000a). But GAO recommendations were not followed. The United States and other donors, when dissatisfied with the Haitian government's performance, tended to channel assistance through NGOs rather than imposing conditions. One consequence of avoiding conditionality in favor of NGOs was that it precluded interactions between Haitian officials and USAID, which might have led to partnership opportunities.

An exception to this hands-off stance was aid tying.

AID TYING

Aid tying—the requirement that recipient countries purchase services, technical assistance, or goods from the donor country—was a widely imposed conditionality in Haiti, as it is in most countries receiving aid. Perhaps the most extensive use of aid tying was in food provision. U.S. aid required that a country buy food products grown and processed in the United States and transported on American ships or carriers.[18] Technical assistance was another use of aid tying. Presumably, the recipient country likely benefited from technical assistance provided by a donor. But this practice can have negative consequences: donor services may be much more expensive than those available from other vendors—11 to 30 percent more so, by some estimates. The actual amount of aid available, then, was reduced by these percentages, as was its potential impact. Tying also may have thwarted efforts to build partnerships among donors. And it contributed little to much-needed government capacity building.

ALIGNMENT

Alignment refers to the alignment of donor programs with country goals, objectives, and strategies, so donors and recipients do not pursue projects at cross purposes. The Canadian assessment of aid to Haiti from 1994 to 2004 noted "insufficient coordination of international aid, the rise of parallel structures, and growing mistrust between the donor community and the Government" (Canadian International Development Agency 2004, p. 13). The failed decentralization project is illustrative of a lack of alignment between donor and recipient goals. An assessment (ARD, Inc. 2000) of the project reached the following conclusions: "There remains . . . a great deal of indifference or even resistance to decentralization within the central government and among the social and political elite. Further advances in decentralization will require a revival of interest and support for decentralization among those who are now indifferent or hostile. The project's relative inability to engage national-level power brokers, both within and outside government, seriously impeded the possibilities of achieving decentralization objectives" (p. 38). According to some observers, the reason decentralization was not welcomed by the government was that Aristide was not about to transfer any power to the administrative level of the province, where he might lose control.

Another example of nonalignment was privatization. Donor countries, and the World Bank in particular, have pressured developing countries into privatizing state-owned enterprises, not only because, they feel, private companies are more efficient and responsible, but also because state-owned enterprises serve as a source of patronage jobs for political cronies. President Préval attempted to privatize Haiti's state-owned enterprises and failed: the Haitian people believed he was transferring the companies to the rich or to foreign owners, none of which would benefit Haitians. Aristide appeared to oppose and undermine Préval's efforts at every turn. Some believe that Aristide, as in the case with the civil service, wanted to protect this source of patronage employment for his party loyalists; the more jaded thought he might be saving them for his paramilitary operatives. Even the World Bank (World Bank, Operations Evaluation Department 2002) concluded that privatization in Haiti was premature or, in the recent past, inappropriate: "The norms of behavior of the private sector and the degree of corruption and cronyism within and between the private and public sectors may be such that privatization may well not enhance the prospects for sustained, equitable development, and may even make them worse" (p. 7).

Throughout the documentation on foreign assistance to Haiti, donors suggested that they had worked with the government and received approval for aid projects. For example, in the 1980s, USAID staff stated in their country review that the government appeared to support their assistance plan for Haiti. Then donors went on to complain about lack of country "ownership" when projects went awry. This was not a paradox. Haitians had no money, and so were likely to agree with almost anything donors proposed, so long as aid flowed. Donors had considerable power over government to get the latter to agree to what they wanted. But securing a commitment did not in any way guarantee follow-through.

PROGRAM DESIGN

Program design is critical to the successful delivery of foreign assistance. In November 1994 USAID funded the International Organization for Migration (IOM) to demobilize the Haitian army and reintegrate soldiers into civilian society. In the short term demobilization was intended to protect U.S. occupation forces; in the long term it would reduce potential disruptions to the restored Aristide government. Ex-soldiers received a stipend for attending vocational training sessions and had access to an employment service to help them find jobs. The program concluded in November 1996. Some 5,500 of 6,250 soldiers registered with IOM; IOM trained 5,200 soldiers, and 4,600 participated in the job service. Around 304, or 6 percent, obtained a job. Only one officer participated in the program.

The IOM program may have succeeded in its short-term goal of neutralizing the army to provide a secure environment for U.S. troops who were there to ensure the restoration of Aristide to power, and it may have stabilized Haiti for two years into the Aristide and Préval presidencies (Dworken, Moore, and Siegel 1997). But it failed to reintegrate ex-soldiers into society. Program evaluators did not perceive this as a problem, since ex-soldiers represented only a "vague threat" to the government. In 2004, seven years later, these ex-soldiers overthrew Aristide for a second time.

Why did reintegration fail? First and foremost, the program offered reintegration as an amorphous, ill-defined goal—almost a wish, according to those who evaluated it. It was unclear whether this was intentional. But program design failed to take into account reintegration problems. Businesses were loath to hire ex-soldiers, many of whom had human rights abuse records and were known to have terrorized the population. Even businesses

---

Box 6-1. *Disarmament, Demobilization, and Reintegration Program (DDR)*

The DDR program is a key element of the Préval-Alexis government's drive to restore security in the slum areas of Port-au-Prince as a precondition for promoting socioeconomic development. The DDR addresses the short-term stabilization objectives by dealing with moderate armed gangs that can be encouraged to enter a DDR process, while building the base for a longer-term sustainable solution to the problem of armed violence by developing capacity in each community to tackle it. This involves community-level social and economic investment and job creation. DDR is also pursuing a policy of constructive engagement with the former military. Currently, the thrust of DDR is on the negotiated disarmament and reinsertion into civil society of gangs throughout the country, with a focus on the urban areas of Port-au-Prince, in order to reduce crime and violence and build community confidence for development. DDR is implemented through the National Commission for Disarmament and offers individually designed support for up to 6,000 high-priority people (those posing a threat) for engagement in education, skills training, apprenticeships, job placements, and micro-entrepreneurial support, based on detailed profiling and personal capacity, assessed in a residential Reintegration Orientation Center. Beneficiaries are monitored and mentored for a period of up to eighteen months to offer the optimum chance of realizing a livelihood sustainability.

Source: World Bank (2006a).

---

that might have hired ex-soldiers did not do so, out of fear of retaliation from Aristide's paramilitary Chimères, because most ex-soldiers likely were anti-Aristide. For the same reason, the government was unlikely to hire them into the civil service. In any case, civil service jobs were reserved for Aristide supporters. Most important, the program did not engage the officer corps. Officers have leadership skills that enable them to motivate soldiers to revolt or mutiny, which they did.

Observers also criticized projects across the board for being small, short term, and fragmented. Canada's assessment of the 450 projects undertaken in Haiti between 1994 and 2002 concluded that "Canadian projects were widely dispersed and did not seem to provide critical mass (Canadian International Development Agency 2004, p. 12). USAID recognized the problem of a proliferation of multiple small projects in Haiti as far back as 1985: "The proliferation of small projects has strained AID's ability to provide adequate technical assistance and oversight" (U.S. General Accounting Office 1985, p. iv).

CAPACITY BUILDING

As observed earlier, Haiti has always lacked capacity to absorb and manage foreign aid, and when private entities did manage it, the government offered little support. Haiti's lack of capacity made it, in the minds of some donors, a costly proposition with few benefits. If for no other reason, donors had strong management incentives for improving capacity to ensure that aid was not wasted. The World Bank estimated that its average program management costs for Haiti were $33 per $1,000 of net commitment for satisfactory or nonrisky projects, as compared to $10 per $1,000 for Latin America and $16 per $1,000 bankwide (World Bank, Operations Evaluation Department 2002). The reason for this was that the World Bank spent an inordinate amount of time supervising project finances. The World Bank tracks the number of "staff years" devoted to supporting projects in postconflict countries. In Haiti, from 1986 to 1998, the bank contributed 86.5 staff years—an average of 6.7 staff years annually—and this despite the fact that from 1991 to 1994 the bank had no staff in country.

Donors have handled capacity issues in Haiti by either offering programs to build government capacity or by-passing government altogether to work with NGOs who manage projects themselves or through contractors. Neither approach was successful. Capacity building worked poorly, and bypassing government only exacerbated capacity problems in Haiti over the long term.

Some experts believe that aid administration may be so complex for some developing countries with weak capacity that it will always be ineffective.

Capacity-Building Approaches. Nevertheless donors tried various capacity-building schemes. In July 1996, the World Bank partnered with the Préval administration on a capacity-building project, called the Préval-Camdessus Initiative, to help the Haitian government manage foreign assistance and reduce need for outside managers. The project provided $1 million to pay higher salaries to skilled expatriate Haitians willing to return to Haiti to assist the country. Few expats participated, as few were willing to return to Haiti. Representative Charlie Rangel (D-N.Y.) proposed a similar approach under H.R. 1492 in 1993 and again in H.R. 617 in 1995, but neither bill was enacted into law.

Technical assistance (TA) and training are common approaches to capacity building in fragile states. But as practiced in fragile states, including Haiti, it has been an ineffective capacity-building tool. Much capacity building relies heavily on short-term workshops, seminars, and conferences, but many have questioned the effectiveness of any short-term approach, including as an effective capacity-building tool. As observed earlier, efforts to promote rule of law seemed to fail in Haiti, even though the justice system was in crisis—perhaps because the program offered was too little, too short term. The National Center for State Courts (NCSC), an American NGO, offered emergency two-day training sessions to judges in Haiti early in 1995, after the election of President Préval. According to NCSC, judges in the program were clueless as to their role in the judicial system and their powers and responsibilities. Many participants thought the United States was trying to impose its system on them. The Ministry of Justice did not lay out any guidance for the program and was not supportive. The Haitian Judges Association complained that training was not related to the current situation in the country, and did not comply with Haitian law (see National Center for State Courts 1995). The spotty training led to a lack of uniformity in interpretation of law across the country. Apparently, NCSC staff were not given much guidance, either by the government or USAID. Without denigrating NCSC's efforts in any way, many questioned how such a project contributed to promotion of rule of law in Haiti. The initiative to implement a case management system in the courts in Haiti is illustrative. Having not trained local Haitians in the justice system to do case management, the system collapsed once donors left (International Crisis Group 2007a).

The World Bank Operations Evaluation Department (2005b, pp. xv–xvi), too, has assessed its technical assistance (TA) efforts as generally ineffective:

> Where TA has been used to fill the gaps in skills needed to manage Bank-funded projects, it has had little impact on strengthening client capacity. TA has been effective when used for discrete and well-defined technical tasks and in the context of a clear TA strategy that includes a phase-out plan. A majority of the projects reviewed support training individual staff, and projects have usually achieved the targeted numbers to be trained. But public agency staff is often trained for specific tasks before they are positioned to use the training or before measures are taken to help retain them. . . . Programs have focused on the supply of skills in the public sector without ensuring that the skill-building is appropriately synchronized with organizational and institutional changes needed to improve public-sector performance.

Others (Fukuda-Parr, Lopes, and Malik 2002; Boesen 2004) have identified the following possible reasons for technical assistance failure in Haiti:

—Absence of serious commitment by recipient to only formally agreed-to TA objectives.

—Direct or indirect incentives for TA to act as "doers" rather than "trainers"

—Lack of in-depth country knowledge; inexperienced TA staff

—Poor and hurried design of TA operations, including lack of local involvement

—Lack of shared vision of TA among government and donors

—Lower priority given to supervision during implementation

—Weak recipient capacity to use TA

—Use of unsuitable expats to deliver TA; under- or overuse of locals

—Tying of TA to aid

—TA seen as a "free good"

—Sustainability not addressed

—Inadequate monitoring and evaluation

An obvious approach to capacity building worth trying would be to identify civil servants who are qualified, committed, and honest, and build administrative capacity around them. In 1982 USAID helped create "semi-autonomous" project implementation offices within some ministries to develop capacity (U.S. General Accounting Office 1982). It was apparently discontinued after the fall of the Baby Doc regime. We know of no other major attempts to use this approach.

The Role of NGOs. As suggested in the foregoing discussion, NGOs are a major factor in capacity building in Haiti. Channeling aid through the government can be ineffective and monies might be diverted. For example, of the 1991–94 humanitarian effort in Haiti, USAID evaluators suggested: "The injection of food into Haiti's resource-starved economy also created incentives and opportunities for diversion, misuse, political exploitation, and community tensions"—which were reduced by using NGOs (U.S. Agency for International Development 1999, p. 14; Ninic 2006). USAID has for decades tried to move aid funding through NGOs as a matter of policy. In 1982 a Democratic Congress required that USAID funnel foreign assistance through NGOs as much as possible, out of concern for corruption and ineptitude in the Haitian government (U.S. General Accounting Office 1985). About half the aid was diverted from the government. One-third of USAID's funding in 1982 went to NGOs. Other donors followed suit. Beginning in 2000, in response to electoral disputes, the Clinton administration redirected humanitarian assistance away from the Haitian government to NGOs. The George W. Bush administration continued the Clinton policy. The Haitian government has repeatedly complained about being bypassed in favor of NGOs; the government argues that this practice means they are unable to develop capacity.

The dilemma: Should the priority be building capacity or delivering services (Fukuyama 2004)?

Even though channeling aid through the government carries considerable risk—corruption and lack of competency—foreign assistance might fail if NGOs are relied on for service delivery, for a variety of reasons.

1. When assistance was channeled through NGOs, the Haitian government seemed indifferent to the programs—they were someone else's worry. The Haitian government tended not to allocate matching, operating, or maintenance funds to programs it did not manage. Also, the government didn't fund programs that were sustainable over time. NGOs appeared actually to welcome this indifference: it kept them in business, and also helped them raise donations from charitable contributors. CARE, International Red Cross, and Doctors without Borders all benefit greatly from aid and donor dollars.

2. Building capacity in NGOs in Haiti created a brain drain in public-sector employment, as good people were drawn from government to NGOs, where salaries can be higher and mobility was facilitated. This is a problem in developing countries generally, but especially in Haiti because of language issues. Most Haitians speak only Creole—an uncommon language—so NGOs must rely on Haitians to help in service delivery; they find them in government.

3. NGOs tended to be numerous and difficult to coordinate. In 1981 USAID formed the Haitian Association of Voluntary Agencies (HAVA) in response to criticisms by Haitians that aid was uncoordinated. By 1989, HAVA boasted over 100 agency members. At present there are many more times this number. Haiti has been called the "Republic of NGOs."

4. The government's operating parallel service delivery systems likely eroded the legitimacy of government, which already had demonstrated that it could not serve the people (Republic of Haiti 2006). Parallel systems also substantially increased aid coordination needs. But NGOs also ran the risk of loosing their legitimacy in the eyes of Haitians. Those in opposition in Haiti liked to paint NGOs as "tools and fools" of the United States, Canada, and multilateral organizations in particular.

5. Once NGOs obtained power, they resisted ceding it back to the government. Under the military regime in 1991 to 1994, government capacity to administer aid virtually disappeared, and the void was filled by an army of specialized NGOs. On Aristide's return, many NGOs were unwilling to transfer power back to the government, preferring instead to operate "under the radar" in isolated operations as they had during the aid embargo (UN Economic and Social Council 1999, p. 10).

6. Not only were NGOs empowered vis-à-vis the government, but donors also became more dependent on NGOs. This limited donor options and reduced donor control in some ways. For example, numerous studies of NGOs in Haiti in the 1980s showed that corruption was just as rampant in NGO service delivery as it would have been for government (see DeWind and Kinley 1988).

7. NGOs themselves can be corrupted, contributing to the service delivery problem. The International Crisis Group (2007c) reported that about 100 NGOs working in Cité Soleil, Port-au-Prince's massive ghetto, had direct links to gangs who were causing violence in the district. Apparently, these NGOs were not adequately vetted before partnering with donors (p. 6).

8. There was growing concern among donors that NGOs were becoming increasingly politicized, extending their reach well beyond their mandate to deliver service for donors or governments.[19] Many were becoming advocates for causes, tarnishing their credibility. A case that received a great deal of notoriety was that of the International Red Cross, which spoke out publicly against the U.S. government.

The Overseas Development Institute, a British think tank, noted: "Nongovernmental agencies tap into the public's suspicion of bureaucracy as well as its desire for concrete results, and implicitly compete with government agencies for taxpayer resources. However, they remain partially dependent on public aid for funding, guarantees, tax relief and other support that mitigates their risks, so competitive pressure is muted. They can still take strong advocacy positions against a government's policy while accepting its funding support" (Hewitt and Waldenburg 2004, p. 14).

DONOR-ADMINISTERED PROJECTS

Donors felt over time that they had been "burned" by the Haitian government in administering aid programs, especially through corruption and incompetency. So donors, particularly multilaterals, often managed projects themselves. This had several implications for capacity building and aid policy.

1. Haitians had no way to acquire administrative skills if they were not allowed to manage projects. Furthermore, excluding Haitian government officials from managing projects only postponed the inevitable, and likely made it worse.

2. Donor projects tended to be short-term and narrow in focus, because donor project management was expensive to keep in place over longer periods of time (Hassan 2004). Because these projects had little impact, they were wasteful, and the problem of poor government or Haitian capacity remained.

3. Donor administration was several magnitudes more expensive than government management, with the result that aid projects had less impact per aid dollar spent. It may be that such projects have done little to reconstruct Haiti.

Project executing units (PEUs, also sometimes referred to as project management units [PMUs]) are common mechanisms used by multilateral donors to bypass weak-capacity governments, but nonetheless operate parallel to them. PEUs hire anyone they like, pay higher salaries to attract qualified employees, and operate like businesses in executing projects on behalf of multilateral organizations. IABD (2003c) frequently employed PEUs with great success, but states, "These mechanisms must be seen as transition mechanisms, and simultaneous work on strengthening the State must be carried out" (p. iv). In Haiti, however, PEUs turned out to be a long-term tool. The World Bank Operations Evaluation Department (2002) concluded: "The nearly constant state of crisis and recurring instability in the country have blocked any longer term strategy to reduce dependence on Project Management Units (PMUs)" (p. 8).

Some donor-directed programs, because of their complexity, require donor administration. The IMF put into place a staff-monitored program to manage and turn around the economy from April to September 2004. These staff members' mission was to contain or reduce inflation, limit central bank financing, and increase international revenues. By all accounts, they admirably succeeded.

COMPLEXITY OF AID ADMINISTRATION

Working with donors was an increasingly complicated affair (United Nations 2005b, p. 100). Donors expected returns on their investments, and if there were no noticeable returns they might reprogram money or withhold it; enforce strict compliance with myriad regulations, policies, and laws and exert extensive controls over expenditures; and insist on transparency in all dealings. Donors' requirements in these areas varied. Donors had very different development philosophies, administrative cultures, and political concerns, which often conflicted, not only with a country's goals but also among donors. The paperwork required by donors was crushing in its extent and seemed endless; sometimes duplicative, but often unique to a particular donor. When charitable organizations are added to the mix, the numbers of donors become legion. Numerous meetings with donors in consultative groups were time consuming. When donors required extensive citizen input, development administration became even more complicated. In Haiti, where there was little expertise, restricted resources, continual upheavals in political regimes, ebbs and flows of foreign assistance creating and destroying capacity, and a climate where violence and instability took precedence over administration, it was not surprising that even the best intentioned government might fail to hold up its side of the foreign assistance equation. Transaction costs associated with aid were daunting.

The World Bank operation in Haiti is illustrative of these problems. The World Bank requires extensive planning before it extends loans and grants; once they are approved it requires even more reporting, accounting, and evaluation. The more World Bank programs a country participates in, the more planning, reporting, accounting, and evaluation is required. Country officials must work with each World Bank program (or sector or thematic area). Because each program is highly specialized, countries must assign staff with experience in those specialized areas. As donors add more specializations to the aid portfolio, country staff must coordinate with one another, often across ministries. But other multilateral and bilateral entities also have planning, reporting, accounting, and evaluation requirements. Soon, a developing country needs a large aid administration staff to deal with the donors' requirements. The Interim Cooperative Framework involved twenty-six bilateral and multilateral organizations, employed 250 experts, required six months to complete.

HARMONIZATION

Harmonization refers to donor efforts to ensure that their programs complement and supplement one another, and avoid duplication. In Haiti, according to Canadian aid officials, "Lack of harmonization resulted in under-funded sectors and prevented a common framework for investment and practical and complementary division of labor" (Canadian International Development Agency 2004, p. 13). A USAID evaluation in 1998 identified problems associated with lack of harmonization in Haiti: "USAID focuses on the local service delivery through the private sector, whereas other donors, when they fund service delivery, tend to focus on supporting the central Ministry or limited service delivery through regional offices. Although this is, in principle, a reasonable division of labor, in fact, the respective programs do not articulate well together to enhance the general impact of investments in health or to avoid duplication."[20]

Some experts attribute lack of harmonization to aid competition that arises when bilateral and multilateral donors and charities seek individual recognition for their work. Competition may be good for market economies, but in the field of international assistance it produces inefficiencies and waste and undermines attempts at harmonization (Hartford 2004). Competition can cause distortions in commitments and cooperation. For example, the United States, before the Financing Development Conference held in Monterrey, Mexico, in 2002, pledged a certain level of funding for Haiti, but after the conference, as a result of peer pressure and competition from other donors, it pledged a substantially higher level. Ironically, as of 2007 few donor countries had kept their promises to increase aid. Even those that are spending more on aid are counting debt relief as part of the total.

Even though donors have been working in Haiti for years, in December 2006 the World Bank (2006e, p. 17) concluded, "Harmonization of donor procedures is still at an early stage."

POOR COORDINATION

Donors need to coordinate efforts across donors and between donors and the Haitian government. The World Bank organized a Consultative Group Meeting in Haiti in 1997, attended by representatives of NGOs, civil society organizations, and the media, whose result was that lead donors were designated in priority sectors. This process was generally considered a model for other postconflict programs (World Bank 1997; World Bank, Operations Evaluation Department 1998; Hassan 2004). But the failed elections of 1997, precipitating aid suspensions and reductions, unraveled this exceptional consultative effort. According to a 1999 report by the UN Ad Hoc Advisory Group on Haiti, "Decades of institutional instability have adversely affected the coordination capacities of the government accumulated in previous years" (UN Economic and Social Council 1999, p. 10). The Transition Government's Interim Cooperative Framework purportedly was expected to be state-of-the-art in consultation and coordination; time will tell whether it is sustainable, but as of 2008, it continued to attract substantial amounts of funding.

USAID's strengthening-democracy programs in Haiti have not been evaluated, for the most part, but the General Accounting Office assessed similar programs in Guatemala, Nicaragua, El Salvador, Colombia, Peru, and Bolivia from 1992 to 2002, looking at rule of law, governance, human rights, and elections. Presumably, USAID work in these countries should be much more successful than in Haiti, and the GAO did find that important reforms had been undertaken—yet USAID had not effectively coordinated its efforts either with other participating U.S. agencies or with other donors funding similar or complementary projects (U.S. General Accounting Office 2003). It is likely that programs in Haiti manifested the same lack of coordination.

A classic and not uncommon problem with aid coordination was brought to light by the Haiti Support Group (HSG), a British human rights organization: a lack of basic statistics and information. In an April 2005 press release, HSG reported that Prime Minister Latortue had asked for more assistance for the 3,500-strong Haitian police force. The Organization of American States had reported the number of police at 5,500; the International Crisis Group, at 4,000; and the Small Arms Survey, at 5,000. The Transition Government apparently issued 6,000 pay checks. In the press release HSG asked: Why with the hundreds of millions poured into Haiti for police and UN Stabilization Mission in Haiti (MINUSTAH) security, did no one know how many police officers there were in the country?

Coordination of justice system reforms was also problematic. In 2002 the International Peace Institute sponsored a seminar on lessons learned in Haiti from 1990 to 2002 (Hagman 2002). Senior aid personnel from the OAS, the World Bank, the IADB, France, Canada, and the United States attended. France, Canada, and the United States had each sponsored their own judicial reform programs. Participants observed that each initiative was based on different assumptions about what was needed and how it was to be achieved— in short, no coordination occurred. As a result, the projects produced "conflicting and unintentionally self-serving" consequences in the Haitian justice system. The system actually worsened following the assistance effort.

IMPLEMENTATION AND CONTINUITY

Implementing projects has always been challenging in developing countries, especially in Haiti, which represents a case of extreme need and unusually difficult challenges. Perhaps out of a sense of urgency, donors tended to hurry projects to demonstrate immediate results rather than pursuing projects more incrementally and carefully (World Bank, Operations Evaluation Department 1998). The 1995 elections are a case in point. On October 15, 1994, Aristide returned as president of Haiti. Elections were immediately scheduled for December 1994 to comply with constitutional provisions, an impossible time frame for a national initiative, beginning from scratch. A Provisional Electoral Council, the mechanism that manages all aspects of Haiti's electoral process, had not even been appointed. After its members were appointed, the council tried to hold elections on two different occasions, but failed each time. On June 25, 1995, elections were finally held. Among other problems, donors failed to take into account that Haitians were not accustomed to voting in runoff elections, and there was little attempt to educate them about the process. The next elections, in 1997, in which for the first time Haitians were voting for local assemblies as well as for president, had even lower turnouts—5 percent, by some accounts. A Haitian newspaper headline announced in 1997 following the elections: "Democracy on Course without the People" (Mobekk 2001). The same issues reappeared in 2000, 2003, and 2005–06.

Programs sometimes suffer from a lack of continuity when donor organizations set up operations or reorganize them, often in response to events in country. For example, in 1991 the Haiti office of the World Bank was reassigned to another department of the bank, ostensibly to provide better program management, then it was shut down altogether. From 1994 to 1997, the Haiti office had three directors and three country operations chiefs. The bank did not open its own mission until 1997 (World Bank, Operations Evaluation Department 1998, p. 5). (A further issue was that the World Bank's representative came from the Haitian elite, and this may have reduced the World Bank's standing in the country, given the animosity of Aristide's supporters toward the rich; see World Bank, Operations Evaluation Department 2002, p. 2). Similarly, a new USAID country director was appointed in early 2005, just as the Transition Government was spending ICF funds and planning elections.

It should be pointed out that bilateral and multilateral donors will not leave agents in place in highly unstable, violent countries. In October 2004, the UN issued a security advisory whereby nonessential aid personnel were relocated and curfews were imposed and travel was curtailed for UN workers. USAID and the U.S. embassy also were not fully staffed, for fear of street violence; only in November 2005 were diplomatic staff allowed to return to Haiti. Even in 2007 the U.S. embassy still imposed travel restrictions and curfews on employees. Needless to say, it is difficult to run an aid program under these circumstances.

Not only in-country conditions but also the availability of human resources is a staffing issue. Most multilateral and bilateral missions have insufficient personnel to staff country offices, let alone regional offices around the country. This is a significant Achilles heal in foreign assistance: everything focuses on the capital, while contractors or NGOs do the actual work in the field, hence the Haitian phrase, *la république de Port-au-Prince*.[21] The historian Francis Fukuyama (2004) is one who suggests that this problem is endemic to foreign assistance efforts: there is never enough funding to go around and donors tend to focus on big ticket items, which tend to be located in the capital. There are exceptions, though. Big infrastructure projects such as highways, dams, and irrigation projects frequently are implemented in rural areas and attract a lot of attention.

But some implementation problems appeared difficult to account for. Under the Low Income Countries Under Stress (LICUS) program, for example, the World Bank requires countries to codevelop a "comprehensive transitional results matrix," which is an important vehicle and process used by the Bank to track progress on its investments. A review of Haiti under LICUS found that a matrix had been prepared in August 2004, but as of May 2005 the reporting system on matrix results was not functional, which "made it difficult to address problems encountered and to assess actual implementation [of the Bank's strategy]" (World Bank 2006d, p. 39).

LEADERSHIP

The record of foreign assistance to Haiti shows that the only multilateral or bilateral donor who took the lead in trying to reconstruct Haiti was the 1997 World Bank Consultative Group, where donors agreed to divvy up responsibilities and leadership roles over certain sectors. This effort was discontinued. The IADB tried to take the lead using its process, but recently admitted that it too had failed (Inter-American Development Bank 2007a). To be sure, there was a great deal of on-and-off coordination across donors, sometimes effective, sometimes not. But no single donor or consortium took responsibility for making sure the aid effort worked. The reason why no donor took control was that each agency is a sovereign entity and no one has control over another. Further, no donor wanted to be blamed for failure—or fail to get credit in the event of success. Donor competition was yet again another factor (Hartford 2004). All in all, given the compelling U.S. foreign policy interest in Haiti and its aid investments, it is odd the United States elected not to exert as much influence as it could have if it had played a leadership role, except when it came to suspending aid and setting sanctions.

In 1996 the USAID mission in Haiti, becoming increasingly frustrated with the Haitian government's unwillingness to reform its civil service, tried to organize bilateral and multilateral donors to take coordinated action, using aid as leverage. The mission sought to remove phantom employees, reassess pay scales, and redefine job descriptions and vowed to work with NGOs until the government made the necessary reforms (U.S. Agency for International Development 1996a, p. 3). But reforms by the government were halfhearted and ultimately failed.

INAPPROPRIATE CLAIMS OF SUCCESS

Too often, donors may accept as successes projects that produce outputs called for in the project design or proposal, regardless of whether they have actually improved the situation on the ground. For example, if 360 judges were targeted for training and 360 judges received training, the project is considered a success, regardless of whether the delivery of justice was improved as a result. Many donors simply have not looked to see whether their projects or programs made any difference. USAID's Strategic Plan for Haiti—1999–2004 (U.S. Agency for International Development 1998) is a case in point. The "plan" was merely a listing of projects or programs under way, with the annotation that they were "accomplishments." Yet the actual programs, in different policy areas such as environment, privatization, justice, security, fiscal and monetary management, and elections, were disasters that cost billions and produced adverse results.

Another example of "the operation was a success, but the patient died" was the UN Development Program initiative to promote democracy in the 1999–2000 election cycle. UNDP's Haiti office claims that its Common Country Assessment (CCA) provides an example of a positive *process* (United Nations 2000a). UNDP developed a variety of forums to facilitate national debates on election issues relating to the government's poverty reduction strategy as a guide to future development and foreign aid allocations. The intent of the forums was to give voice to hundreds of civil society organizations, political parties, and other groups concerned with Haiti's future. The CCA concluded, "Had civil society representatives not participated in this process, the goal of creating for the first time in Haiti an open forum of discussion about the trends, constraints, assets and perspectives of human development in the country would not have been completed" (UN Development Program 2000a, p. 5). Yet the Aristide government ignored these democratic inputs and held the most faulty elections in the nation's history.

The World Bank also came to similar conclusions, finding that project-by-project evaluations in Haiti were misleading. In two separate reviews in post-1994 Haiti (World Bank 1998, 2006b), project achievements were highly touted as successes when measured against program objectives, but the World Bank went on to point out that the programs overall were failures. Therefore, the Bank rightly questioned the value of a "successful" project embedded in a much larger failure. The Inter-American Development Bank appeared to be much more forthcoming in its reports, regarding project failure, although IADB admits it learned little form these reports in practice (Inter-American Development Bank 2007a; see also chapter 9).

The score card for foreign assistance in Haiti might be even worse if one took into account the fact that even officially labeled "successful" programs probably made little difference. There are those who believe that aid agencies in the mid-nineties were in a hurry to leave Haiti, so they put into place quick fix programs such as electoral assistance that would allow them to exit, leaving Haitians to solve their problems themselves. Donor fatigue had set in.

DONOR FATIGUE

Donor fatigue—a general sense of futility and discouragement—may have been one of the greatest potential drivers of aid failure in Haiti (Canadian International Development Agency 2003, p. 2; Canadian International Development Agency 2004, p. 11).[22] In their retrospective look at aid assistance effectiveness, Canadian aid officials recount how their hopes rose and fell with the politics of Haiti. Aristide's return in 1994 seemed to augur a new era where aid could really help. Then, after spending months putting together the Emergency Economic Recovery Plan, the 1997 election debacle dampened donor enthusiasm. The pattern continued. One wonders whether donors continued to feel enthusiasm for working with Haiti, or were just going through the motions. In 1998 the World Bank concluded: "Lack of progress in reform measures could discourage further investment, reduce donor support, and jeopardize both political and economic recovery" (World Bank, Operations Evaluation Department 1998, p. 61). This is what happened, as it turned out. From 1994 to the 2004, Haiti became an aid orphan, receiving progressively lower amounts of aid, in part because the cost of the failure of the Haitian state was not of sufficient consequence to bilateral or multilateral donors to justify their giving more to avert it (McGillivray 2005).

Some observers see the outcome of the UN's International Civilian Support Mission in Haiti (MICAH) initiative as a case of donor fatigue, but it can also exemplify the lack of donor commitment or poor administration by donors. The United Nations created MICAH in March 2000 to consolidate several programs intended to professionalize and build capacity in Haiti's police force and to engage in a constructive dialogue with disparate political leaders (United Nations 2000b). The UN delayed deploying its sixty-eight advisers because of funding problems. And this was a rather small commitment, given their mission to support the Ministry of Justice, the police, the Prison Authority, the magistrates' school, and regional criminal justice offices; a similar UN effort in Mozambique required over 1,000 advisers. Given that security has always been the highest priority in Haiti, with justice perhaps a close second, the meager UN response is difficult to fathom, but perhaps donor fatigue played a role.

The issue of donor fatigue is becoming even more crucial for countries like Haiti in an era of increased demand for aid and diminishing aid dollars.

Germany announced in January 2006 that it could not meet its commitments to increased foreign aid because of its own budgetary problems.[23]

Provision of aid is after all a competitive market commodity (Klein and Hartford 2005). For example, in 2004 one-third of the aid increases globally went to Afghanistan and Iraq. The United States also committed $2.5 billion to its new Millennium Challenge Account program, an approach excluding countries like Haiti from participation (Millennium Challenge Corporation 2007; Buss 2008). Developing countries generally will have to do better or receive less assistance.[24] At the same time, many observers are asking whether more aid would really accomplish much, even if it were available (see, for example, Dichter 2005).

The Interim Cooperation Framework and Poverty Reduction Strategy Paper may be the last chance for Haiti. We hope not.

Conclusion

None of the factors discussed here is sufficient in isolation to explain or cause foreign assistance failure. But taken together, these failure factors in foreign assistance to Haiti clearly create a failure synergy.

This analysis concerns foreign assistance experiences primarily from 1994 to 2006, with occasional reference to the 1980s where parallels exist. It is hoped that the new constitutionally elected democratic government, elected in 2006, and an international donor community much more savvy about development together provide the conditions so that mistakes of the past will not be repeated.

7 | LESSONS LEARNED: REFORMING FOREIGN ASSISTANCE

International aid is one of the most powerful weapons in the war against poverty. Today, that weapon is underused and badly targeted. There is too little aid and too much of what is provided is weakly linked to human development. Fixing the international aid system is one of the most urgent priorities facing governments at the start of the 10-year countdown to 2015.
—United Nations, *Human Development Report—2005*

There is little agreement about how to make foreign assistance effective, not only in the Haitian context but also in other fragile, postconflict countries and in developing countries generally. Much remains to be learned. In fact, knowledge about what works best in development is currently in flux, judging from the discussions held at numerous aid effectiveness conferences, on everything from harmonization through conditionality to comprehensive assistance models or approaches and creation of new specialized organizations to work on solutions. In the past few years, multinational and bilateral entities have created organizations to work on postconflict issues. The United States created the U.S. Institute of Peace in 1984 as a think tank devoted to the issues; the Carnegie Endowment for Peace has numerous targeted programs; and the World Bank created the Post Conflict Fund to finance innovative solutions. The United Nations, in December 2005, created the global Peace Building Commission.[1] The Bush administration developed the Office of Reconstruction and Stabilization in the State Department to address nation building, and the Office of Transition Initiatives at USAID to work on fragile nations. For FY2006, Congress substantially scaled back funding for the program to $24 million. The ambassador in charge then suddenly resigned.

There are emerging areas of consensus, but not nearly enough. Consensus in the field has changed over time. To compound matters, each country receiving aid may be very different, requiring customized strategies. So it is hoped that case studies like this will continue to inform debate.

The UN Development Program's *Human Development Report* (United Nations 2005a, p. 76) sums up the issues well: "Poor countries need aid that is delivered in a predictable fashion, without too many strings attached and in ways that minimize transaction costs and maximize value for money. All too often they get aid that is unpredictable, hedged with conditions, uncoordinated and tied to purchases in donor countries." This chapter presents lessons learned in Haiti, with wide application not only in fragile states but also in least developed countries as well.

A Unified Process

Aid success is predicated on the need to address and resolve issues of governance and political instability as the highest priority. Achieving good governance and political stability could take years, and thus requires long-term commitments from donors.

Andrew Natsios, a U.S. Agency for International Development (USAID) administrator, aptly summed up the foreign assistance enterprise generally: "Development is not understood, even inside the Beltway in Washington."[2] Donors must understand the entire aid process, and make decisions from a holistic perspective, not in a fragmented, isolated, and unconnected fashion. Issues concerning conditionality, accountability, harmonization, leadership, planning, alignment, country ownership, partnership, implementation, capacity building, performance assessment, compliance, evaluation, coordination, and knowledge transfer all must be addressed and in most cases rethought: much conventional wisdom may not work in fragile states, or at least did not work in Haiti (see also World Bank 2004b). Thus, the first and most fundamental lesson: *Understand foreign aid as a unified process.*

As Natsios's comment suggests, too often in the literature on foreign assistance, researchers and policymakers focus on specific issues without tying them into a larger framework, and the result is a fragmented picture. In the end, if components of the aid process do not fit together, aid likely will be ineffective.

Figure 7-1 lays out a framework for understanding aid's component parts and illustrates that in the aid process all of the parts must work together. Positions of components in the framework are not fixed and may vary depending on the country and its circumstances. But policymakers should take them into account in understanding "tipping points" where aid might fail (see Gladwell 2005 on the general concept of tipping points), and either design programs to avoid problems or take corrective action to keep the assistance process on track.

Figure 7-1. *Aid Flow Process*

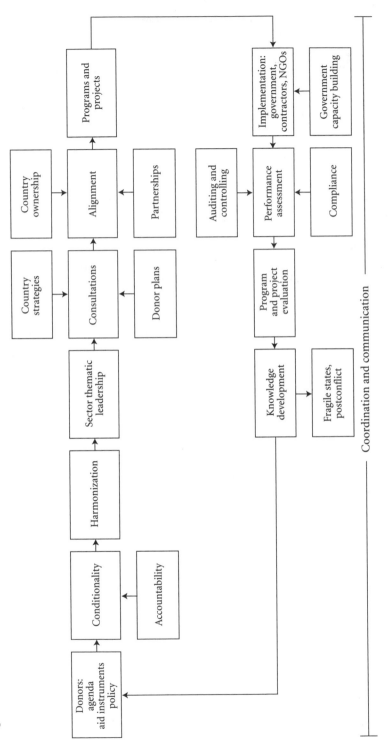

Source: Authors.

AGENDA SETTING

Deal with governance issues first. The top priority for the long-term success of assistance is to resolve governance issues. The experience in Haiti illustrates that failing to address issues of poor governance and political instability jeopardizes an entire foreign assistance effort. Ignoring governance issues or wishing them away only leads to inevitable aid failures. Donors face two choices: either to engage governments or wait until countries resolve their own governance issues (Weinstein 2004). The problem with the latter course of action is that fragile postconflict states are very unlikely ever to resolve their own governance issues without assistance. While they are attempting to do so, economies, societies, and people's lives can be severely damaged. Like it or not, strategic countries like Haiti require intense engagement with good governance; political stability is the highest priority.

Donors now recognize the need to develop good governance capacity as the essential prerequisite for aid effectiveness. They also know good governance takes time—years, maybe decades, to develop (Organization for Economic Cooperation and Development 2005a, 2005b). Nonetheless, they seem to have little patience for such investments (Birdsall 2004; Collier and Hoeffler 2002; Organization for Economic Cooperation and Development 2005a, 2005b). Donor fatigue is sometimes a problem, because aid flows to developing countries through annual appropriations. Bilateral investors are faced with changing priorities and administrations at home, which can translate into reduced or interrupted aid. Multilateral organizations face increasing demand for assistance and diminishing resources, so they increasingly tend to invest where they see the best return. Because results from governance programs are often ineffective or at best invisible, donors get nervous about continuing to pour what they perceive as good money after bad. There is no instant gratification in funding governance programs, whereas there is much gratification in funding humanitarian and infrastructure projects, as one can feel pride in thousands of starving people fed or a highway system completed. Donors must find ways to stay the course in promoting and sustaining good governance. If they do not, aid will continue to fail. Reports by the Inter-American Development Bank show that strides in some democratic Latin American countries are beginning to fade, necessitating more attention to consolidating democratic gains.[3] Since 1999 six democratically elected Latin American presidents have been deposed. One way to persist is to ensure that the donor community commits to long-term, multiyear investments.

Understand what a fragile, postconflict state is and encourage approaches appropriate to it. Donors to Haiti were slow to discover or respond to the idea that even though Haiti is at the center of the Western Hemisphere, where all countries except Cuba are assumed to be more or less functioning democracies, Haiti is not. It is important for policymakers to understand what government is in place and what its circumstances are. Although this looks to be an easy matter, in fairness to donors, it is not. As Fredrik Erixon (2005, p. 21) explains, "The new aid policy implies that the donor is greatly aware of the policy environment and political order in the recipient country. Donors have generally not passed that test." Only in the last few years has the international community tried to understand and focus on the special circumstances of fragile and postconflict states. François Bourguignon, the chief economist at the World Bank, stated in 2007, "The [international donor] community has to some extent been obsessed by the effectiveness of aid and there has been a move toward making aid selective and allocating it to countries where aid would work. But in making progress in that direction, we simply forgot countries where governance is weak. . . . The challenge is now to help fragile states."[4]

There seems to be consensus that Haiti is a fragile state, distinguishing it from other least-developed countries. But there is disagreement at the World Bank as to whether the country is a postconflict country or one in conflict: violence continues and until recently the government was not in control of portions of Port-au-Prince and the outlying regions. Haiti seems to be perpetually in a steady state of conflict, with occasional strong spikes in the violence. The World Bank designated Haiti a postconflict country to qualify it for special funding, but it may not be one. This means that aid is being delivered according to conflicting interpretations. Different models of foreign assistance and attendant uncertainty increase risk of aid failure.

Do not move too quickly from postconflict reconstruction to normalization. Haiti illustrates what happens when impatient donors want to move too quickly from postconflict assistance to normalization (see figure 7-2). Normalization is comparatively easy work, but reconstruction is much harder, yet what goes on during reconstruction determines success of the assistance effort. Some donors seemed to think that if elections in Haiti were held, everything would just fall into place. In reality, elections might actually have made things worse in Haiti; in retrospect we can see that they likely are more appropriate as an aspect of normalization, not reconstruction (though there is will disagreement on this). In any event, donors should front-load assistance for stabilizing a fragile nation—especially a conflict or postconflict one—before assuming it has become normalized. Aid is, or can be, very different under normalization.

Figure 7-2. *Three Stages in Aid Process*

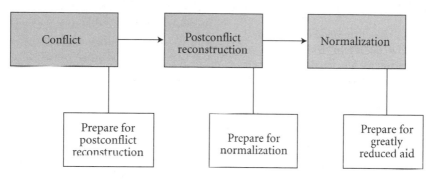

Source: Authors.

AID DEPENDENCY

It is not how much, but how and in what you invest that matters. The premise of this book is that donors have invested a lot in Haiti, but have little to show for it. Perhaps the premise was misstated: it was not the amount of money that was invested but how, when, and in what it was invested. Haiti may be a classic case where too much money actually carried a disincentive for reform. Indeed, research shows that the higher the level of aid, the more likely the quality of governance is to erode, as measured by the functioning of the bureaucracy, the extent of corruption, and the effectiveness of the rule of law (Erixon 2005, p. 20). (Of course, a lot of aid was suspended and restarted, so the amount of aid expended taken out of context can be misleading.)

CONDITIONALITY

Be more flexible in allocating aid, then hold managers accountable. In the U.S. system, Congress tends to appropriate foreign assistance for specific programs—HIV/AIDS, disaster relief, food, democratization—sometimes on its own initiative and sometimes in support of the administration. Even when appropriating according to an administration's plan, Congress expects to allocate funding to specific programs.[5] Congressional and administration aid allocation practices may cause problems throughout the development process. To prevent congressional meddling in aid, the Clinton administration decoupled several aid programs that should have been in USAID's portfolio and placed them in separate agencies, intentionally fragmenting the aid process. Secretary of State Condoleezza Rice in 2006 "clawed" them back, placing them and USAID under the State Department, which gave her direct control of aid as a foreign policy tool.[6] Countries may neither need nor want donor-determined programs (in other words, there may be misalignment). Situations in countries may suddenly and dramatically change, making aid ineffective or irrelevant (a symptom of inflexibility). Donors may duplicate one another's programs and leave gaps in other areas (a symptom of lack of harmonization). Policymakers should consider making aid much more flexible and nonprogrammatic, then hold aid managers accountable for performance.

There seems to be an emerging consensus among donors working in fragile, postconflict countries that conditionality is of limited utility, as it was in Haiti (Canadian International Development Agency 2003, 2004; Department for International Development [U.K.] 2005a, 2005b; World Bank 2005c). Donors have little leverage through conditionality, especially in support of governance, public-sector reforms, and sound economic policies. In many cases, need for assistance is so great that funding flows, even if conditions are less than ideal. Other stakeholders pressure one another politically to provide assistance, even when it might be wasted. Cutting off or slowing assistance can wreck or undo earlier progress. Many regimes simply hold the population hostage, forcing donors to provide assistance. And many regimes care so little about their own people that they are willing to forgo assistance rather than give in to demands for accountability. Many governments will agree to almost anything; whether they support it is another matter. All of these facets characterized Haiti. Conditionality should be employed sparingly or more judiciously.

Multilateral entities are increasingly lobbying against aid tying because of its negative consequences for recipients. Aid tying reduces aid flows to countries, limits options and flexibility in the provision of goods and services, and is politically influenced by powerful vendors such as private companies or NGOs, which may set a donor's aid agenda.[7] Benefits to donors can be significant, but may not be worth the cost to aid recipients. It seems unwise to untie all aid, regardless of the country, the country's circumstances, or the donor's interest. Donors should treat each project or program on a case-by-case basis before tying aid. In general, though, less aid tying will result in greater successes in the country.

Conditionality occurs when donors provide aid only for programs fitting their agenda, and recipient countries must either take it or take a hike. Who determines the aid agenda? It would be nice if donors and governments worked out what needs to be done, but there appear to be many cases where donors are influenced by NGOs, advocacy groups, or industries with agendas that are neither high priority nor desired by the recipient. For example, if an NGO builds capacity for work on the environment, then it will lobby for specific environmental programs, regardless of whether these are the best way to handle the environmental problem or whether other programs should have a higher priority. This appears to be the case in Haiti for some programs funded under USAID. It would be preferable if USAID, the Haitian government, and other donors worked out the aid agenda, then found vendors to deliver services or undertake projects and programs, rather than having vendors and advocates set the agenda, donors fund it, and governments accept it.

ACCOUNTABILITY

Hold government accountable, through incentive-based funding. The Haiti experience shows that even in the best-intentioned governments, officials do not want to be held accountable. They claim that they lack capacity, but argue that they know how to spend wisely. All assistance should be subject to performance-goal attainment and to compliance with regulations, controls, and conditions. Funding should be awarded in tranches based on performance. Many in the international community oppose this; opponents believe that the burdens it places on recipients—compliance, reporting, data gathering— sets them up for failure when they inevitably come up short in meeting development goals. Yet performance management has become virtually universal in its application both in donor governments and for developing countries. For example, World Bank loans often tie future funding to attainment of goals, like the Millennium Development Goal program. But in the case of Haiti, no one believes that the country can come close to meeting MDGs, or even milestones along the way. Rather than using disincentives—aid suspension or reductions—donors should award funding on the basis of incentives for good performance (Boesen 2004; Schacter 2000; Brinkerhoff 1994)

Fund budget support, not just projects. Donors for the most part are suspicious about the ability of Haiti to control aid spending—or any spending— so they channel a lot of funding directly into programs, bypassing government altogether, or treat government as a pass-through agency for funds. Donors are wary of providing direct budget support: transferring funding into the treasury for general use by ministries. Bypassing government is intended to encourage accountability, and hence facilitate more flexible, direct funding. This practice certainly does promote accountability (Department for International Development [U.K.] 2004), but it jeopardizes other aspects of the aid program when viewed more comprehensively. Without direct budget support, countries may not be able to sustain aid investments already made and may be ineffective in managing agencies and ministries where revenue is not available.[8] The problem fragile states face is that they have very scare resources and few options. The extent to which donors provide direct budget support needs to be rethought, because it filters through the entire aid process, affecting success in the long run (Organization for Economic Cooperation and Development 2006).

In the case of Haiti, donors have pledged more in budget support under Préval. In 2006 and 2007 bilateral donors allocated $77.7 million, or 7.6 percent of total assistance, to budget support, and multilateral organizations offered $60.2 million, or 5.8 percent. This seems to be moving in the preferred direction, allowing Haiti to increasingly manage its own affairs.

Be prepared to deal with the consequences of aid suspensions. The Haiti experience has shown that aid suspensions or deep reductions to force accountability are highly problematic. Suspending aid sends a message to government that it needs to reform or comply, or risk loosing future funding. But many governments really do not care whether aid is suspended: they have other priorities—in Haiti's case political power consolidation or individual aggrandizement—or alternative ways of funding their activities, such as drug trafficking. Since 1995, Haiti's government and parliament have engaged in a standoff, while letting the country deteriorate. Haiti's military juntas did much the same. They knew donors would fund humanitarian programs and remittances would continue, perhaps even increase, regardless of what they did. It is an open question as to whether aid should be suspended or reduced to force compliance. Many believe suspensions are largely ineffective and do damage that is expensive to correct.

Regardless of the reasons for or merits of a suspension, if aid is suspended, donors must develop strategies for immediately reengaging a country once a government is ousted or reforms itself. In Haiti's case, donors were too slow to realize the implications of having withheld funds: there were negative effects on donor capacity in Haiti, government capacity in aid administration, and funding for existing or new programs. Planning for reengagement must occur at the point when it appears violence will finally abate. As observed earlier, sensing this point is more art than science, especially in Haiti, where the development context is unclear.

HARMONIZATION

Share credit for aid successes with other donors. Aid harmonization has not occurred in Haiti (Organization for Economic Cooperation and Development 2003b). What seems to occur is that donors meet to share information on what they are doing or intend to do, which is very different from dividing up assistance so that duplication is eliminated, partnerships around common interests are formed, and individual donors are taking the lead in an area. It is no exaggeration to say that in Haiti, every major donor worked on democratization, and yet Haitian democracy was nowhere to be found until Préval's election. Donors have compelling reasons for offering aid, even though it may conflict with or be duplicative of that from other countries. For example, U.S. foreign policy promotes democracy globally, so aid programs tend to focus on democratization in part (De Renzio 2005; Franco 2005b). But other multilateral and bilateral donors have their own aid program agendas, so aid tends to be ineffective because it is not harmonized across donors. It could be that donors do not want to either give up or share credit for reconstructing a country. This has worked to the disadvantage of the United States in Haiti, where its democratization and governance programs have failed, as have similar programs of other donors.

One alternative approach might be for donors to divide up who will get credit for what, and find opportunities for collective credit prior to engaging a fragile country fully so that all donors would be assured of getting some credit. In cases of collective credit, it appears to be in the interest of the United States to be part of a group taking credit because of the tarnished reputation the United States has in Haiti. This strategy should be considered on a country-by-country basis.

One effective mechanism in aid coordination appears to be the Multi-Donor Budget Support (MDBS) approach (see Overseas Development Institute 2007 for an example in Ghana). Donors contribute funding to an account for direct budget support, to be spent against a plan prepared by the recipient country and approved by donors. MDBS promotes not only coordination and harmonization but also country ownership.[9]

Sharing credit is related to the issue of when to take a leadership role in assistance.

LEADERSHIP

Take a leadership role only when it improves aid effectiveness. Donors had numerous issues surrounding whether and when to assume a leadership role in delivering aid. On hindsight it looks as though it may not have been the best approach in Haiti for the United States to take the lead in democratization in all its various aspects—even though every U.S. administration promoted democracy and human rights. But many Haitians and others believed that the United States had meddled in their country, taking sides and imposing its will for over a century. The reality was that the United States had done poorly in its democratization efforts in Haiti. Perhaps the United States, as donor, should have considered taking a leadership role in humanitarian assistance, health care, infrastructure provision, agricultural development and the like, while ceding democratization to others. Again, when it comes to fragile states, this decision should be made on a country-by-country basis.

Some donors may not wish to take the lead in certain sectors, and others may not wish to lead or be permitted to lead a multidonor approach. Ideally, country governments should take a leadership role—a major theme of this work. Failing that, the only viable alternative is a consortium of donors—not a mere collection of parties, but a true consortium. This will be difficult to achieve, but is worth exploring, especially in countries such as Haiti.

PLANNING

Customize planning to meet the needs of a specific country. As observed above, Haiti, like other developing countries, had a plethora of carefully thought-out planning documents, and the planning process consumed a lot of resources of both Haitians and donors. Yet in spite of these planning documents' sophistication and elegance, none of them seemed to pay off in effective aid provision. To be sure, aid failed in large part because of political instability and bad governance. Ironically, these factors were mentioned as issues in every plan, assessment, and strategy document over the past two decades, but then these reports went on to promote other things that should have been of lower priority. One problem may be that planning, especially among multilateral donors, had become so standardized that many plans began to look the same across countries. All had standard sections and issues and common ways of dealing with them.

Obviously, if countries are very different, standardization may be systematically excluding new opportunities not supported in a common product. Plans focus heavily on design but not on context (Brinkerhoff 1994), yet context probably should determine plan design.[10] Plans also seem to take a "blueprint" approach, whereby "good governance" is something that is installed, not developed (Schacter 2000). It might be time to rethink planning in fragile states and postconflict countries.

In January 2006, the Haitian minister of planning announced the creation of a strategic think tank to work on long-term development planning on the technical level in response to the UN Economic and Social Council's criticism in 2005 that Haiti lacked a long-term vision for the country. This think tank, which stands outside the lines of authority in the government, will provide input to the UN and other donors (UN Economic and Social Council 2006, p. 7).

Bear in mind that planning is not management. The World Bank's assessment of its capacity-building efforts in sub-Saharan Africa noted that a major problem with the strategic planning efforts driving aid development, funding, and implementation had little to do with management and service delivery (World Bank 2005b). Perhaps management concerns ought to be much more prominently included in planning processes. Management is all the more important because capacity building has not been done well in Haiti and many other fragile states.

Too often, in the Haitian case, donors saw that projects and programs were unraveling and were likely to be ineffective. Rather than reworking plans to be more realistic for the situation on the ground, donors pressed on with their original plan. This is a classic case of the problem of "sunk costs"—so much effort had been invested in a project or program that many believed the money already spent would be wasted if the rest of the money wasn't spent. Staff of NGOs lobby to keep programs, because their livelihoods are connected to the programs (De Renzio 2005). Others rightly believe that if monies earmarked for a project are not actually spent, they won't get more money for other projects in the future. Some seek to avoid criticism for having to terminate a failing program by keeping the project going and hoping for a turnaround. And others may not recognize failure when they see it (discussed further under "Evaluation"). There is no justification for continuing to invest in hopeless enterprises. Such projects rarely produce results worth the effort, and many seem to have adverse consequences, often worse than the situation before aid intervention. For example, rushing to hold elections when a government is not ready and able to do so leads to flawed and perhaps fraudulent electoral results that in turn cast doubt on the legitimacy of the democratic process—and on donors, too.

Haiti points up the need to establish a physical presence of donor representatives in country early on in the foreign assistance process (World Bank, Operations Evaluation Department 2005a, 2005b). This applies mostly to multilateral organizations, which tend to withdraw entirely when aid is suspended or security is jeopardized. Absence from a country is a problem when countries move into postconflict status and require numerous meetings to prepare plans and loan proposals and coordinate and administer aid. A country presence may be of greater importance to multilateral donors, who do not have embassies, but the admonition applies to bilateral donors as well. In the United States, USAID missions expand and contract depending on circumstances in country, so although there may be a USAID mission in a country, it may not be appropriately staffed to deliver the aid required. Ideally, donors need to begin moving resources into place as soon as security permits, and to do this one needs staff on the ground, already there.

ALIGNMENT

Always align aid. Matching donor programs and country preferences and needs is much talked about in the donor community, but overall still this process of alignments has many shortcomings, especially in fragile and post-conflict countries. There are enough examples of effective alignment practices (Sharpe, Wood, and Wratten 2005; U.K., Department for International Development 2005b) to suggest that it is donors who resist the practice in some countries. Reasons for resistance are legion. Donors often face a dilemma in trying to accommodate a country's needs and preferences while at the same time withholding funding for projects and programs they know will not work or are inconsistent with their agenda (Inter-American Development Bank 2003c). Not aligning aid with a country's agenda has consequences, most often difficulties with developing country "ownership" and having inconsistent, fragmented, or dysfunctional assistance approaches. But another often overlooked negative consequence is legitimacy. On the one hand, if aid is not aligned, good governments may be seen as illegitimate; on the other, aligning aid with bad governments may make them seem legitimate (Canadian International Development Agency 2003, 2004; Leader and Colenso 2005, p. 21). In Haiti's case, issues of legitimacy and foreign intervention were critical but were never addressed in the foreign assistance context. For governments trying to create a good governance environment: "An overarching principle of the harmonization and alignment agenda is that donors should support country-owned strategies for growth and poverty reduction and base their programming on the needs and priorities identified in these strategies" (United Nations 2005a, p. 173). It does not make sense to align with insincere governments unless it serves a donor country's interest to do so.

Alignment issues also relate to country "ownership."

COUNTRY OWNERSHIP

Take country ownership seriously. Benjamin Mkapa, president of Tanzania, in 2004 stated, "We in the developing countries must own the development agenda, and our partners have to align their support to our agenda, our priorities and the sequencing we have set for ourselves. . . . Development cannot be imposed, it can only be facilitated."

Donors tend to pay only lip service to country ownership as essential to aid effectiveness, but not to take it seriously enough. If governments are not committed, they tend to implement programs without enthusiasm and may not invest matching or operational funds in programs; this was the case in Haiti. Donors need to decide whether their programs can be sustainable and effective without government support. If they can, then the present aid system probably works well. If they cannot, then they must move promoting country ownership to the top of the agenda and make tradeoffs to achieve it. Certainly, projects may fail when donors allow government to do things they suspect are risky, but when donors close out government, aid often is ineffective. Donors must take a closer look at the programmatic impact of country ownership before going it alone or operating parallel systems.

Donors often think that they can simultaneously control development and elicit strong country buy-in, but this is unlikely. The very notion of country ownership implies a lessening role for donors and increasing responsibility for governments (Schacter 2000; Brautigam 1996; Sharpe, Wood, and Wratten 2005). Donors must accept the risk.

ActionAid conducted a study of PRSPs (Poverty Reduction Strategy Papers), which was illustrative of the "ownership" issue (as reported in Taft-Morales 2007a, p. 6): "In a review of earlier Poverty Reduction Strategies in seven countries, including Haiti, ActionAid reported that although there was general support for locally generated poverty reduction strategies, the evidence suggested there was little in-county 'ownership' of plans except among some of the bureaucrats that implement them. The study found that 'important constituencies' are being excluded through consultation design or their own lack of capacity."

The donor community is now connecting country ownership and aid predictability as a factor in aid effectiveness: "One reason that donors' commitment to country ownership has failed to improve aid predictability is that it has yet to be put into practice" (United Nations 2005a, p. 99; Bate 2005). Cycles of aid suspensions and reductions, then renewed funding, play havoc with efforts to build country ownership for programs, especially as administrations in the donor country change. Donors typically fail to understand that these cycles affect country ownership enormously and need to be factored in when donors craft a long-term aid agenda (Eifert and Gelb 2005). In the recipient country, changes in regime likely compound the ownership problem, as the process tends to start from scratch with each change of the guard. One alternative is to build partnerships as described in the next section.

PARTNERSHIPS

Be cautious in building partnerships. The Organization for Economic Cooperation and Development's Development Assistance Committee has been exploring the concept of "difficult partnerships" as a feature of their work on fragile states. Of the committee's work the Canadian International Development Agency (2004, p. 4) states:

> A development partnership involves political commitments to poverty reduction as well as financial and technical engagement by all partners. The capability of a developing country government to make such a political commitment depends on its political system—in particular, how responsive the system is to the interests of poor people—and how well authority is consolidated within the state. A lack of political commitment is most often exacerbated by weak capacity in the government to develop and implement policy as well as the institutional weaknesses of non-state actors.

This could be said to summarize the situation in Haiti. Given the uncertainties, some promising models for partnering donors and governments would likely have been high-risk ventures in Haiti. Partnerships should not be developed before donors and countries demonstrate they can work together. Partnerships are based on commitment, trust, and competency, which are scarce in some fragile-state environments (Blagescu and Young 2005). Never build partnerships that will legitimize governments that are not legitimate.

PROGRAM AND PROJECT DESIGN

Fund only sustainable projects and programs that significantly impact the problem. Emergency relief and humanitarian assistance are, by definition, short-term programs to maintain a population in times of crisis.[11] Other assistance should be undertaken only if it is sustainable. Sustainability is likely attainable in one of three ways. The preferred way is to invest in a program that becomes sustainable once aid funding is concluded, for example, creating an irrigation system that helps farmers compete in food markets, the returns from which allow farmers to maintain the irrigation system with their own resources. For other investments, either government or donors must take responsibility for continued maintenance and operations. Donors need to look more carefully at the capacity and willingness of government to pay for maintenance and operations after assistance is withdrawn, by, say, charging user fees. If capacity and willingness are absent, then donors must continue to invest, rethink the investment, or pressure government to take over funding. Too often in the Haiti case, donors seemed surprised that Haitians had not sustained initial donor investments. But donors failed to realize that all of the factors enumerated thus far conspired against the recipients. Poorly governed countries have few resources and many demands on them.

A close examination of donor efforts in Haiti showed a plethora of small projects intended to address big issues—a shotgun approach: throw enough projects out there and something is likely to work. But these small projects tended to be low impact, short term, and labor-intensive to manage. The reason for the shotgun approach in Haiti was that the government lacked capacity to partner with donors for major program initiatives, and donors were suspicious of how Haitians would spend funding on a more massive scale. Being risk-averse, donors tended to opt for small projects where damages of any kind would be minimal. As Canadian aid officials repeatedly pointed out, this strategy produced few positive results. Donors must instead focus scarce development resources on programs and initiatives that will make a difference in post-conflict reconstruction efforts. People in Haiti are looking for positive changes in their lives. A few workshops that serve several hundred people in a democratization program, no matter how well intentioned, are likely to remain meaningless: "Governments and their partners should move from a narrow focus on organizational, technocratic and public management approaches to a broader perspective that incorporates both the political dynamics and the institutional rules of the game with which public organizations operate" (Puri 2004).

Another reason that small projects get done is that NGOs tend to advocate for them in specialized areas where they have capacity—say, workshops for training judges. Few if any NGOs offer "whole of government" approaches.[12] In such a case, donors should, as recommended, define their agendas, then search for a suitable delivery mechanism. It might just be the government (see also "Coordination and Cooperation").

There is a case to be made for small projects in rural villages where any effort at all might make a difference. Indeed, small villages probably require small projects—but village aid was not a focus in Haiti. Much assistance goes to central governments.

CAPACITY BUILDING

Quickly build financial management and aid management capacity. David Hirschmann (1993) advises donors to recognize "the complex interrelationship between weak capacity, task enormity, conditionality, adjustment fatigue, absorptive capacity and sustainability" and suggests that in Ethiopia, another postconflict state, "the very people who were threatened by these policy reforms were the ones who were expected to carry them out." The Addis Ababa principle developed in November 2001 by the Organization for Economic Cooperation and Development (2005b) as part of its Strategic Partnership for Africa Initiative states: "All donor assistance should be delivered through government systems unless there are compelling reasons to the contrary; where this is not possible, any alternative mechanisms or safeguards must be time-limited and develop and build, rather than undermine or bypass, governmental systems" (p. 3). Richard Manning (2005), sums up capacity building and aid: "The history of capacity development mirrors that of foreign aid in general: at different times and different places it has been highly effective, totally ineffective, and everything in between. A new era featuring significant scaling-up of aid presents opportunities for capacity development, but also magnifies the need to learn lessons from experience. What is needed now is a determined common effort, by donors and partner countries, to implement what has been learned and to make good practice common practice."

From Haiti one sees all too well that a country without effective financial management capacity—including accounting, controlling, budgeting, reporting, procurement, and disbursement—will remain dysfunctional until these capacities are acquired (Organization for Economic Cooperation and Development 2005a, 2005b). Financial management must be a top priority within any good governance approach. As already discussed, a good model for this is the Millennium Challenge Account: MCA employs independent evaluators to certify that a country does in fact have financial management capacity in place and that it manages U.S. funds properly over the five years for which aid is granted (Buss 2008). The World Bank also undertakes a periodic procurement review in developing countries, which is a useful tool to keep a focus on good financial management.

In Haiti, lack of capacity in and suspicion of government led donors to administer aid themselves or channel funds through NGOs to deliver services. Expectations were that over time the Haitian government would assume these responsibilities, but it has not done so since 1995, if it ever did, in spite of what now appear to be meager attempts to assist the Haitians. Donors need to make a more determined effort to build capacity in government. Not to do so is in the end self-defeating. How best to do this is a topic of considerable debate, but solutions must be found. Perpetual funding of NGOs and private contractors is not the answer. Extensively bypassing government makes a country a "protectorate"; totally taking control makes it a colony.

One promising approach might be to create "semiautonomous" units in ministries, made up of civil servants who are experienced, committed, and honest, and charge these units with administering programs with minimal interference from what is likely to be an unqualified, uncommitted, and corrupt bureaucracy.

Capacity building is a government responsibility. Too often a lack of government capacity is blamed on donors. In the end, though, it is the responsibility of a fragile state or developing country to develop and refine its own capacity (Edgren and Matthew 2002; Fukuda-Parr, Lopes, and Malik 2002). The Paris Declaration on Aid Effectiveness, agreed to in Paris in 2005 at a conference of donors, states: "This represents a clear agreement that capacity development is the primary responsibility of developing countries, with donors playing a supportive role. Developing countries must lead the process of capacity development through setting specific objectives in their national plans. Donors should mobilize their financial and analytical support around credible partner country objectives, plans and strategies, making full use of what capacity exists" (Manning 2005). Peter MacKay, Canada's minister of foreign affairs (quoted in Sorenson 2006, p. 1), has stated, "Perhaps the most important lesson drawn from past efforts by donors is the need for Haitians themselves to assume the leadership and responsibility for the implementation of their development agenda."

Donors in Haiti effectively bypassed the bureaucracy and political leadership in delivering aid, because they wanted to implement quickly, promote accountability, reduce effects of corruption, pressure government to reform, and retain aid through tying. Although there is a case to be made for parallel or shadow aid systems, their presence makes capacity building in the recipient country much more difficult, and may even make the situation worse (see box 7-1). Donors need to work within and with government, not outside it (World Bank, Operations Evaluation Department 2003; Boesen 2004). Donors always walk a thin line between supporting government or supporting programs. There are, unfortunately, no good rules of thumb for deciding what to do. Each case must be evaluated on its own merits.

Capacity building requires a whole of government approach in fragile states. In 2005 the World Bank's Operations Evaluation Department (2005a, 2005b) did the international community a great service by showing why most capacity-building efforts are woefully inadequate (see also Boesen 2004) when it studied the World Bank's sub-Saharan African capacity-building efforts; lessons learned there apply also in Haiti and other fragile states. The study delineated some important points about capacity building:

—It is not a collateral activity, it is a core goal and high priority in its own right.

—It is the underpinning of good governance.

—It must be integrated government-wide, across all sectors, ministries, and institutions, because weakness in one area affects the rest adversely.

Box 7-1. *How to Make Fragile States Worse*

—Adding to inconsistency of policies and fragmentation of implementation through a proliferation of projects.

—Poaching government staff for parallel project and program units.

—Distorting salary schemes through creation of special aid agency labor markets and in "enclaves," creating strong disincentives for others.

—Creating multiple distorting incentives for civil service.

—Creating procedural bypasses of institutional bottlenecks rather than removing them.

—Bypassing normal budget and accounting procedures, instead of strengthening them.

—Undermining national political accountability mechanisms.

—Replacing institutionally demanding domestic taxation with "easy" aid funds, thereby avoiding pressure to create transparent and rule-bound revenue institutions.

—Establishing parallel monitoring systems.

—Initiating uncoordinated, overlapping, and underused studies, planning processes, and even capacity-building studies and processes.

—Encouraging rent-seeking behavior.

Source: Based on Boesen (2004, p. 10).

—It must have clearly defined purposes, objectives, and strategies, just like projects and programs.

—It must be seen as part of a broader, comprehensive approach to human resource management and a human capital strategy for a country.

—It must switch from a focus on individual training and technical assistance to a "whole of government" needs assessment and strategy.

In addition, capacity building should be built into development plans, a practice not yet common in the field (United Nations 1997).

The Canadian Parliament and government have also come to the conclusion that a "whole of government" approach to foreign assistance is the only way to reconstruct Haiti. In 2005 the Canadian International Development Agency began taking the lead among donors in implementing this approach (Sorenson 2006, p. 3). Canada established the Stabilization and Reconstruction Task Force to provide overall policy leadership and coordination of its "whole of government" responses to failed or fragile states such as Afghanistan, Sudan, and Haiti. Also in 2005, the Organization for Economic Cooperation and Development (2005c) published *Principles for Good International*

Engagement in Fragile States, which it has adhered to in structuring its aid program in Haiti.[13]

Many individual donors, such as the United States, are struggling with this issue of how to make the best use of human capital in the federal system.

Many analysts have pointed out that when building capacity, donors must understand that although civil servants are being trained and technical assistance is being offered, others in the bureaucracy will have to fill these roles. Because these temporary replacements will likely be untrained and in need of assistance, donors will have to provide them with support as well. Thus, capacity building is a Catch-22: To create capacity where it is insufficient, a great deal of excess capacity must be present in both government and donor agencies to plug gaps left by those undergoing training (Andersson and Isaksen 2002).

Evaluations of capacity building in the literature are overwhelmingly negative, finding failures and shortcomings and few positive examples (Boesen 2004). There is a tendency in crafting capacity building programs to assume that undertaking the opposite of a failed effort will lead to success, but often a totally different approach is required. Foreign assistance for capacity building is still in its infancy and there are many unknowns.

Use the people of the Haitian diaspora to assist development. There is something appealing about engaging the diaspora of fragile states in their reconstruction and development. After all, expatriates contribute a great deal to developing country economies through remittances, they maintain ties with relatives, and some own businesses or have business relationships in country. Expatriates generally are concerned about their home countries. Haitians, in partnership with the World Bank, tried to bring Haitians living outside the country back to work in Haiti under Préval's first administration,[14] and some members of Congress tried to legislate appropriations for similar projects. Canadians held national conferences of Haitian expatriates to help with Haiti (see Wah 2005; International Crisis Group 2007d). None of these approaches has yet to produce results. It appears that Haitians in Haiti may not be enthusiastic about expatriate Haitians returning. During Préval's second administration, parliament rejected an Inter-American Development Bank grant that would have covered salaries of Haitians returning to work in government, then reversed itself when members realized it might be beneficial for the country. But donors continue to try to find some mechanism that would have impact (on best practices see World Bank 2005a; Catanese 1999).

There is a downside though for Haitians in the Préval government in 2008: Aristide continues to enjoy considerable popularity among many factions in the diaspora, potentially complicating the efforts of a new government. The real contribution of the diaspora probably lies in developing economic and business ties between themselves and Haiti rather than actually trying to enter the government. One of the drivers in the rapid growth of India in information technology has been the forward and backward linkages of Indian entrepreneurs in IT in the United States to their home country. So the diaspora represents not a way to build capacity in governance but a component in an economic growth and development strategy. Many Haitians told us that they believed that the so-called rich elite were actually not all that rich, so Haiti must turn to the rich among the diaspora for help.

In November 2007, Haiti's parliament reached out to the Haitian diaspora to learn their views on constitutional reform.[15] A high-level nineteen-member Haitian delegation visited Miami, Chicago, Boston, Orlando, and West Palm Beach in an effort to reach out for counsel and support.

PERFORMANCE ASSESSMENT AND EVALUATION

Build performance assessment and evaluations into aid programs to improve effectiveness. The art and science of performance assessment remains in its infancy, even though the concept has been around now for years. Performance measurement, if treated either as a compliance exercise or punitively, as in an audit, probably reduces rather than enhances performance and accountability. All performance measurement systems have the potential for misuse or abuse. Nonetheless, they are powerful systems when properly used (for an overview see Redburn, Shea, and Buss 2008). Performance assessment, when properly deployed, has been shown to improve management, performance, accountability, and transparency. The international community does not yet have adequate performance assessment system models or applications in place for developing countries, although work is progressing in leaps and bounds.

The Bush administration's Presidential Management Agenda, a program created in 2004, sets goals and looks carefully at program performance among federal agencies using a common framework, the Program Assessment Rating Tool; only four years old, the program is enjoying considerable success (see especially Redburn, Shea, and Buss 2008).[16] Another, earlier, effort, the Government Performance Results Act of 1993, promoted strategic planning in federal agencies. The Canadian International Development Agency has taken the lead in performance-based management in foreign aid. In the 2005 International Policy Statement, the agency called for "regular evaluation and, where possible, 'action research' processes to gauge relevance and effectiveness of Canadian programs and approaches." The World Bank is an international leader in efforts to build performance assessment models.

Apparently, signing performance-based contracts or agreements is easy; enforcement is not. A 2005 analysis of the Pentagon's incentive fee program showed they paid out incentive fees regardless of vendor performance. The cost to taxpayers: $8 billion (U.S. Government Accountability Office 2005a).

Performance assessment systems are only as good as the data they produce. Data must be pertinent, accurate, timely, usable, and credible. Even in developed countries, this has been a tall order, not fully attained. In countries such as Haiti, where government resources are scarce even for basic minimal operations, imposing and funding a data-gathering system might be perceived as a low priority. Yet if aid programs are implemented and cannot be assessed, there is no way to keep them on track, let alone determine how well they have performed. Donors should consider building a component for generating performance data into administrative costs of programs. In the long run, such expenditures should pay off in increased government capacity.

It is typical for Haitian projects to result in documents that begin by saying that a democratization program was a success, but then state that specific projects and programs essentially did not work: "The operation failed, but the patient recovered anyway." Such reports are symptoms of donors' failure to understand they are in business to improve governance. A program cannot be successful if governance is not changed for the better; nor can a program be considered successful if governance improves on its own in spite of the program or would have improved without the program (see Redburn, Shea, and Buss 2008). Reports like these have consequences, not the least of which is to detract from seriousness, credibility, and legitimacy of an assistance effort. Naturally, donors are likely to continue to put the best face on their efforts, hence the need for independent evaluations.

This book is possible because of the honest work of bilateral and multilateral donors in Haiti who not only publicize their successes but also analyze their failures. The international community has learned a lot from these efforts. Some programs were not evaluated and others were more of a public relations effort rather than a serious look at what worked and why. Donors should do a better job of funding and conducting evaluations that contribute to knowledge about aid provision. Only in this way can policymakers make corrections and others learn from successes and failures.

Most donors post project and program evaluations on websites; access is easy, but the information there is often of poor or uneven quality, fragmented, and not all that useful in informing others. Even when information is available, it is often a nightmare to assemble and synthesize, despite the substantial expenditures made to produce the information. The World Bank is an exception: it makes a lot of worthwhile information available, at both the country and system level. In 2006, for example, the World Bank and the UN Development Group Office conducted an assessment of progress in Haiti as a "platform for post-conflict recovery and reconstruction planning" (UN Economic and Social Council 2006b, p. 1) presenting critical lessons.

Much more could be done and needs to be done. The United States has perhaps the worst record in conducting assessments and evaluations of assistance projects. Knowledge development needs to move up on the U.S. aid agenda.

COMPLIANCE

Do not waive sound financial control practices for expedience. Donors are under enormous pressure from one another and from recipients to relax financial controls to expedite allocation of foreign assistance, but to give in to this pressure is a bad idea. Even in countries and international organizations with strong controls, extensive transparency, and accountability mechanisms in place, money attracts corruption when controls are waived, ignored, or not enforced.[17] In Haiti, where insufficient financial controls exist or are likely to be weak, aid is likely to be wasted. This problem is endemic in fragile states.

COORDINATION AND COMMUNICATION

Take donor-to-government and donor-to-donor coordination seriously. Ironically, Haiti became a model of aid coordination for a short time under Aristide's second administration (Hassan 2004), and in our view an apparently effective model under the ICF. In spite of these admirable efforts, aid coordination remains a problem. As noted, donors have different agendas, cultures, politics, and capacity, which inhibits cooperation, either intentionally or inadvertently. Until relatively recently, donors failed to coordinate their assistance in developing or transitional countries, which sometimes led to poor results. For example, it was not unusual during the post-Communist era in Eastern Europe for U.S. embassies to have little idea what assistance might be flowing to a country. This might be understandable where private organizations and foreign governments are active in a country—they are not required to coordinate their activities with the United States. But it was often the case that U.S. government agencies working in developing countries were unaware of one another's presence or activities. Recently, international organizations have been doing a better job of coordinating assistance, but much more needs to be done. Lack of coordination contributes to aid failure. Donors need to revisit the reasons for coordination failures and eliminate them.

As of spring 2008 there were about twenty-five major donors in Haiti, not including private charities. This presence represents a heavy burden on country policymakers. At a 2005 meeting on aid to fragile states, the former finance minister of Afghanistan, Ashraf Ghani, remarked that he spent 60 percent of his time coordinating donors. Freeing him from that burden would have allowed him to actually carry out targeted reforms (Organization for Economic Cooperation and Development 2005b, p. 6).

Aid coordination is difficult enough when multiple donors pursue multiple projects and programs, but these difficulties are exacerbated in a system where donors systematically set up independent parallel structures, competing or supplanting those of the government. NGOs, again, are problematic. When dozens of donors deliver services through hundreds of organizations acting independently, problems will occur within and across donor operations and within and across ministries, and a real mess can result. Donors and governments should work to build one coordinated system with shared missions, goals, and strategies.

Donors need to build knowledge of and support for aid programs not only with the government but also with the people. In fragile nations such as Haiti, where over half the people are illiterate and uneducated and few people have access to electronic or print media, and where many in the population are easily led astray by manipulators, the task will not be easy. Nevertheless, ways for donors and the people to communicate with each other must be developed.

8

LESSONS LEARNED: GOVERNANCE AND DEMOCRACY PROGRAMS

It is the policy of the United States to seek and support the growth of democratic movements and institutions in every nation and culture, with the ultimate goal of ending tyranny in our world.
—George W. Bush, Inaugural Address, January 20, 2004

Haitians who seek no political power, wishing only to lead normal lives—and this undoubtedly includes the overwhelming majority of the people—are disgusted with the unending political crisis and would welcome meaningful assistance to help build true democracy in their country.
—Ambassador Terence Todman, April 14, 2004

Failure of democratization programs in Haiti suggests that donors ought to rethink assumptions under which civil society organizations (CSOs) are developed, elections are offered, grassroots participation in politics is promoted, individuals are supported over institutions, and legitimacy in government is spawned. Rule-of-law programs are most effective when courts, prosecution, law enforcement, and prisons are treated as a justice system within a larger set of executive- and legislative-branch reconstruction and reform. National reconciliation and justice following conflict must be effectively pursued. And reform of the civil service, decentralization, and privatization should be delayed until normalization has been achieved, and should not be pursued during reconstruction. Anticorruption programs should be pursued as soon as possible (World Bank 2006f).

As important as governance and democracy issues are in assisting fragile states, they must be understood in a much broader context. First and foremost is the issue of security: without it, nothing else will likely be accomplished. Ravaged economies, especially those that have malfunctioned for years, must be jump-started so that the private sector engages, investments flow, and public revenues expand. In fragile countries there are legions of poor people without work; providing jobs must be a top priority for both humanitarian and political-economic reasons. Regional issues such as securing borders, improving diplomatic relations, promoting trade, and participating in regional and international organizations are important, but less so than the issues just enumerated. Regional actors can hamper advances in fragile states by destabilizing them; if this is occurring they must be neutralized early on.

Democracy and Governance Programs

Democracy and governance programs have become the centerpieces of donor assistance efforts in fragile states.

Haiti raises some troubling issues about the attempt to democratize countries that have no tradition of democracy, have leaders who value democracy only to the extent that it serves their political or individual interests, and are impoverished. There are no good answers about how to use foreign assistance to promote democracy in these countries, but it is time to start asking tough questions. What is the role of these entities and processes in promoting democracy?

—Civil society organizations
—Elections
—Grassroots participation
— Institutions and individuals
—Legitimacy

Donors cannot buy democracy, capitalism or reform. The magnitude of aid funding invested in Haiti suggests that donors may have thought they could buy or install reforms, rather than building them (Erixon 2005). This does not work. Unless a country's leaders believe in reform, they will either take the aid and do what they want, or stand by indifferently.

CSOs are often the problem, not the solution. In many ways civil society organizations are the foundation of modern democracy. Political scientists tell us that CSOs are responsible for aggregating the interests of their constituents, then articulating them to people who are in power or are seeking power. Mothers Against Drunk Driving, the National Rifle Association, and La Raza—an immigrant's rights advocacy group—are CSOs that have played a constructive role in the United States. But in Haiti there is one dominant, and dysfunctional, party and dozens of loosely tied factions and interests; there is no consensus on limits of incivility, and violence is the preferred method of resolving disputes. In such an environment, there are many reasons why funding CSOs may not be a good strategy.

CSOs in Haiti, and in other fragile states, have many negatives that become exaggerated in such states. They claim to speak for the people whose interest they purport to represent, but often either they do not represent these interests or they dictate what the interests should be. CSOs tend to be dominated by elites, or people who soon become elites, who use CSOs to further their own political careers. Because they set the agenda and have the wherewithal to participate, they tend to shut out the common people. CSOs composed only of a handful of people can exert power and influence considerably out of proportion to the size of their membership. Often they are used by political actors as surrogates, while the actors themselves appear to remain at arm's length from the political arena. Once CSOs develop, there are few if any controls that can be used to leverage CSOs in democratic discourse. They can say or do whatever they like, and can cause great havoc in the political system.

For these and other reasons, donors need to think more carefully than they have in the past about when and how they promote CSOs, especially during the postconflict reconstruction phase of an assistance effort. The United States has been widely criticized for appearing to use CSOs to undermine governments, under the guise of democratization.[1] It will be difficult to reduce the influence of CSOs in development assistance. The CSO approach must be revisited.[2]

Do not rush to hold elections, especially if they are serving as a pretext to cut and run. Elections are the mainstay of democracy, but elections do not equal democracy: nearly all countries hold elections, even authoritarian states such as Cuba and the former Soviet Union. What makes elections important to democracy is that they are legitimate, free, and fair, and that people and political parties and actors accept their results. Haiti in the past fifteen years demonstrated that it could hold elections, but they were not viewed as legitimate. The Haiti expert Henry Carey (1998, p. 142) observed mordantly, "The 1987 election massacres were a tragedy, while the 1990–91, 1995 and 1997 elections were farce." Another Haiti expert, Robert Maguire, has offered this analysis: "The principal factor undermining external efforts over the past decade to transform Haiti into a stable, functioning, inclusive and modern democratic state that serves all its citizens, has been the tendency to seek a quick exit. Policy makers today must resist the temptation to intervene only when a crisis reaches a boiling point, stabilize the country and hold an election, and drastically reduce their presence and engagement" (quoted in Sorenson 2006, p. 24). To make matters worse, countries and regional organizations accepted illegitimate election results in Haiti that they probably shouldn't have, and failed to accept legitimate results when they should have.

This politicizes elections even more. The United States needs to rethink the importance of equating democracy with elections during a postconflict reconstruction period.[3]

Terence Todman (2003), ambassador from the Organization of American States to Haiti, after assessing the situation in 2003, reached a similar conclusion: "Elections anytime within the next few months are likely to do more harm than good because the security situation in the country would not permit full participation in safety; opposition parties would be grossly unprepared; participation would be very limited; there would very likely be violent clashes; the result of the elections would be unrepresentative of popular will; and, such solutions not under Resolution 822, probably would not be recognized as valid" (p. 1).[4] Robert Miller, of the Canadian Parliamentary Centre, cautions that "elections should never be viewed as an exit strategy for external actors, because they are only the beginning of a long, arduous process of democratization" (quoted in Sorenson 2006, p. 22). Many international organizations have arrived at similar conclusions. Gerard Le Chevalier, head of the UN electoral assistance mission, had even stronger words about the impending 2005 elections: "The idea that hit-and-run elections will overcome a crisis is wrong—more often than not elections generate civil wars rather than solutions. What Haiti needs is a process of negotiation and dialogue and democratically elected authorities who behave democratically."[5]

The UN's Human Development Report of 2002 stated: "True democratization is something more than elections. Granting all people formal political equality does not create an equal desire or capacity to participate in political processes—or an equal capacity to influence outcomes. Imbalances in resources and political power often subvert the principle of 'one person, one voice' and the purpose of democratic institutions" (p. 10).[6]

Many commentators suspect that elections have become an "exit strategy" for the international community, who might be accused by some of wanting to invest aid in countries that are more deserving. According to this speculation, the rush to hold elections is a way for donors to announce success and then leave reconstruction to a newly elected but inexperienced government. If this is true, it is a great disservice to democracy (Orr 2002, p. 142).

Father Jacques Mesidor, an influential leader of the Society of Saint Francis of Sales (many Catholic priests in Haiti are Salesians), summed up the situation in Haiti succinctly back in 1987: "There are more urgent problems here than having elections!"

Expand opportunities for poor people to participate in the political system. In 1991 Renaud Bernadin, planning minister in Aristide's first administration, observed, "Every so-called professional politician in Haiti creates a political party on paper, but has nothing at the grassroots. These politicians make decisions without consulting the people. They distribute jobs and money to their clients" (as quoted in McFadyen 1995, p. 55). Many informed observers suggest that poor people in Haiti would like a voice in the country, having grown tired of being exploited by a small economic and political elite and a larger cadre of people who would like to become elites.[7] Aristide was and remains popular among the poor because he stood for political participation of the poor. So far, democratization efforts have focused on elections and CSO formation, but elections have made little difference in poor people's lives and CSOs are dominated by elites who may not represent or even care about the poor. What is needed in Haiti and other developing countries is much expanded opportunities for poor people to participate directly in politics. There are many effective models for achieving this, and they ought to be considered in fragile, postconflict countries.[8]

Rather than trying to mobilize the poor through CSO activity, donors might want to consider creating an "enabling environment" in which the poor are given incentives for collective action and mobilization, especially removing obstacles to participation (Moore and Putzel 1999). In mature Western democracies there are few "programs" to create CSOs and other voluntary organizations, because people who believe their interests are not adequately served in the political system find ways to organize themselves into groups.

Support democratic institutions rather than individuals. The rise and fall and rise and fall of Aristide is controversial: Was he a truly democratic figure under assault by reactionary, undemocratic elite forces who ought to have been supported, or was he another in a long line of rulers who talked about democracy but were tyrants and therefore should have been eliminated? The fact that so many believe one way or the other, and the fact that Haiti is in a shambles, indicates that it is time for a more careful reconsideration of supporting specific country leaders versus supporting democratic institutions. Foreign assistance was used both to support and to unravel Aristide's regime—sometimes simultaneously—and so is tied to the controversy surrounding him.

The historian Robert Orr (2002) has written, "Arguably, the single most important factor that determines the success or failure of a post-conflict reconstruction effort is the extent to which a coherent, legitimate government exists" (p. 132). As events in Haiti so clearly demonstrate, even the most corrupt, dysfunctional, autocratic government seeks legitimacy if it can get it. Constitutions, elections and foreign assistance all can legitimize really bad governments. When this occurs, donors have the worst of all worlds: they give legitimacy to the illegitimate and likely fail in the end in their ambitions for democratization. Orr emphasizes that legitimacy should be of much greater concern in aid provision than it is.

RULE OF LAW

Rule of law is too complicated an issue to fully explore here, but the Haitian experience suggests several points of relevance for those attempting to assist fragile states (see International Crisis Group 2007b).

The judicial system — law enforcement, prosecution, courts, prisons—must be reengineered in its entirety, not piecemeal. The rule of law is the mainstay of good governance and as such undergirds democracy, and must be a high priority in foreign assistance. In Haiti, a lot of funding was allocated to establishing the rule of law, but the judicial system appears to have made only marginal gains. One reason for this was that assistance was fragmented across donors and myriad small projects and thus lacked coherence. Many projects were too limited to achieve the donor's policy goals. Furthermore, the government's commitment to the rule of law was weak. The rule of law is another sector where donors must harmonize and align with the government if results are to be achieved.

All legal institutions must be reconstructed. The judicial system is only part of the system of governance. In order for it to be reengineered, operations of the executive and legislative branches must also be reconstructed. One necessary condition is that the executive and legislative branches commit to judicial reform and provide leadership, policy, and funding to make it work.

Reform should change the political culture to one where legal norms prevail over personal political authority. A critical factor in successfully bringing a country under the rule of law is to build a culture where legal norms prevail over individual authority. This is extraordinarily difficult in fragile states, where political leaders promote democratic principles only so long as they themselves benefit personally. In Haiti, presidents who found institutions inconvenient created new ones or ignored existing ones. Unless donors or leaders find a way to break this pattern, rule of law and democratization will be only a dream.

JUSTICE AND RECONCILIATION

Pursuing justice for those killed or wronged during conflict may have no solution. The rule of law rests on the bedrock concept that no one is above the law. But what happens when people break the law to overthrow a government that has not established much legitimacy and behaves lawlessly? Are the law breakers really freedom fighters and perhaps immune from prosecution? What happens if law breakers take over the government and eventually become legitimate? Many sub-Saharan Africa and Middle Eastern countries have leaders in power who got there through revolution and insurrection, mostly violent, and this has occurred repeatedly in Haiti, too. Aristide punished Duvalierists who opposed him, but did not bring his own followers to justice. Apologists seriously contended that this was acceptable because the opposition did it first. The Transition Government in turn tried to bring Aristide and his supporters to justice but not those who opposed him. Some credible political leader needs to break the cycle of violence and one-sided retribution in Haiti.

Like South Africa, Aristide initiated a national reconciliation effort to reduce violence and promote healing to allow recovery to begin, and smaller efforts at conflict resolution have been funded by donors, but these efforts have been poorly conceived or poorly supported. Not surprisingly, nothing has worked. The importance of the rule of law means that donors must determine why programs failed and improve them.[9]

Some Haitians have pointed out to us the necessity of resolving this "unfinished business," not only in relation to Aristide but also to the military juntas and the Duvaliers, and others as well. They feel that this culture of lawlessness and retribution is a ticking time bomb in Haiti. They feel national reconciliation conferences are a waste of time and instead suggest a solution drawn from the voudou practice of a *queckou*. *Queckou* means bringing together the spirits of the past who wronged others or were wronged with people in the present who have grievances or who have caused grievances. This kind of caucus is intended to negotiate a peace between past and present so that people can move on. This suggestion offers an interesting insight into reconciliation issues in the Haitian psyche; since it draws on their belief system it may be a promising basis for a reconciliation program.

President Préval has tried to keep awareness of the atrocities of the past from being swamped by an apparent wave of nostalgia for the Papa Doc and Baby Doc regimes. He has ordered that one of Haiti's most notorious prisons, well known for its torture chambers, be converted into a museum dedicated to memorializing the horrors of the Duvalier regimes.[10]

PUBLIC-SECTOR REFORM

Do not confuse civil service reconstruction with civil service reform. Civil service *reconstruction* means rebuilding the civil service to restore lost capacity to govern, whereas civil service *reform* means improving the effectiveness, efficiency, ethics, and operations of the bureaucracy. In Haiti, as in other fragile states, donors appeared to equate civil service reconstruction with civil service reform.[11] It may have been wrong to do so. Haiti's civil service—characterized by phantom employees, incoherent human resources policies, unskilled personnel, rampant corruption, low salaries, political influence, and under- and overstaffing—was and remains much in need of reform. Yet as dysfunctional as the civil service is, it remains the only mechanism to administer the country during the postconflict era. Reforming the civil service during the reconstruction phase in foreign assistance greatly disrupts an already bad situation, making aid administration and general management all but impossible. As a result, donors will bypass government for the delivery of aid programs, which denies opportunities for capacity building. Donors should try to work within the existing bureaucracy to determine who can do the job, and ignore or marginalize dysfunctional elements until reforms can be put in place. Few bureaucrats will participate in a reconstruction program to redevelop capacity while their jobs are being eliminated under reforms.

Institute anticorruption programs immediately. Governance in Haiti unfortunately seems to have been built on corruption because of conditions that encouraged corruption: low civil service salaries; the ubiquity of bribes and embezzling; lack of transparency and accountability; opportunities for corruption; ineffective legal systems and enforcement that are impediments to investigations and prosecutions; possession of undue political influence; pervasiveness and thus culture of corruption; tolerance of corruption and lack of commitment to put an end to it. Generally, the more corruption there is the less effective aid is (Kaufmann 2005).

Donors must make it a high priority that developing countries end corruption. The international community is in fact becoming increasingly adept at helping reduce corruption in developing countries (Organization for Economic Cooperation and Development 2003a; see also especially Nelson 2007), and some countries have made major strides in reducing it. The foundations of anticorruption efforts are a sincere commitment by country leadership not to tolerate corruption and, when corruption is exposed, to bring perpetrators to justice swiftly and publicly. This requires a well-functioning judicial system (see the section on the rule of law). (In fairness to developing countries it must be noted that many first world countries have their own problems with corrupt politicians, lobbyists, and officials.)

Postpone decentralization initiatives until postconflict reconstruction is well under way. Decentralization—transferring power and resources from national government to local communities—is a cornerstone of foreign assistance efforts in most developing countries. Decentralization can be fiscal, administrative, or political. Like other reforms, decentralization during postconflict reconstruction is highly problematic.[12] Given that the civil service at the national level in Haiti was unable to do its job, imagine how difficult it would be for thousands of local officials, many without experience or resources, to manage villages, cities, and regions. After Aristide's ouster in 2004, local officials discovered that government offices had been ransacked of everything, including desks, file cabinets, and anything of value. To complicate matters, thugs and opportunists roamed the streets with impunity, and no security forces, either local or international, were to be found. How could dedicated local officials possibly manage their departments when they lacked the resources locally to do so and were ignored by the national government? Rushing into decentralization may be ineffective until a country becomes normalized.

Now that Haiti is moving into reconstruction, it is time for policymakers to start thinking about decentralizing government, and some Haitians already have begun: in August 2007, four mayors of cities located on the border with the Dominican Republic developed a cooperative strategic plan to manage the region. This is a great start.[13]

The number of developing countries that have pursued decentralization and actually achieved it is surprisingly low, in light of the attention given to the issue by the donor community (Jutting 2005). So there are few models of best practices that donors can draw on to effect decentralization in fragile states.

Pursue privatization programs only if there is popular and governmental support for privatization. Privatization of government enterprises is a high priority, especially for multilateral donors. Government enterprises are inefficient, encourage rent seeking, and are politicized. They should operate like businesses. Haiti illustrates the necessity of laying the groundwork among people and leadership before attempting wholesale privatization. Premature privatization efforts will tend to be ineffective, or, as in Haiti, they will never really get off the ground (see chapter 9 for a discussion of Haiti's privatization program under Préval).

IMPLICATIONS FOR COUNTRY DEBT AND ACCOUNTABILITY

Debt relief and forgiveness is appropriate in the context of aid failure. In Haiti, as in many developing countries, loans are a mixed blessing: Haiti has experienced difficulties managing its external debt. In September 2003, Haiti's external debt was $1.3 billion, 49 percent of GDP, most of it owed to multilateral lenders. Some of its debt for which payment was in arrears was forgiven by donors, primarily by Canada. Haiti, in spite of its problems, has as of 2007 qualified for debt forgiveness under the World Bank's Highly Indebted Poor Countries program (see chapter 4 for details).[14]

The jury is out on the extent to which Haiti or donors have contributed to aid failures, but it does raise a question about the extent to which fragile countries deserve debt relief if aid failures are attributable to some extent to the actions of donors.[15] Some aid flows to fragile nations in the form of grants, but other flows are loans. Why should a fragile nation pay debt service on a loan that funded a project that failed because of actions of donor lenders? If, say, donors design a poor election program, why should a fragile nation have to repay its debt to that donor? In the case of Haiti, some donors, such as the World Bank, did not offer debt relief until 2007. Canada and the United States have paid Haitian debt service as part of their aid programs. A strong case can be made that fragile nations should not have to pay for the failures of donors' ideas. This should be considered along with other issues in the debt forgiveness debate now under way in the international community.[16]

Aid in Broader Context

Democratization and public-sector reform cannot be successful unless much broader issues are addressed—they simply cannot work in a vacuum. There are at least four areas of broad concern in Haiti, as in all fragile states, that are relevant to the aid context:
—Security
—Growth and development
—Jobs
—Regional issues

SECURITY

Make security in the postconflict country a high priority. Security was and is an important issue in Haiti, though it was not a focus of our attention for this report.[17] The World Bank's Low Income Countries Under Stress (LICUS) group concluded that the donor community had given inadequate attention to even minimum security requirements in Haiti, which precipitated problems in reconstructing the country (World Bank 2006d). As of the end of 2005, USAID had yet to deploy its full resources in Haiti because of security concerns. U.S. diplomats only returned to Haiti in November 2005. Multilateral donors also had difficulty coping with the threat of violence: Doctors without Borders, CARE, and the International Red Cross all lost personnel or curtailed operations for security reasons. Foreign assistance efforts will be jeopardized if violence in Haiti is not reined in.[18]

The United Nations often takes responsibility for securing a country in a postconflict era (Malone and von Einsiedel 2006; Law 2006). In Haiti, the UN peacekeeping force was too small and ill equipped to secure Port-au-Prince, let alone the whole country. In the February 2006 elections, no polling stations were placed in the poor district, Cité Soleil, home to 200,000 people, for fear of the violence their presence might precipitate and which the UN force might not be able to deal with.[19] In both 1994 and 2004 the multinational force exited Haiti within a few months, which was odd since past experience suggested that an intervention would last for years, not months (Dobbins 2003). Donors to the UN must provide the funding necessary to secure the country if they expect their aid programs to work. In addition to providing security, donors must ensure that security is integrated within the rest of the reconstruction effort—the so-called "whole of government" approach (Ottaway and Mair 2004; Organization for Economic Cooperation and Development 2005a, 2005b). As Caroline Anstey, director of the World Bank's Caribbean unit, rightly observed, "Better security would have meant faster development results on the ground. Faster development would have contributed to better security."[20]

GROWTH AND DEVELOPMENT

Ensure that pro-growth and pro-development policies are in place. In the long run, Haiti's future depends on structural adjustment and stability, encompassing reforms in ten areas often referred to as the Washington Consensus (Williamson 2003, p. 10):

Fiscal discipline
Reordering public expenditure priorities
Tax reform
Liberalization of interest rates
Competitive exchange rates
Trade liberalization
Foreign direct investment liberalization
Deregulation
Property rights
Privatization

Imposition of this agenda on developing countries has been controversial and in some cases counterproductive (Ortiz 2003).[21] Critics of the approach point out that pursuing the Washington Consensus has lead many countries to ruin (a Web search on "Washington Consensus Haiti" yielded 46,000 hits, mostly negative). They believe the one-size-fits-all approach fails to take into account culture and context. But there is another explanation for the failure, one closely related to the theme of this book: donors have focused too much on structural adjustment, and not nearly enough on capacity building that would achieve structural adjustment. The historian Francis Fukuyama (2004, p. 5) makes this point:

> In retrospect, there was nothing wrong with the Washington Consensus per se: The state sectors of developing countries were in many cases obstacles to growth and could only be fixed in the long run through economic liberalization. Rather, the problem was that although states needed to be cut back in certain areas, they needed to be simultaneously strengthened in others. The economists who promoted liberalizing economic reform understood this perfectly well in theory. But the relative emphasis in this period lay very heavily on the reduction of state activity, which could often be confused or deliberately misconstrued as an effort to cut state capacity across the board. The state-building agenda, which was at least as important as the state-reducing one, was not given nearly as much emphasis.

Haitians, in their public strategic planning documents, know that growth and development will occur only when the structural framework is in place.[22] And they know that this will take time, will be controversial, and will be painful. They also believe that they must go slow on these reforms if they are to be successful in resurrecting Haiti. The poor population just can't take more abuse in the name of neoliberal economics. At the same time, donors, although not in the end responsible for building capacity and likely to bypass government frequently to deliver services, need to work on capacity building with as much vigor as on economics.

JOB CREATION

Promote massive job creation and reduce income inequality. Most Haitians do not have jobs, and those who do likely have unsatisfactory ones, often in the underground economy. Legions of poor people have been promised jobs, but they never seem to get them. Over time, poor Haitians must feel that it makes no difference whether they participate in the political system, for their lives never change. At the same time, donors are caring for many of the basic needs of poor Haitians as resources permit. But this must over time grate on poor Haitians who have become wards of the donor community, or dependent on handouts through remittances. Somehow, aid needs to create a stake in Haiti for poor people. This has never been easy, but the aid community must find ways to accomplish this. The Social Appeasement Program was started to address jobs and income disparities. Unfortunately, as of 2008, the program is just taking off.

One very promising approach to creating jobs, based on Hernando De Soto's innovative ideas on "the mystery of capital" (De Soto 2000), is the "dead capital" project started by the Inter-American Development Bank in 2007 (Institute for Liberty and Democracy 2006). According to De Soto, capital is considered "dead" when the owner lacks proper legal documentation or title to real property or owns an informal business that has never been registered with the proper authorities. As a consequence, poor people in the informal economy who control only this "dead" capital, unlike wealthier people who participate in the formal economy, have difficulty transferring property and participating in the economy. Furthermore, poor people never really accumulate enough wealth to get ahead. The amount of dead capital in Haiti has been estimated at $5.4 billion, a figure 4 times the total assets of 123 of the largest firms in Haiti, 12 times the total savings in Haitian commercial banks, and 164 times foreign direct investment. Two-thirds of Haiti's businesses are dead capital, and 60 percent of this dead capital resides in rural areas. If this dead capital could be "brought to life," it would go a long way toward creating businesses and jobs, and reducing poverty. The Haitian business community strongly endorses the De Soto approach of incorporating the informal economy into the formal economy as a poverty reduction strategy (Inter-American Dialogue 2005).

Microfinance programs have great potential to bring dead capital to life. The Inter-American Development Bank, under its Multilateral Investment Fund, provided Sogebank, Haiti's largest commercial bank, with $300,000 to conduct a market study and develop a strategic plan. So far Sogebank has served 23,000 clients and disbursed $50 million in micro loans. Acción International, a nonprofit, also invested $195,000 in the venture. In 1998 the International Finance Corporation (IFC), a member of the World Bank Group that finances and provides advice for private sector ventures and projects in developing countries, invested $500,000 to create the first financial institution for micro-entrepreneurs in Haiti. MicroCredit National, IFC's first capital markets project in Haiti, continues to operate on a commercial basis, so it can be considered sustainable. In addition, USAID has funded the international development consulting firm Chemonics to offer technical assistance to the Haiti Development Credit Authority under USAID's Accelerated Microenterprise Advancement Project.

Another initiative, sponsored by the Inter-American Dialogue, Inter-American Development Bank, and the Canadian Investment and Development Agency, tried to find ways to get the private sector more involved in rebuilding Haiti through a roundtable of Haitian business leaders, including members of the diaspora. The roundtable focused on expanding the private sector and using the private sector to improve government capacity. Haiti's business community wants to initiate a continuing dialogue between business and government leaders, and they want to be involved in donor foreign aid conferences. In a meeting in October 2005 in Brussels the private sector was for the first time asked to participate in a planning conference on foreign assistance for Haiti.

The Haitian business community believes that it can supplement or complement management capacity in government. It touts the highly successful HIV/AIDs treatment and prevention program administered by the SogeBank Foundation. It also notes that public management might be greatly improved by creating private-sector advisory boards or even comanagement options.[23] Other public services might be privatized under this model. The private sector supports the privatization of public enterprises generally and desires that the regulatory environment in the country be improved so that privatized firms will not run amok. The private sector observes that a lot of ICF funding goes unspent. Business leaders would like to take those funds and invest them in improved education to build human capital in the country.

Although the Washington Consensus has been roundly criticized for being too harsh on fragile states, Haitian business leaders support its tenets as necessary for achieving growth and development.

REGIONAL CONTEXT

Promote regional solutions. The Dominican Republic has furthered Haiti's instability, often in significant ways, over time. This contributes subtly to aid ineffectiveness. Haiti shares the island of Hispaniola with the Dominican Republic, so their fates are intertwined; shopping districts on the Dominican border draw hundreds of thousands of Haitian shoppers, and 500,000 to 1 million Haitians live in the Dominican Republic, most of them illegally. But there has always been animosity between the two countries, regardless of who is in power in either country. For years the Dominican Republic has served as a staging ground for rebels organizing coups in Haiti, and some claim that the

Dominican Republic has armed and supported some rebels. The Dominican Republic has been accused of facilitating smuggling and drug trafficking.

The Dominican Republic requires armies of Haitian field hands to work its vast sugarcane and coffee plantations; reportedly, many Haitian workers are poorly paid and physically abused. When Dominican leaders wish to make a "statement" about Haiti they often expel large numbers of Haitians living or working there. In the most extreme case, under Aristide's first administration, the Dominican Republic suddenly expelled 50,000 Haitians to embarrass him. In December 2005, the Dominican Republic created a special military border unit of 1,000 men to patrol the 243-mile-long border to control illegal immigration.[24]

Some of this animosity toward Haitians may seem justified to Dominican Republic advocates. When Aristide was overthrown, the Dominican Republic had to absorb thousands of unwanted Haitian migrants and beef up border security. In the aftermath of the coup, GDP in the Dominican Republic fell precipitously over the next two years, which it blamed on Haiti.

USAID has a conflict-reduction plan in place between the two countries, but it is not working, because the Dominican Republic, holding all the cards, has no incentive to cooperate with Haiti. On the contrary, it has every incentive to maintain the status quo. It is the Haitians who need a peaceful neighbor. In light of Haiti's strategic importance, the United States may wish to rethink its Dominican Republic policy.

RENÉ PRÉVAL'S FIRST TWO YEARS IN OFFICE: 2006–08

The next four months of the Préval administration are critical. Over this period, it is essential that the Haitians observe visible improvement. If this doesn't occur, critics of the new president will be able to feed off public disillusionment and the country will fall back again, and as that happens, an enormous amount of investment money, ours included, will have been lost.

—John Graham of the Canadian Foundation for the Americas,
in Kevin Sorenson, *Canada's International Policy Put to the Test in Haiti* (2006)

The preceding chapters recount the seemingly endless problems Haiti must solve if it is to become a well-functioning democracy, and shed its designation as a fragile state. Haiti did not become a fragile state overnight, and in spite of everyone's best efforts, it will not evolve into a well-functioning democracy any time soon. In the meantime, is Haiti on the right track in the short term to achieve its goals in the future? Here we look at President René Préval's first two years in office (he was elected on February 21, 2006). How is his administration doing as this relates to foreign assistance? How effectively is foreign aid being delivered? Next we look at three tough choices to be made in the areas of security, rule of law, and privatization, which all will be critical to Haiti's reconstruction. Then we examine the relationship between the United States and Haiti. Though much of our analysis is speculative, we attempt a prognosis for Haiti's future.

The First Two Years: A Work in Progress

In a May 2007 meeting sponsored by the Inter-American Dialogue on progress in Haiti that was attended by widely respected experts on the country, all were cautiously optimistic about its prospects; major accomplishments in five specific areas were mentioned (Neeper 2007):[1]

—Improved security

—Political moderation

—Independence from Aristide

—Economic stabilization

—Foreign policy successes

There seems to be a strong consensus about these achievements expressed in the popular press, in comments by donors, and on organizational websites with interests in Haiti, but most are guarded in their optimism, given the gravity of Haiti's problems, its capacity, and its history (see, for example, Inter-American Dialogue 2007; Zartman 2007). Murilo Portugal, the deputy managing director of the International Monetary Fund, summed up progress in Haiti under Préval as of July 2007: "Haiti has made commendable progress on its path of economic and social stabilization. Significant economic reforms have been implemented, and the security situation has improved markedly. The government is also building on earlier efforts to improve governance, including through transparency in public sector operations and improved public financial management. A full poverty reduction strategy is being developed, based on a broad participatory process."[2]

IMPROVED SECURITY

By all accounts, Haiti's security problems are decreasing, although there remains much to do to make the country safe. Unlike his predecessors, Préval has called for peace in very public ways, and he appears to have had some success. The U.S. Department of State's Bureau of Democracy, Human Rights and Labor (2006), in its *2006 Country Report on Haiti,* concludes that the Haitian state is no longer a sponsor of violence. This is highly significant in a country in which since the 1960s, and even before, political disputes have been solved by violence, often perpetrated by semiofficial gangs such as the notorious Tontons Macoutes and Chimères. These groups still exist, but they are not acting on behalf of the state.

In a statement to the UN Human Rights Council on June 12, 2007, Jan Levin, the U.S. representative to the council, stated that antigang programs in Port-au-Prince were paying off: many gang leaders have been arrested along with 700 gang members. Claudio Magno, the head of the UN Stabilization Mission in Haiti, stated in February 2007 that much progress has been achieved.[3] In December 2006, there were 129 kidnappings, but this figure had declined to 9 by May 2007.[4]

Several international organizations monitor violence around the world. Amnesty International, the International Committee of the Red Cross,

Human Rights Watch, Doctors Without Borders, Oxfam, and CARE on their websites in August 2007 reported on violence in Haiti, but the accounts were not nearly as extreme as they were in 2004, under Aristide, and 2005, under the Transition Government. The *Los Angeles Times,* too, reported that traffic was beginning to flow in Port-au-Prince, tangible evidence that security had markedly improved.[5]

Not all observers are quite so sanguine. The Haiti Democracy Project website still expresses grave concerns about violence and how it is being managed under the new government. In December 2006, Secretary-General Jose Miguel of the Organization of American States decried the 100 kidnappings that took place that month in Haiti. Also in December 2006, the Catholic Bishop's Conference of Haiti was compelled to condemn the violence and kidnappings in Port-au-Prince. In spite of progress, as of 2007 the State Department maintains a travel warning for U.S. citizens traveling to Haiti. U.S. embassy personnel are under curfew to remain in their homes, and travel in country is limited. In July 2007, the top UN official in Haiti, Edmond Mulet, denounced the sharp increase in lynchings and mob violence. The UN estimates that 105 people were lynched between 2005 and 2007.

In July 2007, the International Crisis Group, in its assessment of the Disarmament, Demobilization and Reintegration (DDR) project, stated that it believes the program is a failure. Haiti is awash in arms, and community violence reduction programs have not gotten off the ground. One reason is that donors and DDR managers are not coordinating their efforts effectively (International Crisis Group 2007c).

Haiti's fate in part hinges on getting control of violence.

POLITICAL MODERATION

Préval has not sought to attack factions that were aligned against Aristide and then his current presidency. Rather, he has taken a much more conciliatory approach, asking for unity. When that hasn't occurred, Préval remains silent. The opposition seems to have toned down its rhetoric as well. Is this the political honeymoon that most national elected figures enjoy, or the beginning of an era of good feeling?

INDEPENDENCE FROM ARISTIDE

By all accounts, Préval has placed considerable distance between his presidency and Aristide. Aristide has not publicly announced his intention to return to Haiti, as he did under the Transition Government.[6] In July 2007, the periodic demonstration of Aristide supporters in Port-au-Prince, calling for his return, numbered only about 1,000, a sign that they have lost their momentum and people are no longer paying attention. Ironically, pro-Duvalier factions continue to march as well, in equally small numbers, demanding the return of the former dictator from France. If Aristide announces his intention to return, will the international community pressure Préval to prevent him from doing so, or will they allow him to handle the situation as a purely Haitian affair?

STABILIZATION OF THE ECONOMY

Most observers would caution that it is way too early for either the Transition Government's prior efforts or Préval's more recent initiatives to demonstrate economic success. It can take several years before the economic impacts of policymaking take effect. Astonishingly, when data for FY2004 were compared with estimates for FY2006, there was a dramatic turnaround in every major economic indicator (see table 9-1; Fasano 2007). The Haitian economy was performing so well as of April 2008 that the Préval administration will meet economic targets under the World Bank's Heavily Indebted Poor Countries (HIPC) initiative, allowing Haiti to receive debt forgiveness in the amount of $525 million. Few would argue that Aristide's policies spawned the turnaround, so full credit must go to his successors.

Good economic news should not be taken to mean that the lives of Haitians have substantially improved—economic indicators show merely that Haiti is finally on the right track for growth and development, but getting there will take time, and meanwhile there are clear signs of continuing problems. In December 2006, health workers at the General Hospital in Port-au-Prince went on strike to protest the fact that they had not been paid for over six months by the Ministry of Health. Strikers chose the most macabre means to draw attention to their cause: they placed the bodies of eleven infants who had died, presumably for lack of care, on a table for all to see.[7] There were disturbing reports that some poor people have resorted to eating dirt in an attempt to fill empty stomachs.[8] The U.S. Coast Guard reports having intercepted some 1,500 boat people fleeing poverty in Haiti in 2007. Food riots broke out in Haiti in April 2008, forcing President Préval to cancel several visits abroad. The riots followed after news reports publicized that thousands of pounds of food had rotted in Port-au-Prince, likely because of regulations imposed by donors on food aid (Katz 2008, p. A14). Préval's prime minister, Edouard Alexis, was forced by the opposition to resign on April 11, 2008. On April 14, 2008, the World Bank pledged $10 million in emergency food aid to help Haiti.

Table 9-1. *Economic Progress, 2004–06*

Country indicators	FY2004 actual	FY2006 estimate
GDP at constant prices (annual percentage change)	−3.5	2.3
Real GDP per capita (annual percentage change)	−5.4	0.6
Consumer price inflation (percent, end of period)	21.7	12.4
Central government overall balance (percentage change)	−2.5	−1.2
Total public sector debt (as percent of GDP)	40.8	32.0

Source: International Development Association (2007a, 2007b).

The good economic news should also not be taken to mean that Haiti finally has the capacity to manage its own economic affairs. By all accounts, Haiti has improved, but it has a long way to go before it is capable of self-government.

FOREIGN POLICY SUCCESSES

From his first appearance on the national and international stage in Haiti, Aristide spent a great deal of energy intentionally antagonizing the United States, Canada, and France, even when it was not in Haiti's interest to do so and even when it harmed his supporters in Congress, U.S. administrations, and donors. For example, he reached out to Cuba and Venezuela for assistance as an act of defiance, knowing this would gain little but would jeopardize aid from the international community.

Préval, by contrast, has shown considerable skill in juggling sensitive relationships with a number of international partners. He knows that Haiti's future depends on striking a balance between courting the United States, Canada, and France on the one hand and nations in the Caribbean and Latin America, including Cuba and Venezuela, on the other. Préval has not engaged in anti-American rhetoric or championed communist causes, but instead has tried to partner with the West. He also knows that Haiti is part of the Caribbean and Latin American community (he is well respected in Caricom), regions increasingly populated with anti-American factions, many of them holding socialist or antidemocratic ideologies. Miraculously, Préval managed to meet with Cuban, Venezuelan, and Bolivian leaders at the 2007 Latin American Summit, held in Chile, and seemingly gaining their praise without precipitating a negative response from the United States.

In March 2007, President Hugo Chavez of Venezuela visited Haiti. Préval reached an agreement to join Petrocaribe, an oil pact that would allow Haiti to pay only 60 percent of the cost of fuel. Additionally, Chavez promised to donate $21 million to be used to pay 800 Cuban physicians to work in the rural regions of Haiti, a program reminiscent of Préval's first presidency, in which a similar agreement was reached with Fidel Castro. Although the United States is not happy and has chided Préval about this, the United States has let it pass, at least for now.

On August 1, 2007, UN Secretary-General Ban Ki-moon visited Haiti to see how the UN might better help. The secretary-general met with business leaders, civil society organizations, and political parties to encourage development of a unified partnership to reconstruct Haiti. This is a good sign for Haiti: to gain a priority spot on the UN's crowded agenda.

In January 2007, Préval did attack the United States on drug-trafficking policy. In an address to parliament he suggested that drug trafficking was in part responsible for violence in Haiti, and that this was the fault of drug users in the United States who created such a large demand that Haitians responded. He called on the United States to provide more funding to fix "its" problem. Préval is right, but the United States still continues to admonish Haiti for drug trafficking. In the March 2007 State Department report *2007 International Narcotics Control Strategy Report* the agency still considers Haiti the major trans-shipment point for cocaine headed for the United States (Perito and Maly 2007). The report cites weak institutions, corruption, and a dysfunctional police and judicial system as factors enabling drug trafficking to continue. The U.S. Joint Interagency Task Force South has found that the number of drug-smuggling flights from Venezuela to Haiti increased by 167 percent from 2005 to 2006. Drugs from Haiti and the Dominican Republic account for 10 percent of illegal substances reaching the United States. From the U.S. perspective, corruption among the Haitian police and government officials is a major issue.

There were some initial issues with Préval's state visit to Canada in April 2006. Most of his entourage were prohibited from accompanying Préval on the visit because they were on a Canadian security watch list and thus were barred from entry. The Canadians were not especially welcoming, by some reports. But on July 20, 2007, the prime minister of Canada, Stephen Harper, visited Haiti to see its problems firsthand. He was the first foreign leader to visit Cité Soleil, the massive slum in Port-au-Prince where poverty and violence reign. The Canadians continue to offer strong foreign aid support to Haiti.

One curious foreign policy issue arose with Haiti's relationship with Taiwan. Taiwan has contributed foreign assistance to Haiti on a regular basis, although in relatively small amounts compared to other donors, and Taiwan was the only donor that offered aid during the nineteen months following the May 2000 elections when other donors suspended aid. Haiti's partnering with Taiwan poses problems for the United States because of its delicate foreign relations with the People's Republic of China, a country intent on annexing Taiwan. In June 2005, China initially used its veto in the UN Security Council to block the extension of UN peacekeeping forces in Haiti. Out of respect for Préval's efforts thus far in Haiti, the Bush administration has not publicly sanctioned or pressured Haiti on the issue to refuse aid from Taiwan.

Further evidence of Préval's skillful foreign policy initiatives came from meetings in 2006 and 2007. In March 2006, Préval met with U.S. and multilateral donor officials, where he made a convincing plea for a new beginning for Haiti. In March 2007, Assistant USAID Administrator Adolfo Franco stated before the House Committee on Foreign Affairs that the Préval government's "willingness to undertake reforms has caught the attention of the international donor community and that there is a window of opportunity to reverse the cycle of violence and instability." He also stated that the United States is committed to helping the Haitian people during this critical time" (Taft-Morales 2007a, p. 1). Following this vote of confidence, Préval met with President Bush in May 2007, who lauded him for his efforts in the first year of his term.

Préval's first foreign visit after being elected president was to the Dominican Republic, in recognition of that country's importance to Haiti. In November 2006, Dominican Republic and Haitian officials met to devise a strategy for patrolling the shared border, which has always been a problem as officials in both countries accept bribes to allow people to pass. As of January 2007, the Dominican Republic had not set up the border patrol, and the head of the armed forces announced that it could take six more months at least. In the meantime, the Dominican Republic has expelled hundreds of illegal Haitian immigrants. Préval visited the Dominican Republic in 2007 to learn more about its successful tourism sector. During this visit, the Dominican Republic indicated that it would not grant citizenship to babies born of Haitians living illegally in the country.

Perhaps Préval's crowning foreign policy achievement was the state visit to Port-au-Prince by First Lady Laura Bush in March 2008. Although entirely symbolic, Laura Bush's visit supported the perception that progress was being made in Haiti, and also that it was now safe enough for a first lady to visit.

By nearly all accounts, Préval has been successful in conducting foreign policy, and it remains to be seen whether his successful balancing act can be sustained. It could be that donors and others are giving Préval some space to get Haiti on track, or perhaps they are ignoring him and paying attention to bigger issues, or they do not want to be the first to take an adversarial approach vis-à-vis Haiti, as has been the case in the past.

At a State Department press conference on April 4, 2007, Secretary of State Condoleezza Rice summarized the current state of affairs with Haiti when she told Haiti's visiting prime minister, Eduoard Alexis: "You will have a friend in the United States as you make the journey toward greater stability and prosperity of Haiti's democracy" (quoted in Perito 2007, p. 9).

Hard Choices

Préval faces numerous issues in getting Haiti back on track, of which three—security, the rule of law, and privatization—seem to be central.

SECURITY

Security is the major issue facing Haiti (International Crisis Group 2006, 2007a, 2007c, 2007d; Malone and von Einsiedel 2006), and it does appear to be improving; nevertheless, it looms large in Haiti's recovery because the Haitian government will have to provide its own security when the UN peacekeeping force leaves, most likely at the end of 2008. Haiti has no army, and its National Police is completely unreliable. In June 2007, Préval created a commission to study whether Haiti ought to have an army or just a special military unit to support the National Police. To an outside observer it seems as though the Haitian government should be much further along in taking over security than just discussing options. Even when the government decides on a course of action, implementing it will take time. This does not bode well for the future, in our view. Perhaps Préval expects to lobby the UN to extend its peacekeeping mission yet again, as he did in 2007.

THE RULE OF LAW

Judging from all accounts, it sounds as though the judicial system is still a shambles. Past efforts to remake it have not been successful (see International Crisis Group 2007b, 2007c). Because the justice system undergirds democracy, it needs to be fixed. Since it appears that the system is so far gone and will need to be reconstructed from scratch, Haiti is in jeopardy of loosing any gains toward achieving democracy that it may have made. According to a local news service, "Haiti's top priority in 2007 is reforming its judicial system, the UN's special representative for Haiti, Edmond Mulet, said during a visit to Washington. The judicial system in Haiti is extremely corrupt, Mulet told reporters. I think to begin with the reform of the judiciary . . . [is] absolutely fundamental. He said he was concerned that the pace of reform was not meeting UN expectations."[9] Unfortunately, donors trying to reconstruct the justice system continue to pursue small-impact projects that are having little effect on the big picture.

Another rule-of-law issue is the constitution. As noted previously, Haiti's constitution has always existed for the convenience of its rulers, as evidenced by their willingness to change it—there have been thirty constitutions in 200 years. On October 17, 2007, Préval caused raised eyebrows when he proposed major amendments to the 1987 constitution, the most significant one being to allow the president to serve for a second consecutive five-year term, instead of two nonconsecutive five-year terms.[10] Préval believes that a single-term presidency greatly limits the power of the president to get things done. In an effort to defuse any concerns about his personal ambitions to seek a second consecutive term as president, Préval promised that he would only serve for one term. There has not been a great deal of backlash, but the amendments proposed were risky, given Haiti's history.

PRIVATIZATION

A make or break issue for Préval is privatization of state-owned enterprises. Aristide resisted privatization to such an extent that it cost him the support of the Clinton administration. Aristide undermined Préval's efforts at privatization in the latter's first term as president. And privatization led to considerable unrest in the country, including worker strikes, protests, and violence. Now, privatization is back on the national and international agenda.

This time around Préval has been much more clever in his privatizing efforts. In February 2007, the Haitian government entered into an agreement with the World Bank's International Finance Corporation (IFC) to act as its adviser in privatizing nine state-owned firms in the areas of electric power, telecommunications, transport, banking, construction, and agribusiness. These firms are the heart of the Haitian economy. The agreements calls for the IFC to support Haiti's Asset Democratization Program, in which blocks of shares are reserved for special populations, such as the victims of past regimes. In July 2007, the government gave job termination notices to several thousand workers in Teleco, Haiti's public telecommunications company, demonstrating the seriousness with which Préval is privatizing government enterprises. Préval can always blame the donor community if privatization fails. But he also created a program wherein Haitians will seemingly benefit. Will this be enough?

The major issue to be resolved is who will end up owning the privatized firms? If it is the Haitian elite or foreign investors, trouble could be on the horizon, yet these appear to be the only groups with experience and capital. It is not clear how this careful balancing act will play out.

Rare Bipartisanship in the United States

Astonishingly, despite the acknowledged gridlock in the U.S. Congress and the administration, Congress has come together with the Bush administration in an unprecedented way in support of trade preferences for Haiti, which have been the bone of contention for years (see U.S. Trade Representative 2005 for an overview of trade issues with Haiti; see also Taft-Morales 2007a).

On December 9, 2006, the 109th Congress passed the Haitian Hemispheric Opportunity through Partnership Encouragement (HOPE) Act, which allows trade preferences for Haiti, an effort not only to help stimulate economic revitalization but also to reward and assist President Préval (Sullivan 2007).[11] HOPE allows apparel imports from Haiti to enter the United States duty free if at least 50 percent of the value of the inputs or costs of processing are from any combination of U.S. Free Trade Agreement and regional preference program partner countries. HOPE also removes duties from other products; for example, Haiti would be able to ship textiles made in China to the United States duty-free.[12]

According to Senator Tom Coburn, HOPE was a genuine bipartisan effort on the part of Congress and the Bush administration in support of Haiti and represented a compromise reached over a previous failed bill, the Haiti Economic Recovery Opportunity (HERO) Act of 2005, which did not pass the House but did the Senate in July 2004.[13] Passage of the bill was significant given the opposition of many Democrats who are protectionist and Republicans who are swayed by lobbyists representing especially the textile industry. Representative Charlie Rangel (D-N.Y.), a longtime supporter of Haiti, was able to marshal sixteen members of the Congressional Black Caucus to vote in favor of the bill, including House Speaker–elect Nancy Pelosi (D-Calif.).

Passage of HOPE was not a foregone conclusion. U.S. textile manufacturers, always under competitive pressure from abroad, and U.S. companies with interests in Asian textile manufacturing were strongly opposed to lowering duties for Haiti, which could reduce their own imports.[14] An earlier version of the legislation had more restrictive country-of-origin rules for apparel components. Those in favor of trade preferences were U.S. companies with business in Haiti, a large contingent of groups interested in social justice for

Haiti, and of course Haitian manufacturers whose businesses had been destroyed during the embargo in the 1990s; the last group saw HOPE as a way to start up again.[15] Estimates of new jobs to be created in Haiti ranged from 20,000 to 100,000. At the end of 2007, there were 20,000 textile workers employed in seventeen factories, demonstrating the Haitian spirit of entrepreneurship.

The question for Haiti is whether bipartisanship in the United States will be sustainable. In 2009 a new U.S. president will take office and there will be changes in the makeup of Congress in ways that could affect policy toward Haiti. And, of course, bipartisanship could deteriorate any time before January 2009.

Foreign Assistance

It is too early to tell what bilateral and multilateral donors have learned from their experience in assisting Haiti in the past. Donors have not evaluated their programs recently, although many are starting to. A report published by the Inter-American Development Bank in 2007 evaluating its assistance programs in Haiti from 2001 through 2006 suggested that many of the issues plaguing aid in the past continued right up to 2006, when Préval took over the government, and were likely to continue their impact in 2007.

The IADB reported that it had assumed a de facto leadership role in Haiti in the decade from 1996 to 2006 (we here paraphrase principal points made in the report). IADB normalized business with Haiti under the conviction that its continued involvement in Haiti was the most effective contribution the institution could make to support the country at this difficult juncture. This assertion needs to be qualified. A continued involvement per se is not sufficient, as it needs to be coupled with solid and relevant nonfinancial products to provide the necessary analytical elements to inform policymaking under difficult circumstances. Although this was recognized in formal strategies, IADB did not generate a relevant body of knowledge on the development challenges for Haiti. The Economic and Sector Work (ESW) studies financed by IADB were lacking. Whereas the presence and engagement of the IADB should have generated a solid body of knowledge on the Haitian challenges, ESW was limited to two fiscal studies and a general assessment of sources of growth. Key studies were missing, for example, data on the funds needed to attain desirable levels of investment in infrastructure and services in key areas such as health, education and transportation that could inform policymaking, or the long-terms prospects of a sustainable fiscal system in Haiti.

Although the "crux" of the strategy was to provide "budgetary support to help finance improvements in public finance and fiscal management along with associated technical assistance and required analytical work," IADB and other donors have not followed through and have continued to work through project executing units, a practice that is in part justified by the lack of confidence in the public management system that was the target of reform efforts supported by the policy-based loans. In addition, technical assistance and analytical work required to tackle the root causes of the problems faced in terms of public finance and fiscal management have been insufficient.

During 2005, IABD outlined seven dimensions on which to assess these documents: diagnosis, analysis of previous programming cycle, objectives, logical consistency, risks, indicators, and monitoring and evaluation.[16] Against these guidelines, IADB's strategies failed to present a proper diagnosis of the situation beyond a description of some of the many problems. This failure resulted in the inability to effectively prioritize among the different pressing needs that the country faces. The analytical background for the strategy, if it existed, was not reflected in the document. The results from previous programming exercises and from recently closed projects were omitted, and nothing was reported to have been learned from the past. This is a major omission, for at that time several project completion reports were either available or under preparation for the projects that were canceled in August 2002. The common findings in all of these reports was that IADB's assessment of the projects was very negative.

Individual IADB reports provide useful insights on what went wrong and how to avoid the same outcomes in the future, and some of these considerations were taken into account in new projects approved in 2003 and 2005. However, the IADB in its 2004 *Country Strategy* did not acknowledge these poor results or general findings in individual reports.

Although *Haiti: Bank's Transition Strategy* (Inter-American Development Bank 2004a) represents a step forward by IADB in the midst of a difficult and unique situation, it shares most of the flaws of other country strategies reviewed.

On the evaluability dimensions of country strategies, the second transition strategy achieved better results than its predecessor, partly because it drew on the work of the Interim Cooperation Framework, which served as an umbrella for all donor activities in Haiti. The diagnosis was still inadequate in that it described situations without a thorough analysis of the root causes of the problems. Taking the ICF as the equivalent of a national development plan, the IADB's *Country Strategy* was tautologically related to the country's priorities, but there is no discussion on the strategic considerations that led IADB to support the activities it engaged in. The previous strategy was acknowledged and lessons learned from it and from past donor activity in the country (discussed also in the ICF) were explicitly considered, but there was still silence of past IADB involvement in Haiti. The logical consistency of the strategy was based on that of the ICF.

This strategy included a "strategy matrix" with more than forty indicators, a mix of activities, outputs, and outcomes linking IADB's intended actions to the ICF. Some indicators were meaningful and well defined, and although recent baseline information was missing and targets are not provided, they could have been useful to assess program impacts. Data gathering was not undertaken to any great extent. All of the indicators were from individual projects; there were no strategic indicators.

Although the declared criteria for strategy were flexibility and a strategic focus and selectivity assistance and donor coordination, there were no elements to substantiate them. It is not clear why IADB decided to participate in the sectors it did (higher rates of return? more value added?), or how those operations had strategic synergies or complementarities. Hence, the current portfolio lacked a strategic perspective. This could be explained by the use of the ICF as an umbrella for the IADB's participation, and thus reflects weaknesses in the ICF. It could also be the result of its transitional nature and the lack of a solid counterpart in the government with a long-term development strategy in mind.

The accumulated experience in Haiti over the last twenty years, which shows that donors do not know how to work to tackle the country's development challenges in face of the implementation challenges, suggests that operations should be meticulously drafted with a demonstrative design in mind. Yet the current portfolio does not reflect these considerations. For example, in the Vocational Education Program, the viability and assumptions of the model could have been tested in some regions first, and then if the model worked, could be expanded to the whole country. Also, operations should be framed in a way to facilitate lesson learning and identify key conditions for replication. For example, the urban rehabilitation component in the town of Carrefour should be used as a pilot program for other slum-upgrading operations.

The issue of coordination among donors and with the government is central, and it is directly related to the evaluation of the coherence of IADB's Haiti program. Although the creation of the ICF was an important positive step, the task of coordination among donors is still a pending issue. Progress-tracking mechanisms were established to follow up on the ICF agreements, with mixed results in terms of their effectiveness in coordinating donor activity. Coordination, always complex, has been complicated by the lack of a solid planning partner within the government, particularly under the Transition Government. Ideally, the government should be responsible for setting its development agenda and determining the proper role for each donor, and donor coordination would not be an issue for donors.

Has the donor community correctly assessed the situation under Préval, and are donors launching the appropriate foreign assistance response?

Prospects for the Future

As just about every authority writing or speaking about Haiti has pointed out, the country is at a critical juncture. The game is set with many of the critical pieces in place, and much goodwill and consensus exist. As might be expected, the election of one man, René Préval, cannot solve Haiti's problems, yet many people are acting as though it will. President Bush noted that President Préval might have the toughest job in the world.

As of August 2007, Préval had garnered somewhat mixed reviews. He was tackling corruption, yet holding back on tackling drug trafficking. He was promoting economic development, but publicly stated that Haiti was not yet open for business. He courted the donor community, but perhaps went too far in befriending Venezuela and Cuba. He has spoken of reconciliation, yet thousands of prisoners languish in jail without due process. He has followed up on the positive things put in place by the Transition Government, but has not yet found his own strategy. The rest of his term of office, which ends in 2011, may be problematic, but certainly is not hopeless.

The international community cannot abandon Haiti, for too much is at stake—not least the fate of the Haitian people. If Préval does not turn Haiti around, then it is very likely that the international community will take over and move from assistance to occupation.

AFTERWORD

Edward J. Perkins

Terry Buss and Adam Gardner have presented a clear and compelling review of the sometimes tragic development efforts directed toward Haiti and of the concept of foreign aid and development in this history. This book contains findings that illuminate successes and failures and the reasons for each. This does not mean that a panacea for all times is offered, but clearly it does represent a path whose guideposts will lead to better and more effective foreign policy and attendant development policies. The important contribution in these pages is how to achieve development for the most needy and seemingly the most impossible to develop, or help develop. Straight away, I think it is important to state that, on a nation-to-nation basis or a nation-to-people basis, any foreign assistance, offered for whatever reason, must be seen as being in the American national interest.

I applaud the work done by the authors. I commend it to foreign policy analysts and development actors. It will provide a pathway to better understand the processes that have been in operation since the period immediately following the end of World War II. With Haiti as the operational example, I think some foreign policy and development points made in the book should be amplified and reemphasized.

The authors note the critical necessity of understanding the foreign assistance and development playing field—the essential nature of the developing country and its capacity, the probability of success, and whether the target country or people are looked upon by the United States or the donor country as being within the national interest or of meeting overall foreign policy objectives. An ancillary question would be, "Does the probable donor community believe the target country worthy of receiving assistance?" Will it be able to make use of the assistance such that the donor or donor community can expect returns: economic stability, social growth, increased GDP and GNP? And is there the expectation that the receiving nation or people will become responsible members of the world community of nations?

In the case of Haiti, I would make two observations that are relevant in this context. The first question is whether the probability of success of Haiti has been influenced toward assisted development because Haiti is a black nation. The second observation I would make is that the view among some analysts that Haiti should be treated as an African country rather than a hemispheric nation should be enlarged in terms of realistic expectations. I would posit that these two views have in the past, and even now, contributed to unintended evaluations of Haiti as a contender with high probability of success. No doubt numerous decisions on the part of the United States government have been influenced by whether Haiti was considered a desirable developing nation with potential.

The authors discuss foreign assistance as a unified process. This is very important. I would add that the policy analysts and donor administrators need to observe this as a unified process with a clear, no-nonsense understanding of the "grassroots" nature of the ground in front. I am persuaded that the sociological concepts in Philip Selznick's *TVA and the Grass Roots* (Selznick 1949) constitute a reference point in preparing to work the foreign assistance ground.

The authors emphasize leadership as an important element of consideration. It is more than important. It is a concept that portends life or death, depending on the capacity. The authors suggest and I emphasize that leadership is a quality often overlooked by foreign policy practitioners and development planners. Leadership is often misunderstood in terms of the receiving nation's understanding of what leadership means to the giving nation. If the two do not travel along the same track, looking out the same window, the probability is that they will see a different scene and react or operate accordingly.

All elements should be used in the evaluation process. The authors provide useful analyses and paths toward appropriate guidelines. I urge that this book be used by political analysts in both the donor and receiving nations, so that they can see the fault lines and the benefits. I am also painfully conscious of the gap often found between the thinking of foreign policy analysts or planners and that of those who initiate and administer aid programs.

The promotion of democracy has for some time been a part of United States foreign policy planning. Administrations since Harry Truman's have approached the concept of democracy and foreign policy differently. The authors highlight representative institutions that are a natural part of democratization such as civil society organizations, elections, grass roots participation, institutions, and individuals, plus legitimacy. Emphasis on these important institutions once again should be a part of analysis in foreign policy and policy planning. At the very least, it reduces the dangers inherent in reinventing the wheel.

The authors highlight job creation as a necessary follow-on to development processes. Job creation ensures self-actualization possibilities. Thus it is essential in ensuring that the citizens of the receiving nation feel good about themselves and therefore more inclined to support the nation. The authors are right to see job creation as an essential part of institution building. Working with the recognized leadership often is not an easy matter. Quite often policymakers and assistance administrators look for leaders who fit a preconceived model. But sometimes, those leaders fitting the mold are resented by others who perceive them as fitting a different mold.

To sum up, my view is that the National Academy of Public Administration has fostered a publication that examines fault lines, failures, and successes. The authors have effectively used Haiti as a case study. Policy planners and assistance administrators, as well as donor nations and receiving nations, would do well to use this book as a tool for successful development administration.

APPENDIX A
PRESIDENTS OF HAITI,
1804 TO PRESENT

President	Year(s) in office	Term in office
Jean Jacques Dessalines	1804–06	Assassinated
Henri Christophe	1807–20	Suicide
Alexander Petion	1807–18	Died in office
Jean Pierre Boyer	1818–43	Overthrown
Riviere Riviere Herard	1843–44	Overthrown
Philippe Guerrier	1844–45	Died in office
Jean Louis Pierrot	1845–46	Overthrown
Jean Baptiste Riche	1847–47	Died in office
Faustin Soulouque	1847–59	Overthrown
Fabre Nicholas Geffrard	1859–67	Overthrown
Sylvain Salnave	1867–69	Executed
Saget Nissage	1870–74	Served full term
Michel Domingue	1874–76	Overthrown
Canal Boisrond	1876–79	Overthrown
Lysius Felicite Salomon	1879–88	Overthrown
Francois Legitime	1888–89	Overthrown
Florvil Hyppolite	1889–96	Died in office
Tiresias Simon Sam	1896–1902	Served full term
Alexis Nord	1902–08	Overthrown
Antoine Simon	1908–11	Overthrown
Cincinnatus Leconte	1911–12	Died in office
Tancrede Auguste	1912–13	Died in office
Michel Oreste	1913–14	Overthrown
Oreste Zamor	1914	Overthrown
Davilmar Theodore	1914–15	Overthrown
Vilbrun Sam	1915	Assassinated

President	Year(s) in office	Term in office
Sudre Dartiguevave	1915–22	Served full term (1st U.S. Occupation)
Louis Borno	1922–30	Served full term (1st U.S. Occupation)
Eugene Roy	1930	Temporary
Sternio Vincent	1930–41	Served full term (occupation until 1934)
Élie Lescot	1941–46	Overthrown
Franck Lavaud	1946	Provisional
Dumarsais Estimé	1946–50	Overthrown
Paul Eugène Magloire	1950–56	Overthrown
Joseph Nemours Pierre-Louis	1956–57	Provisional
Franck Sylvain	1957	Provisional
Executive Government Council	1957	Provisional
Antonio Thrasybule Kebreau	1957	Chair, military council
François Duvalier	1957–71	Died in office
Jean-Claude Duvalier	1971–86	Overthrown
Henri Namphy	1986–87	Served full term
Lesli Manigat	1988	Overthrown
Henri Namphy	1988–89	Overthrown
Prosper Avril	1989–90	Overthrown
Etha Pascal-Trouillot	1990–91	Served full term
Jean-Bertrand Aristide	1991	Overthrown
Joseph Nerette	1991–92	Provisional
Marc Bazin (acting prime minister)	1992–93	Interim
Émile Jonassaint	1994	Interim
Jean-Bertrand Aristide	1994–96	Finished remainder of term
Rene Préval	1996–2000	Served full term
Jean-Bertrand Aristide	2000–04	Overthrown
Boniface Alexandre	2004–06	Provisional
Rene Préval	2006–	Elected February 7, 2006

Source: Compiled by the authors from multiple sources.

APPENDIX B
THE HAITI TRANSITION
INITIATIVE: A CASE STUDY

In August 2006 USAID published an evaluation of a project that in our view represents many of the failed aspects of foreign assistance summarized. Our aim is not to criticize the Americans and Haitians on the ground who tried to make it work, rather we question the assumptions and implementation issues in the project. The initiative did accomplish many positive things for some communities.

USAID's Office of Transition Initiatives (OTI) launched the Haiti Transition Initiative (HTI) in May 2004 to deal with political instability surrounding the exit of Aristide as president in February 2004. The program ended in May 2006, when René Préval assumed the presidency. Some $22.3 million was budgeted. HTI's goals were the following:

—Enhance citizen confidence and participation in a peaceful political transition

—Empower citizens and the Haitian government to meet community needs

—Build cooperative frameworks between citizens and government

—Promote peaceful interaction among conflicted populations

HTI partnered with the International Organization for Migration (IOM) and OTI to implement the project. HTI assigned small grants to 440 projects in an effort to create quick-impact projects. (IOM claims on its website that there were 618 projects.) Initially HTI opened offices in Port-au-Prince, Petit Goâve, and Saint Marc, followed by offices in Cap Haïtien and Les Cayes. Project funding was awarded on the basis of community need, which had to be agreed on by the Haitian government, the community, and HTI. A wide variety of projects were funded. Projects generally did not exceed $50,000, with the average project receiving $23,500. One of the program's design features was its flexibility: the direction of the overall program seems to have changed four times during its tenure in response to situations on the ground. Additionally, projects varied greatly depending on location and need, so many projects were unique.

Did the program have the impacts intended? According to the independent contractor evaluating HTI and HTI officials, projects themselves were less important than the new working relationships established between government and communities (U.S. Agency for International Development 2006a, p. 4). They stated that this is the importance of "process over product" (p. 4). Thus, they seemed to claim program success without actually demonstrating success. The evaluation component of the project offers some clues.

Projects had a built-in evaluation assessment component, but these were framed as outputs: number of people served, number of meetings held, number of people employed. There were no measures intended to determine the projects' actual impacts (see Redburn, Shea, and Buss 2008 for a general discussion of performance management). Instead, much of the impact data were anecdotal—reports by satisfied community members who benefited from a project.

HTI was an attempt to foster country ownership by asking the government to approve local projects, to provide resources in some cases, and to develop partnerships. From the evaluation, HTI claims that the new working relationship between communities and government was a positive outcome. But the absence of government ownership seemed apparent. Various ministries involved in the projects did not hold up their end of the agreement, except to approve projects. In addition to reflecting poorly on country ownership, HTI became another example of a donor program bypassing government for expediency's sake, rather than seizing an opportunity to build capacity. Also in 2006, the government tried to launch a similar initiative, the Inter-Ministerial Commission for Neglected Neighborhoods, to work in conflict zones at the neighborhood level. This initiative, too, failed because ministers were unmotivated, lacked authority, and had divided agendas.

Recurring violence reduced the impacts of individual HTI projects, and the evaluator cautions that projects need to be undertaken in more secure venues. In fact, MINUSTAH had to provide security to keep gangs at bay. This seems an odd thing to say, given that the projects were intended to reduce violence in the first place. HTI found that the Haitian National Police had become so corrupt that they could not provide the security necessary for projects to succeed. HTI, then, bypassed government creating a parallel security operation. HTI illustrated the difficulty in determining whether projects are appropriate to the conflict, post-conflict, or normalization phases.

Coordinating with MINUSTAH proved difficult at times, so much so that HTI had to protest to the UN to get their attention. This seems to reflect the occasional turf battles that occur when donors need to cooperate. But MINUSTAH is given much credit for supplying the security to make projects possible.

Opponents of the project claimed that HTI, in its efforts to thwart violence, was interfering in Haitian politics. Gangs and thugs presented themselves to the people as political entities so that they could continue their criminal activities. These activities are dangerous for the U.S. aid efforts because political opposition groups are constantly seeking ways to discredit the United States or the Haitian government or derail projects that benefit the people—the evaluation calls them "spoilers." Although USAID does not discuss the "Play for Peace" massacre in its reports, the August 2005 killings in Port-au-Prince were intended to embarrass the United States on the world stage.

HTI projects were small and the resources available from communities themselves were minimal, especially in rural areas. Underresourcing projects is just as problematic as overresourcing them and wasting money. Because HTI did not measure the impact of its work, its difficult to see how these projects could have had sustainable results, given the poor track record of small projects executed in previous assistance efforts. It may be that these projects had short-term benefits, but they were undertaken in violent places where they may fail once the UN pulls out.

There is no evidence presented that HTI tried to coordinate its programs with those of other donors, although many donors were funding similar projects. Coordination seems to have been restricted to the Haitian government, MINUSTAH, and USAID.

Is this program sustainable? HTI was handed over to the USAID mission for future implementation, possibly aligning it with the Haitian government's flagging Social Appeasement Program (failing in part because donors have not funded it). It is difficult to see how the mission could manage this with all of the other tasks it has. OTI was unable to keep a representative in the field to work with HTI; instead, a series of temporary managers worked on the project over two years. USAID was short-staffed because of personnel evacuations during the political crisis. As a result, there was no mutual understanding of how HTI was supposed to work with reduced coordination. If this is the case, it is difficult to see how Haitians were supposed to share the vision.

NOTES

Chapter Two

1. It occurs to the authors in writing this sentence that they have seen this information in virtually every news story, academic book, donor document, and advocacy piece concerning Haiti. One can only imagine how demoralizing this must be to the Haitian people. Haiti's unfortunate distress is documented in World Bank (2006a, 2006b) and Maureen Taft-Morales (2007a, 2007b).

2. See Felicity Barringer, "U.S. Ranks 28th on Environment," *New York Times*, January 23, 2006. In fairness, some environmental groups have criticized the index as highly subjective and ideological. Nonetheless, Haiti's environment is in bad shape by any measure.

3. The entry "Haiti" in the 1947 *Encyclopedia Americana* states, "The interior consists of heavily timbered ranges which cover 8,000 sq. mi. of the entire area of the republic" (s.v. "Haiti"). See Richard Hosier and Mark Bernstein (1992) for a review of energy issues.

4. The Turks and Caicos islands have a population of 20,000, one-half of whom are Haitians. The Bahamas, only ninety miles away from Haiti, in recent times has absorbed between 30,000 and 75,000 illegal Haitian immigrants. The Bahamas has a population of 310,000. The influx of illegal aliens became a major campaign issue in the Bahamian presidential race in 2006. Benedict Mander, "Political Instability in Haiti Rocks the Idyllic Bahamian Boat," *Financial Times*, November 28, 2005.

5. The Haitian constitution is available online at www.haiti.org/official_documents/87constitution/doc_constitution_en_preamb.htm.

6. The Transparency International rankings are based on surveys estimating the perception of corruption in a country. See www.transparency.org.

7. See http://siteresources.worldbank.org/IDA/Resources/2004CPIAweb1.pdf.

8. Scores available at www.heritage.org/research/features/index/countries.cfm.

9. The World Bank maintains a website on fragile states and development assistance. Go to www.worldbank.org, click on "projects," then "strategies."

10. The methodology and database can be found at www.fundforpeace.org/programs/fsi/fsiindex.php.

Chapter Three

1. Conspiracy theories in writings about Haiti abound, and ideology is rampant. Readers will likely have to read widely from numerous sources, then decide for themselves what might be true.

2. Just to put this in perspective, the Dominican Republic has had eighty-nine "presidents" since 1844, when it became independent from Haiti.

3. In the 1700s, society became stratified into French colonists, Creoles (whites born in Haiti), freed blacks, and black slaves. Between blacks and the French and Creoles were mulattoes, whose social status was indeterminate. When Creole planters of French descent sought to prevent mulatto representation in the French National Assembly and in local assemblies, mulattoes revolted, destroying the rigid structure of Haitian society. Blacks formed a rebel army under L'Ouverture. Some historians credit Toussaint L'Ouverture with being Haiti's first and, sadly, only great leader (Bell 2007). Two interesting books on this period are James (1989) and Dubois (2005).

4. In February 2004, President Aristide, exiled to the Central African Republic, used similar words as he deplaned there (see Amy Wilentz, "Coup in Haiti," *The Nation*, March 22, 2004).

5. Some historians plausibly claim that Emperor Napoleon of France sold the Louisiana Purchase lands to the United States because he feared slave uprisings and unrest emanating from Haiti. Hugh Thomas (1999) argues that Napoleon, deeply engaged in a European war at the time, was not confident that "Emperor" Dessalines would be anything more than trouble for the struggling empire. On route to Louisiana after Napoleon extorted Louisiana from the Spanish, soldiers of the French army contracted yellow fever after stopping over in Haiti, further dampening France's enthusiasm for the region.

6. An excellent commentary on the U.S. presence in Haiti in 1914 can be found in James Johnson, "Self-Determining Haiti" *The Nation*, August 28, 1920 (www.thenation.com/doc/19200828/johnson).

7. A widely quoted book on the period is St. John (1886).

8. Two classic books about the Marine Corps occupation of Haiti are Craige (1933) and Davis (1928).

9. "Why and How to Help Haiti," *The Economist*, February 26, 2004; Spector (1984).

10. *Time* reported in its August 27, 1965, issue ("Haiti: Crushing a Country," p. 10) that Papa Doc had sent a secret emissary to the gravesite of President John F. Kennedy to gather soil to be used in a voudou ceremony to capture the soul of the deceased president. Papa Doc hoped to use this to influence U.S. State Department policy.

11. An excellent study of migration can be found in DeWind and Kinley (1988).

12. An excellent review of the corrupt regime under Baby Doc is found in Bella Stumbo, "Millionaires and Misery," *Los Angeles Times,* December 16, 1985. Some have commented that Baby Doc occasionally extorted a share of ownership in prospective new businesses in exchange for locating in Haiti. Some left or never came rather than pay up.

13. Mary Carmichael, "Haunted by HIV's Origin," *Newsweek,* November 3, 2007.

14. Voodoo, or voudon, or voudou is an officially recognized religion in Haiti, along with Roman Catholicism. Voudou plays a role in Haitian politics and society (Garrison 2000). Some scholars claim that voudou, an African religion originating in Benin, got a bad reputation because Haitian slaves resorted to it in trying to overthrow the French colonists and army ("Voodoo Still Wins," *The Economist,* January 26, 2006). Voudou appears occasionally in the news. In February 2006, a Haitian woman was arrested in Miami International Airport when baggage screeners found the head of a woman in her luggage. Apparently she was carrying the head around to ward off evil.

15. Joseph B. Treaster, "Haiti Vows Irresistible Democracy," *New York Times,* September 30, 1988, p. A3.

16. Dan Coughlin, "Haitian Lament: Killing Me Softly," *The Nation,* March 1, 1999.

17. An interesting firsthand account of Haitian politics from 1990 to 2004 can be found in Klarreich (2005).

18. Bazin was a candidate for president under the Transition Government, representing, of all things, Aristide's political party Fanmi Lavalas.

19. Socialist and leftist supporters of Aristide long campaigned against the development of assembly plants in Haiti, claiming they paid too little. The effect of this over time has been to drive away foreign investment. Because USAID spent millions trying to build assembly plants for unemployed Haitians, leftist organizations conveniently tied this to anti-Americanism, charging that the United States wanted to exploit the Haitian poor (see Pierre-Yves Glass, "US Viewed with Resentment," *International News,* February 19, 1987).

20. Matthew Cooper and Hannah Taylor, "Fear and Loathing in Haiti," *USNews.com,* September 26, 1994.

21. Colin Powell (1995), in his autobiography, recounted his meeting with General Cédras. In Cédras's office hung the portraits of the six American generals who administered Haiti during the American occupation 1915 to 1934. When Powell asked why the portraits were there, Cédras replied, "We always remember our history" (p. 597).

22. *Time* magazine reported on Aristide's first day in office, October 17, 1994. Aristide made a public plea for calm, standing behind a bullet-proof shield, as his enraged supporters killed one man and torched fifteen buildings the night before. A false rumor also had a former Duvalierist general, Claude Duperval, leading a coop against Aristide in Gonaïves, a city in the north. Aristide asked Duperval to raise the Haitian flag over the National Palace as a symbol of national unity and reconciliation, which he did.

23. "Sins of the Secular Missionaries," *The Economist*, January 27, 2000; "Fear of the Vote," *The Economist*, May 11, 2000.

24. "A Vote for Misrule," *The Economist*, July 23, 2000; Dailey (2003a); Erikson (2004a, 2004b).

25. Daniel Whitman (2005), a U.S. embassy official, reported seeing a sign on a local Port-au-Prince Western Union office: "Remittances to Colombia limited to $1,000 U.S. per person, per day" (p. 47).

26. There is disagreement as to whether the National Palace assault was a coup, and if so, whether it was sponsored by the opposition. An OAS investigation concluded that neither was the case.

27. Michael McCarthy, "United States Can't Let Haiti Slip into Abyss," *Los Angeles Times*, February 15, 2004; Ruder (2004).

28. Amy Wilentz, "Haiti's Collapse," *The Nation*, March 1, 2004, "Coup in Haiti," *The Nation*, March 22, 2004, and "Haiti's Occupation," *The Nation*, April 22, 2004.

29. "Did He Go or Was He Pushed?" *The Economist*, March 4, 2004.

30. Indira Lakshmanan, "In Struggling Haiti, Some Long for Ex-Dictator," *Boston Globe*, October 27, 2005; Palmer (2003).

31. Ibid. France offered to send French troops from Martinique to restore order after Aristide's departure, but the United States rejected the offer (Babbin 2004). See also Fenton and Engler (2006) for a view of the coup from the left.

32. Republic of Haiti (2004a, p. 4); "If at First . . . ," *The Economist*, March 4, 2004; "pariah state": Fatton (2003).

33. See Haiti Democracy Project (2005, 2006), Haiti International Assessment Committee (2005), and Dupuy (2007) for different interpretations of this period.

34. Taft-Morales (2007a); "Haiti's Interim Government Sues Aristide," *Washington Post*, November 3, 2005; Raoul Peck, "Jean-Bertrand Duvalier," *Wall Street Journal*, December 3, 2005; World Bank (2006a, p. 40).

35. "Another Martyr?" *The Economist*, May 12, 2005.

36. See U.S. State Department, Bureau of Democracy, Human Rights, and Labor (2005); see McCalla (2005) for a review of these issues from an opposition viewpoint.

37. For a review of events in Haiti in 2005 see Haiti Democracy Project (2006).

38. Reed Lindsay, "Massacre Erupts at USAID Game," *Washington Times*, August 30, 2005.

39. Alfred de Montesquiou, "14 Haitian Officers Face Charges in Deaths," *Washington Post*, November 8, 2005.

40. See "Haitians Strike to Protest Gang Kidnappings," CNN.com, January 9, 2006; see also "The Death Squads Return," *The Economist*, September 1, 2005.

41. About 1 million Haitians work in factories, plantations, and cattle ranches as temporary laborers. There are numerous reports that these laborers have been abused. In February 2006, the Dominican Republic government issued contracts guaranteeing a minimum wage and improved living conditions.

42. American Airlines, fearing that violence was likely to erupt during the impending February 2006 elections, canceled its flights to Haiti. The airline was probably right to do so.

43. "Haiti: Electoral Mirage," *The Economist*, January 5, 2006.

44. "Haiti Election Headed Toward Runoff," February 13, 2006; "Rubbishing of Haiti's Crucial Vote," *The Economist*, February 16, 2006; Joe Mozingo, "Barricades Go Up in Haiti to Protest Vote Tallies," *Miami Herald*, February 13, 2006; Manuel Roig-Franzia, "Haiti's Preval Claims Fraud Spoiled His Win," *Washington Post*, February 15, 2006.

45. Ginger Thompson, "After Volatile Election, a Smooth Vote Count in Haiti," *New York Times*, February 9, 2006, p. A10; "Candidate of Haiti's Poor Leads in Early Tally With 61% of Vote," *New York Times*, February 10, 2006; and "Haitians Dance for Joy as Preval Is Declared Winner," *New York Times*, February 17, 2006, p. A8; Jose Cordoba, "Haitian Officials Declare Preval Wins Presidency," *Wall Street Journal*, February 17, 2006.

46. "Rubbishing of Haiti's Crucial Vote"; Stevenson Jacobs, "Vote Dispute Seen as Possible Preval Liability," *Miami Herald*, February 20, 2006.

47. Mary O'Grady, "Haiti's Future: Democracy or Mobocracy?" *Wall Street Journal*, February 17, 2006, p. A13.

48. Philippe Girard (2005) explores the legacy of racial tension in *Paradise Lost*. See also Fatton (2003) and Bell (2007).

49. The titles of two early works on Haiti illustrated the fixation on race and Haiti: Sir Spenser St. John's *Hayti, or the Black Republic* (1886), and H. P. Davis's *Black Democracy* (1928). In 1947 the *Encyclopedia Americana* entry on Haiti began: "Known as the Black Republic, Haiti is one of the few independent Negro nations of the world."

50. Andres Oppenheimer, "Make Haiti a U.N. Protectorate—But Don't Call It That," *Miami Herald*, December 2, 1992; Vasquez (1992).

Chapter Four

1. For a review of the issues in computing aid flows see Nowels (2006).

2. See "Transparency: An Antiseptic for Corruption and Waste," American Enterprise Institute online newsletter, July 2, 2007 (www.aei.org/publications/filter.all, pubID.26422/pub_detail.asp).

3. See the MINUSTAH website for documents on peacekeeping in Haiti, past to present (www.un.org/Depts/dpko/missions/minustah).

4. See chapter 9 for President Préval's view on the issue.

5. H.R. 522, 110th Congress, 1st session.

6. Not included in aid spending totals were insurance subsidies that were offered as inducements to attract foreign businesses back to Haiti. In 1994 the U.S. Overseas Private Investment Corporation promised up to $100 million to support companies locating to Haiti.

7. See Uribe and Buss (2007) for a discussion of remittances and development.

8. See www.padf.org.

9. Go to www.cida.gc.ca, click on "Haiti" link, then "overview."

10. Go to www.worldbank.org/ht, then click on "CCD" link, then "Haiti: Building

the Foundation for CD."

11. European Commission, "Country Overview: EU Relations with Haiti," June 29, 2005 (http://ec.europa.eu/development/geographical/regionscountries/countries/country_profile.cfm?cid=HT&type=short&lng=en).

12. See www.padf.org/COUNTRIES/Haiti_e.aspx.

13. See www.padf.org/COUNTRIES/DR_e.aspx#our_border.

14. See www.care.org/careswork/countryprofiles/61.asp.

15. See http://haiticci.undg.org/index.cfm?Module=ActiveWeb&Page=Web Page&s=introduction.

16. See Republic of Haiti, *Interim Cooperative Framework,* Port-au-Prince, 2004, p. iii.

17. To qualify, Haiti had to demonstrate positive movement on key decision points: (1) its status as a PRGF-eligible and International Development Association (IDA)–only country; (2) its NPV of debt-to-exports ratio, which is above the indicative threshold of the HIPC Initiative even after the application of traditional debt relief mechanisms; and (3) satisfactory performance under the two comprehensive Emergency Post-Conflict Assistance (EPCA) programs (October 2004 to September 2006) and the IDA-supported Economic Governance Reform Operation (EGRO) I (since January 2005), with important achievements in the areas of macroeconomic stabilization and structural reforms. Directors also agreed that Haiti could reach its decision point before the end of 2006, together with the approval of a Poverty Reduction and Growth Facility arrangement by the IMF board, provided that (1) the country remains on track with its macroeconomic program, supported by EPCA; (2) an agreement is reached on appropriate completion point triggers; and (3) the Interim Poverty Reduction Strategy Paper (I-PRSP) is finalized. Directors supported the possible triggers and key policy measures outlined in the preliminary document.

Chapter Five

1. Some claim that nonhumanitarian aid was relabeled "humanitarian" so that aid would continue to flow to Haiti in greater amounts (Rotberg 1988b).

2. An example of the chasm between left and right is found in Neumayr (2004).

3. U.S. Department of State, dispatch, October 7, 1991, p. 749.

4. Crandall (2006) analyzes the U.S. invasions of the Dominican Republic, Panama, and Grenada.

5. Howard French, "Land and Health Also Erode in Haiti," *New York Times,* January 28, 2002, p. A3; Lee Hochstader, "For Haiti's Rulers, a Key Signal," *Washington Post,* February 5, 2002, p. A26, and "Embargo Translates into Ecological Disaster for Haiti," *Washington Post,* May 31, 2002, p. A1; Gibbons (1999).

6. French, "Land and Health Also Erode in Haiti"; Hochstader, "For Haiti's Rulers, a Key Signal," and "Embargo Translates into Ecological Disaster for Haiti"; Canute James, "Haiti: A Theatre of the Absurd," *Financial Times,* March 10, 1992.

7. Brian Duffy, "A Question of Options," USNews.com, May 23, 1994.

8. U.S. embargoes of Latin American countries appeared to have been ineffective—viz. Cuba and Panama. In fact, the Haitian embargo may have added substantially to the wealth of Haitian elites; they owned companies importing humanitarian-aid-related goods, so they benefited from both military rule and the embargo. For an analysis, see Kenneth Freed, "Rich Get Richer Flouting U.N. Sanctions on Haiti," *Los Angeles Times,* May 13, 1994.

9. See Theodore Sorensen, "Read Carefully: 10 Reasons to Invade Haiti," USNews.com, June 27, 1994; George Church, "Threat and Defiance," *Time,* July 25, 1994; Smith (1994); Halberstam (2001); and Pezzullo (2006).

10. Michael Tarr and Linda Robinson, "Haiti's Bloody Message to Clinton," USNews.com, October 1993.

11. Naomi Klein, "Aristide in Exile," *The Nation,* August 1, 2005.

12. See Ginger Thompson, "After Volatile Election, a Smooth Vote Count in Haiti," *New York Times,* February 9, 2006, p. A10, "Candidate of Haiti's Poor Leads in Early Tally with 61% of Vote," *New York Times,* February 10, 2006, and "Haitians Dance for Joy as Preval Is Declared Winner," *New York Times,* February 17, 2006, p. A8.

13. Clinton's commerce secretary, Ron Brown, had been a lobbyist for Baby Doc from 1982 to 1986 and influenced, among others, the Congressional Black Caucus to view Haiti favorably; see Peter Stone, "Helping Out a Dictator," *National Journal,* January 1, 1994).

14. Ironically, in November 1995, one year after Aristide had been restored to power, widespread protests against the United States broke out in four major cities in Haiti.

15. For differing views of Clinton's Haiti policy see Bruce Nelan, "Cops for Democracy," *Time,* October 17, 1994; Robert Lawless, "Books by Aristide, Farmer, Plummer and Trouillot," book review, 1994 (www.webster.edu/~corbetre/haiti/haiti.html); Council on Hemispheric Affairs (1994); Palmer (2006); Dupuy (2007), Rotberg (2003).

16. See Albright (2005); Clinton (2005); Corry (2003). Some on the left argue that even through Aristide turned out to be a total failure, Clinton was justified in restoring him to power (see Adam B. Kusher, "Restorative Powers," New Republic Online, March 1, 2004, https://ssl.tnr.com).

17. See, in *The Economist:* "Where Racketeers Rule," January 31, 2002; "Help in the Right Places," March 14, 2002; and "A Fresh Start," March 22, 2002.

18. See "Another Half-Chance for Aristide and Haiti," *The Economist,* February 8, 2001; see also Fauriol (2001).

19. Joanna McGeary, "Did the American Mission Matter?" *Time,* February 19, 1996.

20. "A Tidal Wave of Drugs," *The Economist,* June 22, 2000.

21. See Walt Bogdanich and Jenny Nordberg, "Mixed U.S. Signals Helped Tilt Haiti toward Chaos," *New York Times,* January 29, 2006.

22. The president of IRI, Lorne Craner, hotly disputed both the Bogdanich and Nordberg piece (see previous note) and Curran's assertions; see Craner, "A False Picture of Aristide: NYT Gets It Wrong on Haiti," *Washington Times,* February 12, 2006.

23. See "Whose Coup in Haiti?" and "If at First . . ." both in *The Economist*, March 4, 2004.

24. See "Where Racketeers Rule," *The Economist*, January 31, 2002. Some have justified this expenditure by claiming that Aristide encouraged poor homeless children to use his pool, demonstrating that he was a man of the people.

25. This information, originally confidential, became public in Walt Bogdanich and Jenny Nordberg, "Mixed U.S. Signals Helped Tilt Haiti toward Chaos."

26. "Will America Finish the Job This Time?" *The Economist*, March 4, 2004.

27. See Representative Waters's 2004 press releases of March 25 ("The Contemptible Alliance between Haitian Thugs and the Interim Government of Haiti"), March 26 ("Rep. Maxine Waters Intercedes to Keep President Aristide in Caribbean"), and May 5 ("Congresswoman Waters Denounces Illegally Appointed Prime Minister). Several members of the Congressional Black Caucus introduced a bill to support an independent investigation into the U.S. role in the ouster of Aristide in February 2004 (109th Congress, U.S. House of Representatives, HR 946, February 17, 2005). In February 2006 Aristide supporters filed a petition for an investigation with the Inter-American Commission on Human Rights.

28. See Buss (2005) for more details; see also Smith (2005).

29. For an overview and summary of congressional activity re Haiti, see Taft-Morales (2007a, pp. 21–23).

30. HR 351, 110th Congress.

31. General Cédras bided his time knowing that political jockeying in America would prevent action against him. The strategy worked for three years.

32. Ira Kurzban, "Stop Interfering in Nation's Politics," *Miami Herald*, February 20, 2006.

Chapter Six

1. Important reports on these issues are United Nations (2000a, 2001) and UN Commission for Latin America and the Caribbean (2005).

2. See also Inter-American Development Bank (1994) for additional insights.

3. See World Bank (1985, 1987, 1988) for key reports on Haiti also conducted during this period.

4. World Bank, Operations Evaluation Department (1998); see also Jagdish Bhagwati, "A Noble Effort to End Poverty, Bono, but It Is Misdirected," *Financial Times*, February 28, 2006.

5. Public officials created front organizations, then pressured the Treasury to issue checks to them. Officials then cashed checks and pocketed the cash or transferred it overseas.

6. See Knack (2000); see International Crisis Group (2007a) for a detailed analysis.

7. U.S. General Accounting Office (2000b, p. 5); see also Stromsen and Trincellito (2003).

8. Empirical studies on the issue are reviewed in Radalet, Clemens, and Bhavnami (2005).

9. The authors asked to meet with regional and municipal leaders to discuss their needs. About twenty leaders from around the country attended our meeting. One of our recommendations was for them to form an association to lobby the central government for more resources in the regions. In July 2007, we learned that these leaders had formed an official association and were becoming active under the new government.

10. "If at First. . ." *The Economist,* March 4, 2004, and "Misery Upon Misery," *The Economist,* May 27, 2004.

11. Jeffrey Sachs, "Take the Guessing Out of African Aid," *Financial Times,* March 2, 2007, p. 10.

12. See "The World Bank and Civil Society," http://web.worldbank.org/WBSITE/ EXTERNAL/TOPICS/CSO/0,,pagePK:220469~theSitePK:228717,00.html.

13. Michael McCarthy, "United States Can't Let Haiti Slip into Abyss," *Los Angeles Times,* February 15, 2005, p. 1.

14. For a comprehensive review of performance management and budgeting see Redburn, Shea, and Buss (2008).

15. In order to increase accountability, coordination, and policy consistency, the State Department is merging USAID into its core operations rather than having it stand alone as an independent agency (Nowels 2006).

16. Nicholas Kralev, "US Reverses N. Korean Policy," *Washington Times,* April 11, 2007, p. 1; Steven Erlanger, "Aid to Palestinians Rose in '06 Despite International Embargo," *New York Times,* March 21, 2007, p. A1.

17. We do not include suspension of aid as a condition, as in the case of the Dole-Helms Amendment.

18. Celia Dugger, "African Food for Africa's Starving Is Road-Blocked in Congress," *New York Times,* October 15, p. A4.

19. "Sins of the Secular Missionaries," *The Economist,* January 27, 2000; "Fear of the Vote," *The Economist,* May 11, 2000; "Counted Out," *The Economist,* June 22, 2000.

20. See www.usaid.gov/policy/ads/200/200sad.pdf.

21. The Haiti Transition Initiative case study illustrates these staffing problems (see appendix B).

22. One columnist, Georgie Ann Geyer, in 1992 called for a recolonization of Haiti (Vasquez 1992). Recently, pundits have proposed creation of a "Haitian protectorate" (Andres Oppenheimer, "Make Haiti a U.N. Protectorate—But Don't Call It That," *Miami Herald,* December 2, 2004).

23. Hugh Williamson, "Germany Doubts Ability to Achieve Aid Target," *Financial Times,* January 20, 2006.

24. David White, "Jump in Pledges of Aid Highlights Its Limitations," *Financial Times,* January 25, 2006.

Chapter Seven

1. Warren Hoge, "U.N. Creates Commission," *New York Times*, December 21, 2005.

2. Krishna Guha, "US Aid Chief Admits Funding System Is 'Dysfunctional,'" *Financial Times*, October 10, 2005. Natsios said this just days before he resigned from the agency, after nearly six years of service.

3. See Payne (2000, 2002) and Valenzuela (2004). See also Roger Noriega, "Good, Orderly Elections are Worth Waiting For," *Miami Herald*, December 30, 2005, and "The Summit of the Americas," American Enterprise Institute, November 2005 (www.aei.org), and "Democracy's Ten-Year Rut," *The Economist*, October 27, 2005.

4. *Financial Times*, April 14, 2007.

5. Guha, "US Aid Chief Admits Funding System Is 'Dysfunctional.'"

6. Carol Lancaster, "Bush's Foreign Aid Reforms Do Not Go Far Enough," *Financial Times*, January 20, 2006; Guy Dinmore, "U.S. Shakeup," *Financial Times*, January 20, 2006.

7. See, for example, "Where Racketeers Rule," *The Economist*, January 31, 2002, and "Help in the Right Places," *The Economist*, March 14, 2002. Some critics contend that multilateral donors have a vested interest in untying aid, because it may put more resources and flexibility in their hands.

8. Direct budget support has once again become controversial. In 2006 Kenya, Ethiopia, and Uganda had direct support cut off or reduced because of corruption. On the positive side, the Afghan government has convincingly argued that it has reformed and built capacity necessary to ensure that direct budget support will work. Its proposal is being taken seriously. So direct support will be difficult to achieve, but we believe it is necessary.

9. See case studies at www.dfid.gov.uk/casestudies.

10. Some will counter this by pointing out that the first chapter of just about any plan typically is devoted to country context. This is true, but linkage of context directly to program generally does not happen.

11. All too often they were needed over the long term.

12. We would argue that even if NGOs could take such an approach, it would be unwise for them to do so.

13. Sorenson (2006, p. 5) lists the OECD principles:

   1. Take context as the starting point.
   2. Move from reaction to prevention.
   3. Focus on state building as the central objective.
   4. Align with local priorities and systems.
   5. Recognize the political-security-development nexus.
   6. Promote coherence between donor government agencies.
   7. Agree on practical coordination mechanisms between international actors.
   8. Do no harm.
   9. Mix and sequence aid instruments to fit the context.

10. Act fast . . . but stay engaged long enough to give success a chance.

11. Avoid excluding groups in society.

14. For a detailed overview of the Haitian diaspora in Miami, home to nearly 100,000 Haitians, see Sohmer (2005).

15. See chapter 9 for a discussion of this issue.

16. The National Academy of Public Administration has published extensively in this field. See, for example, *NASA: Human Capital Flexibilities for the 21st Century Workforce* (2005); *Transforming the FBI: Roadmap to an Effective Human Capital Program* (2005); *Twenty First Century Manager*, 7 volumes (2004). All available from the NAPA (www.napawash.org; for a list of publications see link at http://71.4.192.38/NAPA/NAPAPubs.nsf?OpenDatabase).

17. A few examples: the U.S reconstruction of Iraq (Scott Paltrow, "Some Iraq Rebuilding Funds Go Untraced," *Wall Street Journal,* January 17, 2006); the recovery efforts after Hurricanes Katrina and Rita (U.S. Government Accountability Office 2005c); the United Nations procurement scandals (a UN investigation showed nearly $300 million in fraud and mismanagement in procurements for peacekeeping; see Mark Turner, "UN Chief Attacks Global Inaction on Haiti Drug Wars," *Financial Times,* January 18, 2006); the UN Oil-for-Food scandal; lobbying under the Bush administration, and before that under the Clinton administration ("Hobbling the Lobbyists," *The Economist,* January 26, 2006); and the corporate misdeeds of Enron, Worldcom, and Tyco. In October 2005, Paul Volcker, appointed by the United Nations to head a major anticorruption initiative in Iraq, released his report on the UN Iraq Oil-for-Food scandal (Doreen Carvajal and Andrew Kramer, "Report on Oil-for-Food Scheme Gives Details of Bribes to Iraq," *New York Times,* October 28, 2005, p. A10). Under a general UN embargo of Iraq, the program allowed Iraq to trade oil only for food. Lax financial management enabled at least 2,000 companies to participate in a complex kickback scheme involving Saddam Hussein, company executives, and public officials. See also U.S. Government Accountability Office (2005b) on UN procurement practices, and see J. S. Watts, "GSEs Need Reform Now," *Washington Times,* November 2, 2005, on scandals in the government-sponsored enterprises Fannie Mae and Freddie Mac.

Chapter Eight

1. Some argued that these programs attracted criticism because they were successful and the opposition wanted them terminated. But they provided the opposition with numerous opportunities to exploit the situation. Perhaps a better way to look at this is to consider the costs and benefits of such programs, before implementing them wholesale. (U.S. assistance to the Palestinian Fatah Party in 2006 ended in an electoral victory for Hamas, a terrorist group; see Steven Erlanger, "U.S. Spent $1.9 Million to Aid Fatah in Palestinian Elections," *New York Times,* January 23, 2006.)

2. David R. Sands, "NGOs Face Hostility Abroad: Democracy Efforts Opposed," *Washington Times,* February 28, 2006, p. A1.

3. Roger Noriega, assistant secretary of state from 2003 to 2005, reported an interesting comment made by a USAID officer in Haiti about the election following Aristide's return: "In the mid-1990s, foreign observers characterized a series of national elections as 'free, fair, and fouled-up' but good enough for Haiti. A U.S. aid officer told me at the time that the mismanagement was a good thing, because it proved that the elections were authentically Haitian. Those statements reflected the desperation to hold elections at any cost as part of a strategy of 'restoring democracy' under Aristide" (see Roger Noriega, "Good, Orderly Elections Are Worth Waiting For," *Miami Herald,* December 30, 2005, p. 11A).

4. Resolution 822 expresses the need for the Organization of American States to work to strengthen Haitian democracy.

5. Quoted in Indira Lakshaman, "In Struggling Haiti, Some Long for Ex-Dictator," *Boston Globe,* October 27, 2005.

6. See Newman and Rich (2004) for reports by researchers at the United Nations University on electoral failure in UN-sponsored projects.

7. See Kathie Klarreich, "Voters Push for Change in Haiti," *Time,* February 13, 2006.

8. For a comprehensive overview see Buss and Redburn (2006).

9. See Flournoy and Pan (2002) and Chapman and Ball (2001). Just days after the February 8, 2006, elections, the Nobel Prize laureate Desmond Tutu, a major player in reconciliation efforts in South Africa after the fall of apartheid, nearly had to be rescued from the Hotel Montana in Port-au-Prince by helicopter, as angry mobs protesting the slow vote tally for president stormed the hotel. Tutu was in Haiti to try to get political leadership to think about reconciliation ("Witnesses Claim Peacekeepers in Haiti Open Fire," CNN.com, February 13, 2006).

10. See Jacueline Charles, "Haiti Keeps Alive the Truth of Past Evils," *Miami Herald,* June 2, 2008.

11. The Inter-American Development Bank has lent Haiti money to implement a human resources regulatory framework and management initiative to rationalize and organize the civil service (2006).

12. See International Crisis Group (2007c) for a review of this issue in Haiti.

13. On our January 2005 visit to Haiti, we had the honor of visiting with twenty mayors from one of Haiti's regions in a day-long meeting. The dedication of these officials was extraordinary. None had been paid at least for months, if ever. Most had no staff support, equipment, or, in some cases, even a building to work in. All were being intimidated by rebels, ex-police or military, or local thugs. In spite of all this, each mayor had stayed on the job, trying to hold communities together as best they could. Each mayor had to brave danger just to attend this meeting. They wanted modest funding from USAID to set up a mayors' association so they could meet, set up training and technical assistance programs, and offer self-help, a wish we conveyed to the U.S. embassy. Sadly, USAID rejected the request for reasons we do not understand.

14. There is considerable debate about the wisdom of debt relief to developing countries; see Andrew England, "Concern Grows over 'No Strings' Debt Relief," *Financial Times,* January 18, 2006.

15. Fareed Hassan at the Islamic Development Bank suggested this important point to us.

16. For a discussion of debt forgiveness issues, see "Economic Policy and Debt," on the World Bank website at www.worldbank.org/debt.

17. See Associated Press, "Protection Is Key Issue in Desperate Haiti," MSNBC, September 30, 2005; Raymond Joseph, "Pay Attention to Security for Elections," *Miami Herald,* January 23, 2006; Ginger Thompson, "Fear and Death Ensnare UN Soldiers in Haiti," *New York Times,* January 24, 2006; World Bank (2006d); Forman (2006); Law (2006).

18. See chapter 9 for an assessment of security issues as of March 2008.

19. The UN has called Cité Soleil the "most dangerous place in the world" (see René Rodriguez, "Ghosts of Cite Soleil," *Miami Herald,* August 24, 2007).

20. See Walt Bogdanich and Jenny Nordberg, "Mixed U.S. Signals Helped Tilt Haiti Toward Chaos," *New York Times,* January 29, 2006. Unfortunately, UN security forces may contribute to problems in the countries they are supposed to secure. In December 2007, 108 Sri Lankan peacekeepers were expelled from Haiti in the wake of a sex scandal (Jonathan Katz, "Haiti's Preval: Make Changes to the Constitution," *Miami Herald,* October 18, 2007). Peacekeepers also must be effectively managed.

21. Argentina blamed its economic collapse in 2001 on its adhering to the Washington Consensus agenda. In December 2005, Argentina paid off its IMF loans (Adam Thomson, "Argentina to Pay off Loans from IMF," *Financial Times,* December 16, 2005). The hard feelings created by structural reform may be driving Argentina to the left.

22. See also World Bank (2004a) for an overview of economic governance reforms in Haiti.

23. Co-management may sound like an unrealistic option, but it is common in the U.S. federal government. A large proportion of the federal workforce are independent contractors or subcontractors working on-site alongside their civil service counterparts.

24. Ramon Almanzar, "Dominicans Will Monitor the Border," *Miami Herald,* December 28, 2005.

Chapter Nine

1. Among those present were Robert Fatton Jr., University of Virginia; Mark Schneider, International Crisis Group; Juan Gabriel Valdés, former head of MINUSTAH; and James Dobbins, Rand Corporation.

2. See Reuters, "Haiti Passes First IMF Review, $11.7 Million Released," *Haiti Analysis,* July 11, 2007 (www.haitianalysis.com/economy/haiti-passes-first-imf-review-11-7-mln-released); see also International Development Association (2007a).

3. Claude Magno, "Building a Reluctant Nation," *The Economist*, February 8, 2007, and "Love and Haiti," *The Economist*, February 16, 2007.

4. Mark Turner, "UN Chief Attacks Global Inaction on Haiti Drug Wars," *Financial Times*, January 18, 2006.

5. Carol Williams, "In Haiti's Capital, Traffic Is a Testament to Hope," *Los Angeles Times*, December 23, 2007.

6. In August 2007, the Haitian embassy in Washington, D.C., still named Aristide as president. As of April 21, 2008, the website lists President Préval.

7. "Striking Workers at Haiti's Largest Hospital," *Haiti Info*, December 14, 2006 (www.haiti-info.com/spip.php?article3545).

8. Jonathan Katz, "Haiti's Preval: Make Changes to the Constitution," *Miami Herald*, October 18, 2007.

9. "Haiti's Top Priority Is Judicial Reform," Caribbean Net News, February 2, 2007 (www.caribbeannetnews.com/cgi-script/csArticles/articles/000057/005718.htm).

10. Jonathan Katz, "Haiti's Preval: Make Changes to the Constitution"; see also Perito and Jocic (2008).

11. Title V, P.L. 109-432; HOPE essentially was an amendment of the Caribbean Basin Economic Recovery Act, Title II, of the Trade and Development Act of 2000, P.L. 106-200.

12. Susan Schwab, "US Trade Representative Schwab Welcomes Bipartisan Senate Vote Approving Key Trade Legislation," press release, December 9, 2006.

13. Ibid.; Senator Tom Coburn, "Congressional Gridlock," editorial, *Wall Street Journal*, December 13, 2006; Jacqueline Charles, "Bush Vows Support for Caribbean Trade," *Miami Herald*, June 21, 2007; Minson (2007).

14. Greg Hitt, "Haiti's Trade Push Hits New Political Head Wind," *Wall Street Journal*, November 27, 2006.

15. Gary Marx, "U.S. Law Renews Hope for Haiti's Garment Industry," *Sun-Sentinel*, June 10, 2007.

16. Inter-American Development Bank (2005).

REFERENCES

Albright, Madeleine. 2003. *Madam Secretary.* Los Angeles: Miramax.

Amnesty International. 2005. "Haiti: Obliterating Justice." *News Service,* May 26 (www.amnesty.org/cn/library/info/AMR36/006/2005/en).

Andersson, Goran, and J. Isaksen. 2002. "Best Practice in Capacity Building in Public Finance Management in Africa." Report. Stockholm: SIPU International and Michelsen Institute.

ARD, Inc. 2000. *Haiti Democracy Enhancement Project.* Report prepared for the U.S. Agency of International Development. Burlington, Vt.: November.

Aristide, Jean-Bertrand. 1990. *In the Parish of the Poor.* Maryknoll, N.Y.: Orbis.

———. 1993. *An Autobiography.* Maryknoll, N.Y.: Orbis.

Babbin, Jed. 2004. "Haiti Connections." *American Spectator,* February 23.

Barry, Tom. 2005. "A Global Good Neighbor Ethic for International Relations." Silver City, N.M.: International Relations Center.

Bate, Roger. 2005. "NGO Threat to African Growth and World Bank Agenda." Washington: American Enterprise Institute, June 6.

Bell, Madison Smartt. 1995. *All Soul's Rising.* New York: Pantheon Books.

———. 2007. *Toussaint L'Ouverture.* New York: Pantheon Books.

Birdsall, Nancy. 2004. *Seven Deadly Sins: Reflections on Donor Failings.* Publication 50. Washington: Center for Global Development,

Blagescu, Monica, and John Young. 2005. *Partnerships and Accountability.* London: Overseas Development Institute, August.

Boesen, Nils. 2004. "Enhancing Public Sector Capacity—What Works, What Doesn't, and Why: A Literature Review." Report. Washington: World Bank, Operations Evaluation Department, January.

Brautigam, Deborah. 1996. "State Capacity and Effective Governance." In Benno Ndulu, ed., *Agenda for Africa's Economic Renewal.* New Brunswick, N.J.: Transaction Publishers.

Brinkerhoff, Derick. 1994. "Institutional Development in World Bank Projects." *Public Administration and Development* 14, no. 1: 135–51.

Buckley, Cara. 2005. "American Deejay Kidnapped in Haiti," *Miami Herald*, December 30.

Buss, Terry F. 2005. "A Symposium on Microcredit in Sub-Saharan Africa," *Journal of Microfinance* 7, no. 3: entire issue.

———. 2008. "The Millennium Challenge Account: An Early Appraisal." In Steve Redburn, Robert Shea, and Terry F. Buss, eds., *Performance Management and Budgeting.* Armonk, N.Y.: M. E. Sharpe.

Buss, Terry F., and F. Stevens Redburn. 2006. *Modernizing Democracy: Innovations in Citizen Participation.* Armonk, N.Y.: M. E. Sharpe.

Canadian International Development Agency. 2003. *Corporate Evaluation of the Canadian Cooperation Program in Haiti, 1994–2002.* Quebec City: May.

———. 2004. *Canadian Cooperation with Haiti.* Ottawa: December.

Carey, Henry F. 1998. "Electoral Observation and Democratization in Haiti." In Kevin Middlebrook, ed., *Electoral Observation and Democratic Transition*, pp. 141–66. San Diego: Center for U.S.-Mexican Studies.

Catanese, Anthony. 1999. *Haitians: Migrations and Diaspora.* Boulder: Westview Press.

Center for International Earth Science Information Network. 2005. *2005 Environmental Sustainability Index: Benchmarking National Environmental Stewardship.* Yale University Press.

Chapman, Audrey, and Patrick Ball. 2001. "Truth Commissions." *Human Rights Quarterly* 23: 1–43.

Clinton, William Jefferson. 2005. *My Life.* New York: Random House.

Collier, Paul, and Anke Hoeffler. 2002. "Aid, Policy and Growth in Post-Conflict Societies." Report prepared for World Bank, Development Research Group. Washington.

Corbett, Bob. 1994. "The Uses of Haiti." Review of *The Uses of Haiti*, by Dr. Paul Farmer (www.webster.edu/~corbetre/haiti/bookreviews/farmer.htm).

Corral, Oscar. 2005. "Migration to U.S. Soared in 2005." *Miami Herald*, December 30.

Corry, John. 2003. "Nation Building Fantasies." *American Spectator*, January 8.

Coughlin, Dan. 1999. "Haitian Lament: Killing Me Softly." *The Nation*, March 1.

Council on Hemispheric Affairs. 1994. "Haiti." Washington: February 3.

Craige, John H. 1933. *Black Bagdad.* New York: Minton, Balch.

Crandall, Russell. 2006. *Gunboat Diplomacy.* Lanham, Md.: Rowman & Littlefield.

Dailey, Peter. 2003a. "Haiti: The Fall of the House of Aristide." *New York Review of Books*, March 1.

———. 2003b. "Haiti's Betrayal." *New York Review of Books*, March 27.

Davis, H. P. 1928. *Black Democracy.* New York: Dial Press.

De Renzio, Paola. 2005. *Incentives for Harmonization and Alignment in Aid Agencies.* London: Overseas Development Institute, June.

De Soto, Hernando. 2000. *The Mystery of Capital.* New York: Basic Books.

Department for International Development (U.K.). 2004. *Poverty Reduction Budget Support.* London.

———. 2005a. *Why We Need to Work More Effectively in Fragile States.* London.

———. 2005b. "*Partners for Poverty Reduction: Rethinking Conditionality.* London.

DeWind, Josh, and David H. Kinley. 1988. *Aiding Migration: The Impact of International Development Assistance on Haiti.* Boulder: Westview Press.

Dichter, Thomas. 2005. "Aiding and Abetting." *American Spectator,* September 16.

Dobbins, James. 2003. "Haiti." In *America's Role in Nation Building.* Santa Monica: Rand Corporation.

Dubois, Laurent. 2005. *Avengers of the New World.* Harvard University Press/Belknap.

Dupuy, Alex. 2003. "Who Is Afraid of Democracy in Haiti?" Haiti Papers, no. 7. Washington: Trinity College, June.

———. 2007. *The Prophet and Power.* Lanham, Md.: Rowman & Littlefield.

Dworken, Jonathan, Jonathan Moore, and Adam Siegel. 1997. *Haiti Demobilization and Reintegration Program.* Alexandria, Va.: CAN Corporation, March.

Eberstadt, Nickolas. 2006. "Haiti in Extremis." Issue paper. Washington: American Enterprise Institute.

Edgren, Gus, and P. Matthew. 2002. "Preliminary Synthesis of Emerging Research Findings." Accra, Ghana: Roundtable—Towards a Capacity Development Agenda. Unpublished Paper.

Eifert, Benn, and Alan Gelb. 2005. "Coping with Aid Volatility." *Finance and Development* 42, no. 3 (September): 1–4.

English, E. Philip. 1984. *Canadian Development Assistance to Haiti.* Ottawa: North South Institute.

Erikson, Daniel P. 2004a. "Haiti: Challenges in Poverty Reduction." Conference Report. Washington: Inter-American Dialogue, April.

———. 2004b. "The Haiti Dilemma." *Brown Journal of World Affairs* 10, no. 2 (Winter): 285–97.

Erikson, Daniel P., and Adam Minson. 2005. "Haiti: Preparing for Elections." Conference Report. Washington: Inter-American Dialogue, August.

Erixon, Fredrik. 2005. "Aid and Development: Will It Work This Time?" London: International Policy Network, June.

Fagen, Patricia. 2006. *Remittances in Crisis: A Haiti Case Study.* London: Overseas Development Institute, April.

Falcoff, Mark. 1996. "What Operation Restore Democracy Restored." *Commentary,* May 1, pp. 45–48.

———. 2004. "Where Does Haiti Go From Here?" Washington: American Enterprise Institute, April.

Fasano, Ugo. 2007. "Haiti's Economic, Political Turnaround." *IMF Survey Magazine,* September 17.

Fatton, Robert Jr. 1995. "Haiti's Road to Democracy." Report 1. Washington: Hopkins-Georgetown Haiti Project, December.

———. 2003. *Haiti's Predatory Republic: The Unending Transition to Democracy.* Boulder: Lynne Rienner.

Fauriol, Georges A. 2000. "The New Haiti End-Game." Report. Washington: Center for Strategic and International Studies, April 12.

———. 2001. "Haiti Alert: Searching for Haiti Policy." *Hemisphere Focus,* June 19.

———. 2005. "Haiti and the Democratic Experience." Unpublished monograph. Orlando: Global Connections Foundation.

Fenton, Anthony, and Yves Engler. 2006. *Canada in Haiti.* New York: Fernwood.

Fischer, Sibylle. 2004. *Modernity Disavowed: Haiti and the Culture of Slavery in the Age of Revolution.* Duke University Press.

Flournoy, Michele, and Michael Pan. 2002. "Dealing with Demons: Justice and Reconciliation." *Washington Quarterly* 25, no. 4: 111–23.

Forman, Johanna. 2006. "The Security System in Haiti." *International Peacekeeping* 13, no. 1: 14–21.

Franco, Adolfo A. 2005a. "Keeping Democracy on Track: Hot Spots in Latin America." Report. Washington: USAID, September 28.

———. 2005b. "Policy Overview of the Caribbean." Report. Washington: USAID, October 19.

Fukuda-Parr, Sakiko, C. Lopes, and K. Malik. 2002. *Capacity for Development.* London: Earthscan.

Fukuyama, Francis. 2004. *State-Building.* Ithaca: Cornell University Press.

Garrigus, John D. 2006. *Before Haiti.* New York: Palgrave Macmillan.

Garrison, Lynn. 2000. *Voodoo Politics.* Los Angeles: Leprechaun.

Gibbons, Elizabeth. 1999. *Sanctions in Haiti.* Westport, Conn.: Praeger.

Gingras, Jean-Pierre. 1967. *Duvalier, Caribbean Cyclone.* New York: Exposition Press.

Girard, Philippe. 2005. *Paradise Lost.* New York: Palgrave Macmillan.

Gladwell, Malcolm. 2005. *The Tipping Point.* Boston: Back Bay.

Gros, Jean-Germain. 1997. "Haiti's Flagging Transition." *Journal of Democracy* 8, no. 4: 94–109.

Gutierrez, Gustavo. 1988. *A Theology of Liberation.* Maryknoll, N.Y.: Orbis Books.

Hagman, Lotta. 2002. "Lessons Learned: Peacebuilding in Haiti." A report on the 25 February 2002 IPA meeting in New York. New York: International Peace Academy (see abstract at www.ipinst.org/our-work/archive/lessons-learned-peacebuilding-in-haiti).

Haiti, Republic of. 1997. *Project Implementation Problems: Managing Development Assistance in Haiti.* Port-au-Prince: Government of Haiti, Ministry of Economy and Finance, January 26.

———. 2004a. *Interim Cooperation Framework: 2004-2006.* Port-au-Prince: Government of Haiti, July.

———. 2004b. Press Release. Washington: Embassy of Haiti, September 9.

———. 2006. *A Window of Opportunity for Haiti: Interim Poverty Reduction.* Strategy Paper. Washington: Embassy of Haiti, September 27.

Haiti Democracy Project. 2005. "Findings and Recommendations." Washington: March 16.

———. 2006. "The Year 2005 in Review." Washington: January 6.

Haiti International Assessment Committee. 2005. "Findings and Recommendations." Committee Report. Washington: International Republican Institute, July 23–24.

Halberstam, David. 2001. *War in a Time of Peace.* New York: Scribner.

Hallward, Peter. 2007. *Damning the Flood: Haiti and the Politics of Containment.* New York: Verso.

Hamre, John J., and Gordon R. Sullivan. 2002. "Toward Post-conflict Reconstruction." *Washington Quarterly* 25, no. 4: 85–96.

Hartford, Tim. 2004. "Aid Agency Competition." Publication 277. Washington: World Bank, Private Sector Development, October.

Hassan, Fareed. 2004. *Lessons Learned from the World Bank Experience in Post-Conflict Reconstruction.* Washington: World Bank, September 21.

Heinl, Robert, and Nancy Heinl. 2005. *Written in Blood.* Lanham, Md.: University Press of America.

Hewitt, Adrian, and David Waldenburg. 2004. *The International Aid System, 2005–2010.* London: Overseas Development Institute.

Hirschmann, David. 1993. "Institutional Development in the Era of Economic Policy Reform." *Public Administration and Development* 13, no. 1: 113–28.

Hosier, Richard, and Mark Bernstein. 1992. "Woodfuel Use and Sustainable Development in Haiti." *Energy Journal* 13, no. 2: 129–44.

Institute for Liberty and Democracy. 2006. *Evaluacin preliminar de la economicá extralegal en 12 paises de Latinoamérica y el Caribe.* [Preliminary evaluation of the unofficial economy in twelve countries of Latin America and the Caribbean.] Lima.

Inter-American Development Bank. 1994. *Emergency Economic Recovery Program in Haiti.* Washington: IADB, Joint Assessment Mission.

———. 2001. *Country Program Evaluation: Haiti.* Washington: IADB, Office of Evaluation and Oversight.

———. 2003a. *Country Program Evaluation: Haiti.* RE-274. Washington: IADB, Office of Evaluation and Oversight, April 30.

———. 2003b. *Haiti: Local Development Program—Loan Proposal.* HA-0079. Washington: IADB.

———. 2003c. *Modernizing the State: Strategy Document.* Washington: IADB, August.

———. 2004a. *Haiti: Bank's Transition Strategy.* Washington: November.

———. 2004b. *Haiti: Rehabilitation of Basic Economic Infrastructure.* HA-0093. Washington: IADB.

———. 2005. *Report on the Evaluability of Bank Country Strategies.* RE-309. Washington: Office of Evaluation and Oversight.

———. 2006. Haiti: Support for Public Sector Human Resource Management—Loan Proposal. HA-L1018. Washington: IADB.

———. 2007a. *Country Program Evaluation: Haiti 2001-2006.* RE-327. Washington: IADB, Office of Evaluation and Oversight.

―――. 2007b. *Haiti Remittance Survey.* Washington: March 6.

Inter-American Dialogue. 2005. *The Role of the Private Sector in Rebuilding Haiti.* Washington: Inter-American Development Bank and Canadian International Development Agency.

―――. 2007. "Haiti: Real Progress, Real Fragility." Washington: November.

International Crisis Group. 2006. "Haiti: Security and the Reintegration of the State." ICG Policy Briefing 12. Washington: October 30.

―――. 2007a. "Haiti: Justice Reform and the Security Crisis." ICG Policy Briefing 14. Washington: January 31.

―――. 2007b. "Haiti: Prison Reform and the Rule of Law." Latin America/Caribbean Briefing 15. Washington: May 4.

―――. 2007c. "Consolidating Stability in Haiti." Policy Briefing 21. Washington: July 18.

―――. 2007d. "Peacebuilding in Haiti." Policy Briefing 24. Washington: December 24.

International Development Association. 2007a. *Haiti: Restoring Hope, Delivering Credibility.* Washington: World Bank.

―――. 2007b. "IDA Country Performance Ratings 2005." Washington: World Bank (http://go.worldbank.org/CRZ73X6680).

International Monetary Fund. 1998. "IMF Approves Emergency Assistance for Haiti." Press release 98/58. Washington: November 30.

―――. 2006a. *Haiti—Enhanced Initiative for Heavily Indebted Poor Countries.* IMF Country Report 06-440. Washington: December.

―――. 2006b. *Haiti: Request for a Three-Year Arrangement and Poverty Reduction and Growth Facility.* Country Report 06-441. Washington: December.

James, C. L. R. 1989. *The Black Jacobins.* New York: Vintage.

Jutting, Johannes. 2005. "Decentralization and Poverty Reduction." Policy Insight 5. Paris: Organization for Economic Cooperation and Development, Development Center.

Katz, Jonathan M. 2008. "Delayed Cargo Keeps Haitians Hungry." *Washington Times,* March 18, p. A14.

Kaufmann, Daniel. 2005. "10 Myths about Governance and Corruption." *Finance and Development* 42, no. 3: 4–6.

Klarreich, Kathie. 2005. *Madam Dread.* New York: Nation Books.

Klein, Michael, and Tim Hartford. 2005. *The Market for Foreign Aid.* Washington: International Finance Corporation.

Knack, Stephen. 2000. *Aid Dependence and the Quality of Governance.* Washington: World Bank.

Kohut, Andrew, and Robert C. Toth. 1994. "Arms and the People." *Foreign Affairs* 7, no. 6 (November–December): 47–59.

Kolbe, Athena, and Royce A. Hutson. 2006. "Human Rights Abuse and Other Criminal Violations in Port-au-Prince." *The Lancet,* August 31 (www.ijdh.org/pdf/Lancet%20Article%208-06.pdf).

Law, David M. 2006. "The Post Conflict Security Sector." Policy Paper 14. Geneva: Geneva Centre for the Democratic Control of Armed Forces, June.

Leader, Nicholas, and Peter Colenso. 2005. *Aid Instruments in Fragile States.* London: Department for International Development.

Lundahl, Mats. 1979. *Peasants and Poverty: A Study of Haiti.* London: Croom Helms.

Maguire, Robert. 2004. "Testimony Before Senate Foreign Relations Committee." March 10 (www.trinitydc.edu/academics/depts/Interdisc/International/Haiti_Publications.htm).

Malone, David, and Sebastian von Einsiedel. 2006. "Peace and Democracy for Haiti: UN Mission Impossible." *International Relations* 20, no. 2: 153.

Manning, Richard. 2005. "Beyond 2005: Changes in Donor Roles and Behavior." *Development Outreach,* September.

McCalla, Jocelyn. 2005. "Haiti: Lurching Toward 2006." New York: National Coalition for Haitian Rights, November.

McCarthy, Colman. 1994. "Classic 27-day Hunger Strike Convinces Clinton." *National Catholic Reporter,* May 27.

McFadyen, Deirdre, ed. 1995. *Haiti: Dangerous Crossroads.* Boston: South End Press.

McGillivray, Mark. 2005. "Aid Allocation and Fragile States." Background Paper for the Senior Level Forum on Development Effectiveness in Fragile States, Lancaster House, London, January 13–14. Helsinki: United Nations University, World Institute for Development Economics Research (www.oecd.org/dataoecd/32/43/34256890.pdf).

Meredith, Martin. 2005. *The Fate of Africa.* New York: Perseus Books.

Millennium Challenge Corporation. 2007. *Building Public Integrity through Positive Incentives.* Washington: MCC, Policy and International Relations Department.

Millett, Richard. 2001. "Panama and Haiti." In Jeremy R. Azrael and Emil A. Payin, eds., *U.S. and Russian Policymaking with Respect to the Use of Force.* Conference Proceedings, publication CR129, chapter 9. Santa Monica: Rand Corporation (www.rand.org/pubs/conf_proceedings/CF129/CF-129.chapter9.html).

Minson, Adam. 2007. "Haiti's New Government." Washington: Inter-American Dialogue.

Mobekk, Eirin. 2001. "Enforcement of Democracy in Haiti." *Democratization* 8, no. 3 (Fall): 173–88.

Moore, Mick, and J. Putzel. 1999. "Politics and Poverty." Background paper, World Development Report—2000. University of Sussex (U.K.), Institute for Development Studies.

Morrell, James R. 2003. "Impact of September 11 on U.S. Haiti Policy." Washington: Haiti Democracy Project (www.haitipolicy.org/content/663.htm.)

Mukherjee, Ranjana. 2003. "Recent Bank Support for Civil Service Reconstruction in Post-Conflict Countries." PREM Notes—Public Sector, no. 79. Washington: World Bank, October (http://www1.worldbank.org/prem/PREMNotes/premnote79.pdf).

National Center for State Courts. 1995. *Haiti Short Term Judicial Training.* Report prepared for USAID, "Development Experience Clearinghouse," PD-ABP-366. Washington.

———. 2005. *Training and Support for Judges and Prosecutors: Final Report.* Report prepared for USAID, December 23 (hhttp://pdf.usaid.gov/pdf_docs/PDACI391.pdf [June 2008]).

Neeper, Kate. 2007. "Preval's First Year Encourages Haiti." Washington: Inter-American Dialogue, May 11.

Nelson, Mark. 2007. "Governance and Anticorruption in Fragile States: The Case of Haiti." Slide presentation. Washington: World Bank Institute, October 17.

Neumayr, George. 2004. "Kerry's Dirty Diplomacy." *American Spectator,* March 2.

Newman, Edward, and Roland Rich. 2004. *The UN Role in Promoting Democracy.* New York: UN University Press.

Ninic, Misclav. 2005. "The Summit of the Americas." Washington: American Enterprise Institute, November.

———. 2006. *Renegade Regimes.* Columbia University Press.

Nowels, Larry. 2006. *Foreign Aid: Understanding Data Used to Compare Donors.* Publication RS22032. Washington: Congressional Research Service.

Organization for Economic Cooperation and Development. 2003a. *Synthesis of Lessons Learned of Donor Practices in Fighting Corruption.* DCD/DAC/GOV NET(2003)1. Paris: OECD, Development Assistance Committee, June.

———. 2003b. *Country Level Harmonization: Emerging Implementation Lessons.* Paris: OECD, Development Assistance Committee, February 22.

———. 2005a. *Senior Level Forum on Development Effectiveness in Fragile States.* DAC/CHAIR(2005)3. Paris: Development Assistance Committee, February 1.

———. 2005b. *Implementing the 2001 DAC Recommendation on Untying ODA.* Paris: OECD, Development Assistance Committee.

———. 2005c. *Principles for Good International Engagement in Fragile States.* Paris: OECD, April 7.

———. 2006. *Evaluation of General Budget Support.* Paris: May.

Organization of American States. 2001. *Third Report: OAS Mission to Haiti.* Washington.

———. 2006. "Renew Our Resolve." Press release. Washington: January 12.

Orr, Robert. 2002. "Governing When Chaos Rules." *Washington Quarterly* 25, no. 4, 139–52.

Ortiz, Guillermo. 2003. "Overcoming Reform Fatigue." *Finance and Development,* September, pp. 14–17.

Osborne, David. 1992. *Reinventing Government.* Reading, Mass: Addison-Wesley.

Ottaway, Marina, and Stefan Mair. 2004. "States at Risk and Failed States." Washington: Carnegie Endowment for International Peace, Democracy and Rule of Law Project, September.

Overseas Development Institute. 2007. *Joint Evaluation of Multi-Donor Budget Support to Ghana.* London: June.

Palmer, David S. 2003. *Breaking the Real Axis of Evil.* Lanham, Md.: Rowman & Littlefield.

———. 2006. *U.S. Relations with Latin America during the Clinton Years.* University Press of Florida.

Payne, Mark. 2000. *Political Institutions, Accountability and Government Performance.* Washington: Inter-American Development Bank, January.

———. 2002. *Democracies and Development: Politics and Reforms in Latin America.* Washington: Inter-American Development Bank, January.

Perito, Robert. 2007. "Haiti: Hope for the Future." Report 188. Washington: U.S. Institute of Peace, June.

Perito, Robert, and Josenka Jocic. 2008. "Paper Versus Steel: Haiti's Challenge of Constitutional Reform." Washington: U.S. Peace Institute, January.

Perito, Robert, and Greg Maly. 2007. "Haiti's Drug Problems." Washington: U.S. Peace Institute, June.

Pezzullo, Ralph. 2006. *Plunging Into Haiti.* University of Mississippi Press.

Pierre, Hyppolite. 2005. *Haiti, Rising Flames from Burning Ashes.* Lanham, Md.: University Press of America.

Powell, Colin. 1995. *My American Journey.* New York: Ballantine.

Puri, Sunetra. 2004. News Release 2005/158/AFR. Washington: World Bank.

Radelet, Steven, Michael Clemens, and Rikhil Bhavnami. 2005. "Aid and Growth." *Finance and Development* 42, no. 3 (September): 1–10.

Redburn, Steve, Robert Shea, and Terry F. Buss. 2008. *Performance Management and Budgeting.* Armonk, N.Y.: M. E. Sharpe.

Rice, Susan E. 2007. "Global Poverty, Weak States and Insecurity." Paper presented at the Blum Roundtable, Aspen. Brookings, August (www.brookings.edu/papers/2006/08globaleconomics_rice.aspx).

R&RS. 1996. *Respect for the Rule of Law in Haiti.* Report PN-ABZ-701. Washington: USAID, December 30.

Robinson, Linda. 1993. "Caught in the Grip of Voodoo Politics." USNews.com, June 28.

———. 2000. "The Cocaine Connection." USNews.com, May 29.

Robinson, Randall. 2007. *An Unbroken Agony—Haiti: From Revolution to the Kidnapping of a President.* New York: Basic/Civitas.

Rotberg, Robert I. 1988a. "Haiti's Past Mortgages Its Future." *Foreign Affairs* 67, no. 1: 93–109.

———. 1988b. "Weariness Greets Latest Coup." *Latin American Markets,* August 29.

———. 2003. "Haiti's Turmoil: Politics and Policy under Aristide and Clinton." WPF Report 32. Cambridge, Mass.: World Peace Foundation.

Ruder, Eric. 2004. "An Interview with Robert Fatton." *CounterPunch,* March 8 (www.counterpunch.org/ruder03082004.html).

Schacter, Mark. 2000. "Evaluation Capacity Development." Working Paper 7. Washington: World Bank, Operations Evaluation Department.

Selznick, Philip. 1949. *TVA and the Grass Roots.* University of California Press.

Sharpe, Sam, Adrian Wood, and Ellen Wratten. 2005. "UK: More Country Ownership." *Finance and Development* 42, no. 3 (September): 1–8.

Smith, James T. 2005. "Implementation of the Micro-enterprise Results and Accountability Act of 2004." September 20. Washington: USAID.

Smith, Tony. 1994. "In Defense of Intervention." *Foreign Affairs* 73, no. 6: 34–46.

Sohmer, Rebecca. 2005. *The Haitian Community in Miami-Dade.* Brookings.

Sorenson, Kevin. 2006. *Canada's International Policy Put to the Test in Haiti.* Ottawa: House of Commons, Standing Committee on Foreign Affairs and International Development, December.

Spector, Robert M. 1984. *W. Cameron Forbes and the Hoover Commission to Haiti.* Lanham, Md.: University Press of America.

St. John, Sir Spenser. 1886. *Hayti, Or the Black Republic.* New York: Scribner.

Stromesen, Janice, and Joseph Trincellito. 2003. "Building the Haitian National Police." Research Paper 6. Washington: Trinity College, Haiti Program, April.

Sullivan, Mark P. 2007. *Latin America and the Caribbean: Issues for the 110th Congress.* Report RL33828. Washington: Congressional Research Service, January 23.

Taft-Morales, Maureen. 2007a. *Haiti: Developments and US Policy since 1991 and Current Congressional Concerns.* Report RL 32294. Washington: Congressional Research Service, January 19.

———. 2007b. *Haiti's Development Needs and a Statistical Overview of Conditions of Poverty.* Report RL34029. Washington: Congressional Research Service, May 30,

Tardieu, Jerry. 1998. *Haiti and CARICOM.* Washington: Center for Strategic and International Studies, October 16.

Thomas, Hugh. 1999. *The Slave Trade.* New York: Touchstone.

Todman, Terence. 2003. "Report to OAS on Haiti." Washington: April (www.reliefweb.int/rw/rwb.nsf/db900SID/KHII-67E65B?OpenDocument).

TransAfrica Forum. 1998. "Fact-Finding Delegation to Haiti." Washington.

United Nations and Government of Haiti. 2004. *A Common Vision of Sustainable Development.* New York: UN (in French).

United Nations. 1997. *Capacity Development.* Technical Advisory Paper 2. New York: UN Development Program.

———. 2000a. *Common Country Assessment for Haiti.* New York.

———. 2000b. *Report to the Secretary General on MICAH.* New York: Office of the Secretary-General, November 9.

———. 2001. *UN Development Assistance Framework—Haiti.* New York: UN Development Program.

———. 2003. *Haiti: Integrated Emergency Response Program.* New York: UN, March.

———. 2005a. *Human Development Report—2005.* New York: UN Development Program.

———. 2005b. *Global Monitoring Report.* New York.

———. 2006. *Human Development Report.* New York: UN Development Program.

UN Commission for Latin America and the Caribbean. 2005. *Haiti: Short- and Long-Term Development Issues.* New York: October.

UN Conference on Trade and Development. 2006. *The Least Developed Countries Report, 2006.* New York.

UN Economic and Social Council. 1999. *Report of the Ad Hoc Advisory Group on Haiti.* New York: July 2.

———. 2006. *Report of the ESC Ad Hoc Advisory Group on Haiti.* E2006/69. New York: July.

———. 2006a. *Haiti Needs Assessment.* New York: UN Development Program, August 16 (www.undp.org/bcpr/iasc/content/docs/Meetings/PCNA/doc_44.doc).

———. 2006b. *BCPR Strategic Review.* New York: UN Development Program, Bureau for Conflict Prevention and Recovery, February.

Uribe, Jose, and Terry F. Buss. 2007. "Remittances, Foreign Aid, and Developing Countries." In Louis Picard, Robert Groelsema, and Terry F. Buss, eds., *Foreign Aid and Foreign Policy.* Armonk, N.Y.: M. E. Sharpe.

U.S. Agency for International Development. 1996a. *Haiti: Results Review and Resource Request.* PD-ABM-581. Washington: USAID Mission in Haiti, March.

———. 1996b. *USAID Monitoring Report—Haiti.* Port-au-Prince.

———. 1998. *Haiti: Results Review and Resource Request.* Washington: USAID Mission in Haiti, June.

———. 1998. *Strategic Plan for Haiti—1999–2004.* Washington: Haiti Country Office.

———. 1999. *Providing Emergency Aid to Haiti.* PN ACA 92. Washington: May.

———. 2005a. *Fragile States Strategy.* PD-ACA-999. Washington: January.

———. 2005b. *Migrant Remittances.* CBJ2006. Washington: August.

———. 2006a. *Haiti Transition Initiative.* Washington: September.

———. 2006b. *Final Evaluation of the Haiti Transition Initiative.* Washington: October.

U.S. General Accounting Office. 1982. *Assistance to Haiti: Barriers, Recent Program Changes and Future Options.* GAO/ID-82-13. Washington: February 22.

———. 1985. *US Assistance to Haiti: Progress Made, Challenges Remain.* GAO/NSIAD-85-86. Washington: June 12.

———. 1988. *Caribbean Basin Initiative: Impact on Selected Countries.* GAO/NSIAD-88-177. Washington: July.

———. 1993. *Haiti: Costs of US Programs and Activities Since the 1991 Military Coup.* GAO/NSIAD-93-252FS. Washington: August.

———. 1994. *Drug Activity in Haiti.* OSI-95-6R. Washington: December 28.

———. 1996a. *Peace Operations.* GAO/NSIAD-96-38. Washington: March.

———. 1996b. *Haiti: U.S. Assistance for the Electoral Process.* GAO/NSIAD-96-147. Washington: July.

———. 1997a. *UN Peacekeeping.* GAO/T-NSIAD-97-139. Washington: April 9.

———. 1997b. *Haiti: US Response to Allegations of an Assassination Plot.* GAO/NSIAD-97-87. Washington: February.

———. 2000a. *Foreign Assistance: Aid to Haitian Justice System.* GAO-01-24. Washington: October.

———. 2000b. *Foreign Assistance: Lack of Haitian Commitment Limited Success of U.S. Aid to Justice System.* GAO/NSIAD-00-257. Washington: September 19.

———. 2003. *Foreign Assistance: US Democracy Programs in Six Latin American Countries Have Yielded Modest Results.* GAO-03-358. Washington: March.

U.S. Government Accountability Office. 2005a. *DOD Paid Billions in Award and Incentive Fees Regardless of Acquisition Outcomes.* GAO-06-60. Washington.

———. 2005b. *United Nations: Preliminary Observations on Internal Oversight and Procurement Practices.* GAO-06-226T. Washington: October 31.

———. 2005c. *Hurricanes Katrina and Rita.* GAO-06-235T. Washington: November 2.

———. 2006. *Peacekeeping: Operations in Haiti.* GAO-06-331. Washington: February.

———. 2007a. *Foreign Assistance: Various Challenges Impede the Efficiency and Effectiveness of U.S. Food Aid.* GAO-07-905T. Washington: May.

———. 2007b. *Peacekeeping: Observations on Costs, Strengths and Limitations.* GAO-07-998T. Washington.

U.S. State Department, Bureau of Economic and Business Affairs. 2002. *2001 Country Report: Haiti.* Washington: February.

U.S. State Department, Bureau of Democracy, Human Rights and Labor. 2005. *Haiti: Country Report on Human Rights, 2004.* Washington.

———. 2006. *2006 Country Report on Haiti.* Washington.

U.S. State Department, Bureau of Public Affairs. 2005. "Foreign Relations, 1964–1968" (www.state.gov/r/pa/ho/frus/johnsonlb/xxxii).

U.S. Trade Representative. 2005. *Sixth Report to Congress on the Caribbean Basin Economic Recovery Act.* Washington: December 31.

Valenzuela, Arturo. 2004. "Latin American Presidencies Interrupted." *Journal of Democracy* 15, no. 4: 5–15.

Vasquez, Ian. 1992. "Doing What We Can for Haiti." Policy Analysis Paper 183. Washington: Cato Institute, November 5.

Wah, Tatiana. 2005. "The Significance of US Haitian Expatriates for Haiti's Development and Their Requirements for Participation." National Organization for the Advancement of Haitians website, March (www.noahhaiti.org/conferences/Jean1.htm).

Wallack, Jessica. 2004. *Disagreement, Delay and Deficits.* Washington: Inter-American Development Bank, September.

Wasem, Ruth Ellen. 2005. *US Immigration Policy on Haitian Migrants.* CRS Report for Congress RS21349. Washington: Congressional Research Service, January 21 (www.ndu.edu/library/docs/crs/crs_rs21349_21jan05.pdf).

Weinstein, Jeremy. 2004. "Which Path to Peace? Autonomous Recovery and International Intervention." Unpublished Paper. Stanford University, Department of Economics.

Whitman, Daniel. 2005. *A Haitian Chronicle.* Victoria, B.C.: Trafford Press.

Williamson, John. 2003. "From Reform Agenda to Damaged Brand Name." *Finance and Development*, September, 10-13.

World Bank. 1985. *Haiti: Policy Proposals for Growth.* 5601-HA. Washington: June 10.

———. 1987. *Haiti: Public Expenditure Review.* 6113. Washington: January.

———. 1988. *Economic Recovery in Haiti.* 7469-HA. Washington: December 23.

———. 1991. "Haiti: Restoration of Growth and Development." 9523-HA. Washington: May 20.

———. 1996. *Country Assistance Strategy: Haiti.* 15945. Washington: August 13.

———. 1997. *Haiti: Consultative Group Meeting.* SecM97-299. Washington: April 21.

———. 1998. *Haiti: The Challenges of Poverty Reduction.* 17242-HA. Washington: August.

———. 2004a. *Project Appraisal Document: Economic Governance Reform.* 30882-HT. Washington: December 10.

———. 2004b. *From Adjustment Lending to Development Policy Lending.* Washington: World Bank, Operations Policy and Country Services, March 15.

———. 2005a. "Engaging the Diaspora to Deal with Brain Drain." Washington: World Bank, Capacity Development Resource Center.

———. 2005b. *Project Appraisal Document: Economic Governance TA.* 32147-HT. Washington: May 13.

———. 2005c. *Review of World Bank Conditionality.* Washington: World Bank, Operations Policy and Country Services, September.

———. 2006a. *Haiti: Social Resilience and State Fragility in Haiti.* 36069-HT. Washington: World Bank, Caribbean Country Management Unit, April 27.

———. 2006b. *Haiti: Options and Opportunities for Inclusive Growth.* Washington: World Bank, Poverty Reduction and Economic Management Unit, June 1.

———. 2006c. *Economic Governance Reform Operation II: Development Policy Grant.* 38235-HT. Washington: World Bank, International Development Association, December 12.

———. 2006d. *Engaging with Fragile States.* Washington: World Bank, Independent Evaluation Group.

———. 2006e. *Interim Strategy Note: Haiti.* 37720-HT. Washington: World Bank, Caribbean Country Management Unit, December 14.

———. 2006f. *Strengthening Bank Group Engagement on Governance and Anticorruption.* Washington: August 17.

World Bank, Operations Evaluation Department. 1998. *The World Bank's Experience with Post-Conflict Reconstruction.* 18465. Washington: June.

———. 2002. *Haiti: Country Assistance Evaluation.* Washington: February 12.

———. 2003. *Toward Country Led Development.* Washington.

———. 2005a. *Improving the World Bank's Development Effectiveness.* Washington.

———. 2005b. *Capacity Building in Africa.* Washington.

Zartman, I. William, ed. 2007. "Haiti: Understanding Conflict 2007." Unpublished Paper. Baltimore: Johns Hopkins University, School for Advanced International Studies.

INDEX

ABOUT THE ACADEMY

The National Academy of Public Administration is an independent, non-profit organization chartered by Congress to identify emerging issues of governance and to help federal, state, and local governments improve their performance. It exists solely to help government achieve excellence in management. The Academy's mission is to provide "trusted advice"—advice that is objective, timely, and actionable—on all issues of public service and management.

The unique source of the Academy's expertise is its membership, which includes more than 650 current and former cabinet officers, members of Congress, governors, mayors, legislators, jurists, business executives, public managers, and scholars who are elected as Fellows because of their distinguished contribution to the field of public administration through scholarship, civic activism, or government service. Participation in the Academy's work is a requisite of membership, and the Fellows offer their experience and knowledge voluntarily.

The Academy maintains a core professional staff that is regularly augmented by study teams recruited for their superior qualifications to contribute to specific projects. Panels composed of Fellows and invited experts from science, business, labor, and other relevant fields direct project and study activities. The business and leadership functions of the Academy are guided by an elected Board of Directors. The president of the Academy is appointed by the board to direct operations.

Since its establishment in 1967, the Academy has responded to a multitude of requests for assistance from various agencies and has undertaken numerous studies on issues of particular interest to Congress. In addition, the Academy has conducted projects for private foundations, states, and other governments and has begun to develop some private sector partnerships.

The views presented here are solely those of the author and do not reflect the views of the Academy as an institution or of its Fellows.